MW00988285

Praise for *Beyond Diversification*

Sébastien Page presents an eclectic blend of theory, anecdotes, and common sense to describe the best practices of investment management. His mastery of the topic, along with his considerable wit, make for a very entertaining way to learn serious finance. Read this book, and without doubt, you will become a wiser investor.

> **—Mark Kritzman**
> President and CEO, Windham Capital Management;
> Senior Lecturer in Finance, MIT Sloan School of Management;
> and author of *A Practitioner's Guide to Asset Allocation*

Sébastien Page presents a rigorous but easy to digest guide to the basics of asset allocation. Whether you invest for fun or profit, his framework for forecasting risk and return to build portfolios will resonate. Clearly written and understandable concepts make *Beyond Diversification* a one-stop choice for any student of investing.

> **—Bill Stromberg**
> President and CEO, T. Rowe Price

In this tour de force, seasoned investor and researcher Sébastien Page provides sophisticated answers to many questions arising in the practice of asset allocation, risk management, forecasting, and portfolio construction. Page has a tremendous sense of what is important in investment management, and this book reflects that wisdom.

> **—Laurence B. Siegel**
> Gary P. Brinson Director of Research, CFA Institute Research Foundation;
> and author of *Fewer, Richer, Greener*

Oftentimes, the powerful ideas of modern finance are obscured by esoteric mathematics and jargon. Not so in this lively and highly readable book by a master of the practice. Sébastien Page brings the ideas of asset allocation to life, especially the debates that continue to animate our profession.

—**Robin Greenwood**
George Gund Professor of Finance and Banking,
Harvard Business School

This is a wonderful book. It represents an authoritative survey of a broad range of recent research on related topics of asset allocation, risk measurement, and return forecasting, with an emphasis on its practical application in asset management. It is thoughtful, well written, and surprisingly entertaining. The author is a thought leader in this area, and his book is a very important contribution.

—**Stephen Brown**
Professor Emeritus of Finance, Department of Banking
and Finance, NYU Stern School of Business;
Executive Editor *Financial Analysts Journal*

Sébastien Page has masterfully woven threads from academia and practice, combining insights from rigorous research and high-bandwidth anecdotes, to provide an amazingly entertaining and informative tapestry of state of the art asset-allocation techniques. This book is a must-have for anyone who has ever been curious on how the very best construct investment portfolios.

—**Vineer Bhansali**
CIO LongTail Alpha, LLC;
Ex-Partner, Head of Quantitative Portfolios, PIMCO;
and author of *Tail Risk Hedging*

BEYOND DIVERSIFICATION

BEYOND DIVERSIFICATION

What Every Investor

Needs to Know About

Asset Allocation

SÉBASTIEN PAGE

New York   Chicago   San Francisco   Athens   London
Madrid   Mexico City   Milan   New Delhi
Singapore   Sydney   Toronto

Copyright © 2021 by McGraw Hill. All rights reserved. Printed in the United States of America. Except as permitted under the United States Copyright Act of 1976, no part of this publication may be reproduced or distributed in any form or by any means, or stored in a database or retrieval system, without the prior written permission of the publisher.

1 2 3 4 5 6 7 8 9   LCR   25 24 23 22 21 20

ISBN   978-1-260-47487-9
MHID   1-260-47487-9

e-ISBN   978-1-260-47488-6
e-MHID   1-260-47488-7

This publication is designed to provide accurate and authoritative information in regard to the subject matter covered. It is sold with the understanding that neither the author nor the publisher is engaged in rendering legal, accounting, securities trading, or other professional services. If legal advice or other expert assistance is required, the services of a competent professional person should be sought.

—From a Declaration of Principles Jointly Adopted by a Committee of the American Bar Association and a Committee of Publishers and Associations

Library of Congress Cataloging-in-Publication Data

Names: Page, Sebastien, author.
Title: Beyond diversification : what every investor needs to know about asset
  allocation / Sebastien Page.
Description: New York City : McGraw Hill, 2020. | Includes bibliographical
  references and index.
Identifiers: LCCN 2020027606 | ISBN 9781260474879 (hardback) | ISBN
  9781260474886 (ebook)
Subjects: LCSH: Asset allocation. | Investments. | Portfolio management.
Classification: LCC HG4529.5 .P334 2020 | DDC 332.6—dc23
LC record available at https://lccn.loc.gov/2020027606

McGraw Hill books are available at special quantity discounts to use as premiums and sales promotions or for use in corporate training programs. To contact a representative, please visit the Contact Us pages at www.mhprofessional.com.

Disclosure: Views expressed are the author's, are subject to change without notice, and may differ from those of other T. Rowe Price associates. Information and opinions are derived from sources deemed reliable; their accuracy is not guaranteed. This material does not constitute a distribution, offer, invitation, recommendation, or solicitation to sell or buy any securities; it does not constitute investment advice and should not be relied upon as such. Investors should seek independent legal and financial advice before making investment decisions. ***Past performance cannot guarantee future results.*** All investments involve risk. The charts and tables are shown for illustrative purposes only.

To Anne, love of my life,
and our wonderful children,
Olivia and Charlie.

———————————

Contents

PART TWO
RISK FORECASTING

PART THREE
PORTFOLIO CONSTRUCTION

Foreword

THERE ARE TWO QUESTIONS I'M OFTEN ASKED ONCE I introduce myself as the head of investments at T. Rowe Price.

First, people are not shy about asking me what markets might do next or where to invest. Second, people ask how to become better investors or, more ambitiously, what makes an investor great.

On markets, I don't have a crystal ball. None of us do. But after decades of investing, I can usually offer an answer that's rooted in experience and informed by the research and insights of the talented investors I'm lucky enough to call my colleagues.

On what makes an investor great, most people don't appreciate how rare truly great investors are. I have been fortunate enough to work with a number of them. I've learned—paraphrasing Leo Tolstoy's principle that "all happy families are alike"—that great investors generally have things in common. Below-average managers are below average in their own way, but that's a subject for another time.

Great investors have an almost insatiable intellectual curiosity. They want to know why things are the way they are and how they might be different. Many people love engaging with capital markets. What sets the great investors apart is their all-consuming passion for uncovering insights.

Great investors are original thinkers. I don't mean just about markets. They are original thinkers in all aspects of their lives. What's also important, though, is that original thinkers value other original thinking. They learn from, and challenge themselves through, a vigorous discourse with other investors. Great investors use that collaboration to arrive at their own original thinking. Our corporate culture at T. Rowe Price empowers these investors to thrive.

Great investors also have a process in which their intellectual curiosity and original thinking are grounded. This process, though differing from investor to investor, usually incorporates a few common traits. A great investor's process is consistently rigorous and disciplined and rooted in deep research. The process is not just capturing lightning in a bottle, but something that is durable and repeatable over the long term.

This leads me to Sébastien Page, my colleague. He is one of the great investing minds on asset allocation, the subject of this book. Sébastien has a nearly unquenchable intellectual curiosity. He devours books, podcasts, studies, the latest thinking from a colleague, reams of data on capital markets. You name it, he's read it, digested it, and thoroughly understands it.

Sébastien is an original thinker. He values, in turn, other original thinkers. Our Asset Allocation Committee comprises many of the most gifted investors at our firm. Sébastien brings their voices into a robust, sometimes contentious, discussion that informs our critical decisions. In this book, count the number of times he reflects on running down the hall to a colleague's office with questions. Those questions so often stimulate informed, original thinking.

Finally, Sébastien and our asset allocation team are grounded in a durable, rigorous process. If you fail to establish a process, you will inevitably succumb to fear or greed. Sébastien's process ensures our asset allocation team balances judgment with data and analysis in a disciplined, respectable way.

Sébastien is a thought leader on asset allocation. He is also an avid (and quite fast) runner, likes the occasional glass of wine, and tells a good story. As to this last point, I think you'll agree as you learn more about him, his story, and multi-asset investing in the pages to come.

Rob Sharps
Head of Investments & Group CIO, T. Rowe Price

BEYOND DIVERSIFICATION

PART ONE

RETURN FORECASTING

Many skeptics will argue that the hypotheses behind the model
can't be verified, and therefore, we can't use it in practice.
But our goal is not to describe all the complexities of real life.
Rather, we want to provide tools to help decision-making.
If the model improves the odds that we'll make the right decisions,
then we should use it.
—JPP

A note to readers: I've included quotes by "JPP" throughout this book. I will reveal this author's identity in the Conclusion.

Several years ago, I was half asleep at a small quantitative research conference when an interesting discussion took place. A fundamental portfolio manager (i.e., a heretic among quants[1]) asked the presenter, somewhat rudely, whether *all* portfolio optimization models were in fact completely worthless, in light of the "GIGO" critique. This question brought an immediate silence to the room. Perhaps the easiest way to annoy a quant is to bring up the GIGO critique. GIGO stands for "garbage in, garbage out." The questioner was arguing that because we can't estimate expected returns with any reasonable level of confidence (garbage in), the output of portfolio optimization models will always be wrong (garbage out). There is validity to this critique in that portfolio optimization models often give a false sense of precision. And ultimately, there's no such thing as financial alchemy—a calculator can't turn bad inputs into the right answer (portfolio optimization models are, broadly speaking, sophisticated calculators).

The presenter was Dr. Bernd Scherer, a highly regarded thought leader who has straddled the worlds of academia and investment practice for many years. Dr. Scherer was jet-lagged. He had just flown in from overseas, and he was not in the mood for a philosophical discussion on the GIGO critique. In one short sentence, he gave the most remarkable rebuttal of the critique I had ever heard. His answer ended the debate before it started, and it has stayed with me throughout the years. I must admit, I've used it a few times myself. He said, "If you don't think you can estimate expected returns, you shouldn't be in the investment business."

Investing is mostly about forecasting returns. Even investors who don't formulate expected returns as a precise number make *implicit* forecasts when they pick stocks or bonds or allocate assets. These implicit forecasts aren't precise, but they require a view on directionality (up or down? outperform or underperform?) and, to a certain extent, magnitude, as reflected in position sizing. Even proponents of risk parity (more on this topic in Chapter 14) make implicit return assumptions when they equalize risk contributions in their portfolio. Of course, there's more to the story. We must balance our return expectations against risk. And we must think about correlations, goals, time horizon, risk tolerance, liabilities, and so on. But to echo Dr. Scherer, it's hard to call yourself an investor if you don't think you have insights about expected returns.

There are many ways to estimate expected returns, from fundamental to quantitative approaches and everything in between. Over the years, I've worked with fundamental investors who broadly dismiss quantitative models as naïve, usually on the basis that the models rely on past data. Also, I've worked with quants who think fundamental approaches lack rigor and amount to a collection of made-up stories. Most successful investors are less dogmatic, and their views lie somewhere between these two extremes. They believe that a combination of powerful quantitative data analysis *and* fundamental, forward-looking judgment leads to the best outcomes.

The challenge, of course, is how to marry fundamental and quantitative approaches. I will make suggestions in this chapter. But first, the criticism that quantitative expected returns are flawed because they use historical (as opposed to "forward-looking") information merits a rebuttal. As for GIGO, the critique used to make my blood pressure spike.

During the first few years of my career at State Street, a significant part of my responsibilities was to help develop quantitative expected returns. Sometimes clients would question the models. They would say, "This approach doesn't work, because it's not forward-looking—it's based on past data, and the current environment is different."

I loved my job at State Street, but the global travel schedule was grueling. So like Dr. Scherer, one day I was jet-lagged and gave a client a curt answer. I said: "I'm sorry. I've looked everywhere for future data, but I can't find any. They're not on Bloomberg."

The salesperson who had invited me to present to this client was not impressed. The point is that historical data are all we have. They are useful *to the extent they help formulate a view about the future*. It's in that context that I review various approaches to expected returns in this chapter.

Note

1. A "quant" is an industry term used to describe those involved in quantitative research and investment management. Quants use computer models and mathematics to predict markets and manage risk.

1

Equilibrium and Something About Quack Remedies Sold on the Internet

The expected return for the market portfolio should be a function of the level of interest rates. When rates are high, investors require higher returns on all tradable assets.
—JPP

A note to readers: I completed this book shortly before the Covid crisis. No model can predict what might come next in the evolution of the pandemic from a public health perspective. If we take a long-term view, I don't expect the estimates provided in this and other sections of the book to be too different from those that we could construct in the postcrisis environment. Methodologies are simple and transparent. They can easily be updated with more recent data.

FOR MULTI-ASSET INVESTORS, A BASIC WAY TO ESTIMATE expected returns is to use the capital asset pricing model (CAPM). *Despite its shortcomings, the CAPM is more useful than most investors think, because it links expected returns to an objective measure of risk and current interest rate levels.* Jack Treynor, Bill Sharpe, John Lintner, and Jan Mossin independently developed this model in the 1960s.[1] Anyone who has taken a basic course in finance knows about the CAPM. I was first introduced to the history behind it as an undergraduate. A professor gave me a copy of the book *Capital Ideas*, by Peter L. Bernstein (1991), a masterfully written account of the beginnings of modern finance. (This book had more influence on my interest in finance and career choices than any other book I've ever read.) In his follow-up book, *Capital Ideas Evolving*, in which he discussed applications of the concepts presented in *Capital Ideas*, Bernstein (2007) concludes that the CAPM "has turned into the most fascinating and perhaps the most influential of all the theoretical developments described in *Capital Ideas*." Similarly, in their ubiquitous textbook *Modern Portfolio Theory and Investment Analysis*, Edwin Elton and Martin Gruber (1995) describe it as "one of the most important discoveries in the field of finance."

However, there are issues with the CAPM. Its derivation relies on a long list of questionable assumptions: investors are rational; taxes and transactions costs do not exist; all investors have the same information; etc. Even Harry Markowitz, father of portfolio theory, has expressed misgivings about the widespread use of the CAPM. In a paper titled "Market Efficiency: A Theoretical Distinction and So What?" published in the *Financial Analysts Journal* in 2005, he writes about the model's "convenient but unrealistic assumptions." He focuses on one of the key, yet rarely discussed, building blocks of the model: the (clearly unrealistic) assumption that investors can borrow all they want at the risk-free rate. Like taking away the wrong Jenga piece will make the tower of blocks collapse, if we take away this important theoretical building block, the CAPM edifice crumbles. Markowitz demonstrates that the market portfolio is no longer "efficient," which means that other portfolios offer a better expected risk-adjusted return, and the key conclusions and applications of the model are no longer valid (an interesting conclusion given the popularity of index funds).

At the Q Group conferences, which bring together academics and investment professionals, we've had the chance on a few occasions to hear Markowitz and Sharpe debate these and related issues. I've felt lucky to be part of an industry group where Nobel Prize winners engage in intellectual debates and exchange ideas with practitioners. It's been clear from these discussions that the two intellectual giants have agreed to disagree on a few topics. But they seem to have maintained a longstanding friendship. When Sharpe received news that he, Markowitz, and Merton Miller had won the Nobel Prize, he said he was particularly happy to share the award with Markowitz: "We're old and very close friends. He was basically my mentor. He so richly deserves it, as did Miller of course."[2]

But if I read between the lines, Markowitz's motivation to critique the CAPM could be that while the model was *derived* from mean-variance portfolio optimization (which is one of Markowitz's most important contributions to the field of finance), it also suggests *there is no need for it*. When taken literally, the model dictates that all investors should buy a combination of cash and the market portfolio, mixed together in proportions consistent with their risk aversion. In his 2005 paper, Markowitz directly questions this conclusion:

Before the CAPM, conventional wisdom was that some investments were suitable for widows and orphans whereas others were suitable only for those prepared to take on "a businessman's risk." The CAPM convinced many that this conventional wisdom was wrong; the market portfolio is the proper mix among risky securities for everyone. The portfolios of the widow and businessman should differ only in the amount of cash or leverage used. As we will see, however, an analysis that takes into account limited borrowing capacity implies that the pre-CAPM conventional wisdom is probably correct.

Ultimately, Markowitz acknowledges the theoretical relevance of the model, but with a great analogy from physics, he argues that we should be aware of its limitations in practice:

Despite its drawbacks as illustrated here, the CAPM should be taught. It is like studying the motion of objects on Earth under the assumption that the Earth has no air. The calculations and results are much simpler if this assumption is made. But at some point, the obvious fact that, on Earth, cannonballs and feathers do not fall at the same rate should be noted and explained to some extent. Similarly, at some point, the finance student should be shown the effect of replacing [the model's assumptions about borrowing at the risk-free rate and shorting] with more realistic constraints.

Other academics have expressed broader misgivings about the model, from both the theoretical and the empirical perspectives. In a 2004 paper titled "The Capital Asset Pricing Model: Theory and Evidence," published in the *Journal of Economic Perspectives*, Eugene Fama and Kenneth French attack the CAPM much more directly than Markowitz:

> In the end, we argue that whether the model's problems reflect weaknesses in the theory or in its empirical implementation, the failure of the CAPM in empirical tests implies that most applications of the model are invalid.

Ouch. For an academic paper, that's an unusually direct attack. To back it up, Fama and French show that individual stocks' CAPM expected returns do not line up with subsequent realized returns. Superficially, they show that the average month-to-month returns of portfolios of individual stocks ranked on the basis of their CAPM expected returns do not line up with the model's predictions. Also, Fama and French explain that other factors add explanatory power to the CAPM, namely book-to-market ratio and size. (However, multi-asset investors should take these tests with a grain of salt, as they are based on a short time horizon and rely on stock-level estimates of the model. These tests say nothing about the validity of CAPM expected returns at the asset class level.)

And then there's Nassim Nicholas Taleb, who never minces words. In his sometimes bombastic but entertaining book *The Black Swan* (Taleb, 2010), he expresses disdain for the work of Markowitz and Sharpe. He almost sounds angry when he discusses their Nobel Prize:

> The [Nobel] committee has gotten into the habit of handing out Nobel Prizes to those who "bring rigor" to the process with pseudoscience and phony mathematics. After the stock market crash, they rewarded two theoreticians, Harry Markowitz and William Sharpe, who build beautifully Platonic models on a Gaussian Base, contributing to what is called Modern Portfolio Theory. Simply, if you remove their Gaussian assumptions and treat prices as scalable, you are left with hot air. The Nobel Committee could have tested the Sharpe and Markowitz models—they work like quack remedies sold on the internet—but nobody in Stockholm seems to have thought of it.

"Locke's Madmen, or Bell Curves in the Wrong Places" from *The Black Swan: The Impact of the Highly Improbable*, with a new section "On Robustness and Fragility" second edition, by Nassim Nicholas Taleb, copyright © 2007, 2010 by Nassim Nicholas Taleb. Used by permission of Random House, an imprint and division of Penguin Random House LLC. All rights reserved.

That's far from Elton and Gruber's description of the CAPM as "one of the most important discoveries in the field of finance." Taleb's concern is that modern portfolio theory and the CAPM were derived under Gaussian assumptions. Essentially, the models assume that investment risk can be represented by the standard deviation of returns. Hence, we must assume that the underlying return distributions are "normal"; i.e., they have no fat tails. In Part Two of this book I'll discuss the limitations of Gaussian assumptions, as well as remedies for multi-asset investors, but for now, suffice it to say that extreme returns—in particular on the downside—are more frequent than the normal distribution predicts. Experienced investors know that in the markets, the tails are always fat. Therefore, exposure to loss can be much greater than expected if one relies on the theoretical foundations behind the CAPM.

To be fair to Markowitz, Sharpe, and other academics, I'm sure they would agree that empirical return distributions are often nonnormal. Markowitz, for example, wrote about semivariance to address nonnormal returns as far back as 1959. It doesn't mean the CAPM and other related models are wrong. To borrow Markowitz's analogy of the physics experiment that shows a feather and a cannonball falling at the same speed under vacuum, it means that *if* the assumptions hold, *then* these models are correct. In this sense, the CAPM is perhaps as close as it gets to a law of motion in finance.

Ultimately, to estimate expected returns is to try to predict the future. It should be hard! In the absence of a crystal ball, any model will have its flaws. *In my view, despite the multidecade academic equivocation on its merit, the CAPM is as good as any other starting point for multi-asset investors, because it relates expected returns to risk.*

From that perspective, while discussions on expected returns often degenerate into never-ending debates about what the future holds, with the CAPM we can make predictions in a somewhat agnostic, less controversial way. It's hard to refute the argument that risk should be compensated: asset classes with higher risk should have higher expected returns than those with lower risk, as least over a reasonably long time horizon. There's an appealing notion of equilibrium behind this approach. But there's an important subtlety: under the CAPM, risk isn't defined as the asset's volatility or exposure to loss. It's defined as its *contribution* to a diversified portfolio's volatility. In other words, expected return on a security or asset class is proportional to its sensitivity (beta) to the world market portfolio.

Let us briefly get into some technical details. To calculate an asset's beta, we multiply (a) the ratio of its volatility to the market's volatility by (b) its correlation with the market. So the formula is

Beta = (asset volatility/market volatility) × correlation

where volatility is the standard deviation of returns, and the correlation is calculated between the asset and the market. Then we define expected return as follows:

Expected return = risk-free rate + beta × (market expected return − risk-free rate)

In their 2004 critique of the CAPM, Fama and French show that high-beta stocks can underperform low-beta stocks during long periods of time, which invalidates this equation. On the other hand, in his excellent monograph, titled *Expected Returns on Major Asset Classes*, Antti Ilmanen (2012) points out that from 1962 to 2009, there is a positive relationship between beta and the relative returns of stocks and bonds. It's obvious: stocks have a higher beta than bonds, and over time they can deliver a higher return. While simplistic, this example suggests the CAPM may work better across asset classes than for individual stocks.

In addition to beta, expected returns depend on the current risk-free rate and the expected market risk premium (market expected return – risk-free rate). Purists will point out that there's no such thing as a risk-free rate. That's correct, as even cash has nonzero volatility, and in theory, there's default risk associated with even the safest of government bonds. However, practitioners aren't purists, and US Treasury bonds are generally used as a proxy for the risk-free asset. (As an interesting side note, for liability-focused investors such as defined benefit plan sponsors, cash is far from the risk-free rate. In fact, on a surplus basis, cash is a high-volatility asset compared with a long-duration bond that matches the duration of the liabilities. I'll discuss liability-driven investing in Part Three of this book.)

To account for the "historical data" critique, our estimate of the risk-free rate must be forward-looking. We can think of the CAPM as a simple building block approach: we start with the current risk-free rate and add a risk premium (scaled by the asset's beta). Suppose we use the three-month US Treasury bill rate as our risk-free rate, and we want to calculate expected return on an asset class with a beta of 1. Also, suppose we estimate the total market risk premium to be 1.9%, and we assume it doesn't change over time. (I'll discuss this total market risk premium estimate in more detail shortly.)

During the first half of the 1980s, the three-month US Treasury bill yield rose above 10%. As of March 23, 2018,[3] it was at 1.7%. If we travel back in time and assume we're in the early 1980s, we'll have to endure bad music and questionable hairstyles. We'll also notice high nominal expected returns. I use the term "nominal" because inflation was also very high, and this simple version of the CAPM doesn't say anything about inflation and real returns. Expected return on our asset class in the early 1980s would have been 11.9%, calculated as follows:

Expected return = risk-free rate + beta × market risk premium

11.9% = 10% + 1 × 1.9%

whereas in the current environment, it's 3.6%:

$$3.6\% = 1.7\% + 1 \times 1.9\%$$

Same asset class, same risk level . . . different starting points. In a low-rate environment, investors should expect low returns across the board. The risk-free rate is the anchor, and when it's low, it holds down expected returns across markets.

Skeptics will say that we've been in a low-rate environment, yet realized equity returns have been very high. In March 2018, the S&P 500 was up a staggering 292% over the previous nine years (12.7% annualized[4]), including dividends. Even when rates are low, it's still possible to see high realized risk premiums. Valuation may be the missing part of the puzzle: nine years earlier, equities were extremely cheap in the wake of the 2008–2009 financial crisis. My view is that in a CAPM framework, the forecast of the market risk premium (which includes both stocks and bonds) should account for whether financial markets are expensive or cheap in general. We can't adjust for *relative* valuations to model each asset class's expected return individually, but a valuation adjustment to the overall market risk premium should improve our forecasts. Investors sometimes use the expression "A rising tide lifts all boats" to describe market rallies. Do we expect the tide to rise or to come down? For the nine years previous to 2018, price-to-earnings ratios (P/Es) rose, and rates declined—clearly a rising tide.

In March 2018, we faced extended valuations across markets. If we want our estimates to be forward-looking, shouldn't we calibrate our CAPM expected returns to be lower than historical averages? "When the tide comes down, we'll see who's been skinny-dipping" is a quote frequently attributed to Warren Buffett. With apologies for my overuse of the tide analogy, my point is that bear (or even just weak) financial markets are harder to navigate for unskilled investors and can make life difficult for plan sponsors, financial advisors, and individual investors.

In the next chapter, we'll review methodologies to forecast returns based on valuations. For now, let us focus on the simplest of models. Jeremy Siegel, Wharton professor and author of *Stocks for the Long Run* (Siegel, 2002), often uses the inverse of the P/E ratio as a back-of-the-envelope forecast of real return for stocks. If we assume a P/E of 20, which is a number Siegel has quoted recently,[5] expected real return for equities should be 5% (1/20). For inflation, we can use a market-implied or "breakeven" estimate, as measured by the difference between the yield of a nominal bond and an inflation-linked bond. In March 2018, 10-year inflation breakevens were around 2%. If we add inflation to the real return estimate, we get an expected nominal equity return of 7% (5% + 2%). Not bad.

On the other hand, Robert Shiller, Yale professor and Nobel laureate, uses a P/E ratio that normalizes earnings over the last 10 years and adjusts for inflation (the cyclically adjusted price-earnings ratio, or CAPE). The 10-year period is meant to represent a full business cycle. His approach yields a meager 1% expected real return for US stocks, or 3% nominal if we assume 2% inflation.[6] The CAPE is higher than the current P/E in part because earnings have increased significantly over the last 10 years. Another reason for Shiller's ultralow forecast may be that he doesn't simply invert the ratio—he adjusts the estimate based on a regression model.

As much as we try to keep it simple, it's never easy to forecast returns. Markowitz and Sharpe seem to disagree on the theory behind CAPM, even though it's one of the most important foundations of modern finance. And here, two equally credible thought leaders disagree, this time on the equity risk premium, a key input to the model. I suspect the Shiller and Siegel estimates represent bookends—from one of the most bearish to one of the most bullish forecasts.

Because we want to build an estimate for global equity markets (CAPE ratios are closer to 20 outside the United States versus 30 in the United States),[7] and for other reasons that I'll explain shortly when we revisit the CAPE debate, my recommendation is to tilt the forecast toward Siegel's estimate. A split of 80% Siegel, 20% Shiller seems reasonable to me, which gives us an expected nominal equity return of

$$6.2\% = 0.8 \times 7\% + 0.2 \times 3\%$$

Some important caveats: This 6.2% forecast doesn't represent T. Rowe Price's view (as a firm, we don't have a "house view") or the views of our Global Multi-Asset Division. It's just meant to be a simple and transparent forecast that uses a single factor, the P/E ratio. And the 80–20 blend is clearly my own finger-in-the air estimate—definitely not "robust" from a quantitative perspective. In fact, my colleagues in our Multi-Asset Division's research team would be embarrassed and worried if I used it anywhere in our investment process. In the next several chapters, I'll review several other methodologies to forecast returns that include more factors and that incorporate judgment in a more tractable way.

Here I use this estimate as a basic input to the CAPM. Is 6.2% reasonable for the world equity market portfolio? Bond managers tend to have a pessimistic bias on risk assets, so perhaps it's not surprising that my old employer, PIMCO, expects equity returns to be quite low going forward. In early 2018, my ex-colleagues Ravi Mattu and Vasant Naik published a valuation-informed view that the equity risk premium should be about 2.5%, with an additional warning: "Equities may deliver even lower excess returns than the current ex-ante equity risk premium (ERP) of 2.5%, since a reasonable fair value for the ERP may be slightly higher."[8] (I assume they mean that in order to get a higher ERP, valuations will have to come down.) If we assume a nominal risk-free rate of 2%, we get an expected return of 4.5%. In contrast, BlackRock expects long-term equilibrium returns to be 7.2% for US stocks and 8.1% for international stocks.[9] Once again, these forecasts look like bookends. In that context, 6.2% seems reasonable to me. It turns out that it's close to estimates published by AQR (6.2%), Northern Trust (6.4%), Aon (6.5%), and BNY Mellon (6.2%).[10]

Is the goal to forecast returns over the next month, year, or longer? The CAPM is a single-period model, so in theory, the question of time horizon is abstracted away. In practice, investors use the model for relatively long time horizons. (I've never come across an investor who uses the CAPM for short-term investment decisions.) Plan sponsors and consultants use it for strategic asset allocation studies, for example. For such studies, the time horizon is usually between 3 and 10 years. And for life cycle investing applications, the investment horizon can be as long as 40 or more years. Similarly, Shiller's and Siegel's equity return forecasts assume a long time horizon. It's my view that this relative consistency in time horizon makes them appropriate inputs to the CAPM.

What About Bonds?

To estimate the total market risk premium, we also need to forecast bond returns. (In theory, we need to forecast returns on all assets, including illiquid investments, but for practical reasons I'll focus on liquid markets.) In fixed income markets, yield to maturity is a reasonably good predictor of future returns . . . better than most people think. In fact, by definition, yield to maturity is a perfect predictor of the buy-and-hold return of a single default-free bond. However, with the CAPM we need a return forecast for the total bond market, which includes credit exposures and is better represented as a constant maturity portfolio, rather than buy and hold.

Nonetheless, ultimately, it's easier to forecast bond returns than equity returns, and the math behind forecasting bond returns is fascinating, at least to a geek like me.

First, the key takeaway is that higher reinvestment rates offset interest rate shocks over time. Suppose a bond portfolio has a duration (interest rate sensitivity) of five years. If rates unexpectedly spike by +0.5%, the portfolio should go down about –2.5% (5 × –0.5%). However, we now earn +0.5% more on the portfolio than we did before the rate shock. If we ignore several less important subtleties, such as yield curve effects and the timing of the rate shock, we can expect to recover the 2.5% over roughly five years (5 × +0.5%). *This offset effect works no matter the size of the rate shock.* It explains why, historically, the initial yield to maturity has been a remarkably good predictor of forward return for bonds, and the sweet spot of our ability to forecast, or close enough, is when the investment horizon matches the portfolio's duration.

Bond investors tend to worry about rising rates because of the short-term losses that occur when the rate hikes aren't already priced into the forward curve. However, contrary to conventional wisdom, this example illustrates how rising rates are good for bonds: higher rates mean higher reinvestment rates and, ultimately, higher expected returns. In an excellent paper titled "Bond Investing in a Rising Rate Environment" (2014), my former colleagues Helen Guo and Niels Pedersen go beyond this simple example. They account for the timing of the rate shock(s), and they model nonparallel yield curve shifts. They find that if rates rise gradually, or if the increase occurs later in the investment horizon, then it takes longer for the reinvestment effect to heal the price shock(s). They derive rules of thumb to predict when the convergence will occur for these special cases. Their results are remarkably intuitive, simple, and quite interesting (again, if you're into geeky bond math). The bottom line is that the impact of rising rates on bonds is both bad (in the short run) and good (in the long run).

In a related empirical study published in 2014, Marty Leibowitz, Anthony Bova, and Stanley Kogelman show that returns for the Barclays U.S. Government/Credit Index have consistently converged toward the initial yield to maturity on the index. Over their study period, the index has had a relatively constant duration of about six years—consistent with the time horizon they used to measure convergence. Therefore, historically, the simplest rule of thumb seems to have prevailed: returns have converged to the initial yield to maturity at a time horizon that matches duration. This result holds across a variety of rate paths. It begets the question, why are bond investors and financial commentators in the media so worried about rising rates? If the horizon is long enough, it doesn't matter whether rates go up, down, or sideways. The starting yield is what matters. As a predictor of the return on bonds, the accuracy of this single, publicly available number is much higher than that of any model we could ever build to forecast equity returns, at least out-of-sample.

As I write these thoughts on the impact of rising rates, the yield to maturity on the Barclays Global Aggregate is a meager 1.9% (yield to worst, as of April 3, 2018),[11] and its duration is about seven years. Therefore, 1.9% is a reasonable long-term estimate of expected return for the bond market portfolio. Earlier I mentioned that stocks appear expensive after a nine-year bull market. But as we stare down the barrel of a *30-year* bull market in bonds, bonds appear even more expensive. Some multi-asset investment firms (not my firm), primarily in Europe, have seduced investors with promises of "stock-like returns for bond-like volatility." Until recently, several of them had been able to deliver on this promise. But from 2000 to 2016, guess what had delivered stock-like returns for bond-like volatility? Bonds.[12] Again, the tired expression "A rising tide lifts all boats" applies. Going forward, it might be more difficult to deliver a stock-like return for bond-like volatility. It certainly was in 2017, as stock markets significantly outperformed bonds, such that any unlevered allocation that was not 100% invested in stocks did not deliver "stock-like returns."

Yields are especially low outside the United States, due to unprecedented monetary easing in Europe, Japan, China, and the United Kingdom. Globally, not only have many central banks driven rates toward zero, but they've also pumped more than USD 20 trillion of liquidity into financial markets, through quantitative easing (QE).[13] Meanwhile, the Fed has started normalizing. As an illustration of the impact of QE and divergence in policies, two-year US Treasuries currently yield more than two-year Greek government bonds (2.3% versus 1.3%, as of April 3, 2018). Yet, clearly, Greek bonds are much riskier.

The Market Portfolio: It's Not What It Used to Be

Now that we have return forecasts for stocks (6.2%) and bonds (1.9%), we must estimate their relative weights within the market portfolio. I exclude private markets for simplicity, but as I mentioned earlier, in theory the CAPM market portfolio should include them. In fact, it should be a weighted sum of all assets in the world. *Forbes* contributor Phil deMuth explains that the market portfolio should include "your human capital, your family business, your wife's jewelry, your house, and the Renoir on your fireplace,"[14] another good example of when theory doesn't work in practice.

Importantly, because I exclude private markets, their correlation with the market portfolio—and ipso facto their CAPM betas—will be biased down. For this and other reasons, such as the smoothing bias, their betas will require separate adjustments. In Chapter 9, I'll discuss methodologies to build risk models for private assets.

Asset weights within the market portfolio should be based on their relative market capitalizations. Theory says these weights represent the aggregate allocation of all investors, a market consensus of sorts. Interestingly, most CAPM research and applications focus on equity-only examples. The stock market is almost always used as the market portfolio, as if other asset classes didn't exist. It puzzles me that so many academic papers gloss over the multi-asset nature of the theoretical foundations of the model, including the paper by Fama and French (2004) I mentioned earlier, as well as most of the prior studies they reference. This omission seems meaningful to me. It raises the question, should stocks be priced based on their beta to the stock market or to the total market portfolio?

In practice, it makes a significant difference. In a 2018 paper titled "Yes, the Composition of the Market Portfolio Matters," Avraham Kamara and Lance Young use 75 years of monthly data on 30 equity industry portfolios. They show that adding bonds to the market portfolio "produces economically large differences in estimated [returns]." It changes the average level of return estimates across industry portfolios, through the combined effect of lower betas and a lower market risk premium. It also changes the relative expected returns, as some high-dividend industries are more bond-like and therefore more sensitive to interest rates (utilities and telecoms), while others have negative duration (financials). From an asset allocator's perspective, clearly we should use the multi-asset market portfolio, not just equities.

Unfortunately, it's difficult to estimate the relative weights of asset classes within the multi-asset market portfolio, due to a lack of reliable data. Overlaps across indexes are also an issue. For example, real estate investment trusts (REITs) are part of most equity indexes, but they invest in real estate, not stocks. Ronald Doeswijk, Trevin Lam, and Laurens Swinkels, in their 2014 paper titled "The Global Multi-Asset Market Portfolio, 1959–2012," make a valiant effort to scrub the best available data, untangle the Russian nesting dolls of asset class exposures, and create a history of asset class weights within the market portfolio. Their analysis reveals that these weights have changed over time. In 2000, the market portfolio was close to 60% stocks, 40% bonds. Good old 60–40. Nowadays, these weights have flipped to about 40% stocks, 60% bonds.[15] The shift has occurred in relatively slow motion. Since 2000, bonds have performed well, and net supply has increased, despite central bank purchases. Meanwhile the supply of publicly traded stocks has shrunk due to corporate buybacks, a reduction in IPOs, and the privatization of an increasing number of companies.

For CAPM purists who believe the capitalization-weighted market portfolio is always optimal, this significant change in its risk level must be a bit of a head-scratcher. To forecast returns, current weights are what matter. After all, we want to be forward-looking. (Or perhaps we should try to forecast the average weights over our time horizon, but that would be difficult, because so many supply and demand factors are unpredictable.)

If we assume the market portfolio is composed of 40% stocks and 60% bonds, our expected total market return is 3.6%, calculated as follows:

Expected total market return = 40% × expected stock market return + 60% × expected bond market return

3.6% = 40% × 6.2% + 60% × 1.9%

If we subtract the current three-month US Treasury bill rate of 1.7% (as of March 23, 2018), we get a market risk premium of 1.9% (3.6% − 1.7%). It's not clear to me whether cash rates are the appropriate risk-free rate for long-term investors. Over a relatively long investment horizon, the cash return depends on rate changes, due to reinvestment effects (i.e., the three-month yield resets many times before the end of the horizon). From that perspective, cash is riskier than a zero-coupon bond that matches the investment horizon. An investor's base currency is another consideration. Here I assume a US investor, but cash rates differ across countries. If they're high, investors should expect high nominal returns on local assets. However, high cash returns usually coincide with high expected inflation.

Some of my colleagues can effortlessly move between nominal and real returns, local and foreign returns, etc. They mentally account for spot and forward rates, interest rate differentials, and inflation differentials on the fly. I've been involved in global macro investing for many years, and I used to oversee a currency overlay business, but I'm embarrassed to say that I still struggle with these problems. I always need to pause and think through them. To make it easy, let's focus on a US investor who wants to forecast nominal returns.

Betas and Depressingly Low Expected Returns

Now that we have estimates for the risk-free rate (1.7%) and the market risk premium (1.9%), all we need are the asset class betas. In Table 1.1, I show betas for 21 asset classes, based on monthly data from February 2002 to January 2017.[16] Also, I show each asset class's CAPM expected return, which I calculate as explained earlier: risk-free rate + beta × market risk premium.

For the market portfolio, I use a blend of 40% world equities (MSCI All
Country World Index), 60% world bonds (Barclays Global Aggregate).

TABLE 1.1   CAPM Expected Returns

	Data Source	Beta	CAPM
US Stocks			
Large cap	Russell 1000	1.4	**4.3%**
Small cap	Russell 2000	1.2	**3.9%**
Value	Russell 1000 Value	1.3	**4.1%**
Growth	Russell 1000 Growth	1.5	**4.5%**
Non-US Stocks			
Large cap	MSCI World ex-U.S.	1.9	**5.2%**
Small cap	MSCI EAFE Small Cap	1.7	**4.9%**
Growth	MSCI EAFE Growth	1.9	**5.3%**
Value	MSCI EAFE Value	1.8	**5.2%**
Emerging Markets	MSCI Emerging Markets	2.4	**6.4%**
US Bonds			
Aggregate bonds	Barclays U.S. Aggregate	0.2	**2.0%**
Treasuries intermediate	Barclays Treasuries Intermediate	0.0	**1.8%**
Treasuries long	Barclays Treasuries Long	0.3	**2.2%**
Credit intermediate	Barclays Corporate Intermediate	0.2	**2.1%**
Credit long	Barclays Corporate Long	0.8	**3.2%**
High yield	ML High-Yield Master Index	0.8	**3.3%**
Leveraged loans	S&P/LSTA U.S. Leveraged Loan Index	0.3	**2.3%**
Non-US Bonds			
Global aggregate bonds (ex-US)	Barclays Global Aggregate ex-US	0.9	**3.4%**
Global government bonds (ex-US)	Barclays Global Government ex-US	0.9	**3.3%**
Emerging markets debt	JPM EMBI Global Composite	0.8	**3.3%**
Emerging markets debt (local)	JPM GBI Emerging Markets (Local)	0.4	**2.4%**
Real Estate			
Wilshire Real Estate Securities		1.3	**4.2%**
World portfolio equities		1.66	4.86%
World portfolio bonds		0.56	2.77%

The return forecasts shown in the table are depressingly low. Yet this shouldn't be a surprise, given the low level of rates and the low expected market risk premium due to high valuations. Following the 2020 pandemic crisis, as panic runs high, valuations have become more attractive, and the equity risk premium has likely increased. US rates have hit their zero bound. As I'm about to submit my manuscript for this book, it remains difficult to assess the impact of the economic heart attack. But it's reasonable to expect that as we recover, risk assets will deliver relatively high returns.

A more surprising outcome may be that the numbers aren't entirely consistent with the return expectations I put in the model for the world equity market (6.2%) and for the world bond market (1.9%). Equity markets have CAPM expected returns in the 4–5% range across US and non-US markets. These numbers can't add up to my initial 6.2% world equity estimate, even after we include emerging markets. Also, US bond returns are lower than expected, given their current yield to maturity. On the other hand, non-US bonds have higher expected returns than their current yield to maturity suggests.

What explains these inconsistencies? The main reason is that I use a valuation approach to determine the market risk premium, while the CAPM is a statistical, risk-pricing approach. In a sense, because it relies on beta as the main driver of relative expected returns across asset classes, the CAPM is valuation-agnostic. As our director of research, Stefan Hubrich, would say: "These are 'unconditional' expected returns. If you were air-dropped into the US and you didn't know what decade it was, how would you invest?"

Consider the example of non-US bonds. Relative to US bonds, they have higher volatility and higher correlation to the world portfolio. Therefore, they should have a higher expected return, without regard to their artificially low yield. (Central bank interventions create an artificially low yield.) The same intuition holds for stocks. To the CAPM purist, it doesn't matter whether equity asset classes have a high or low price-to-earnings ratio. Their betas are all that matter.[17]

From that perspective, CAPM forecasts are most relevant for long investment horizons, say, over 10 years. They're useful as inputs for life cycle investing applications, for example. Also, CAPM results can indicate whether valuation spreads, relative to long-term averages or between asset classes, may be transitory or permanent. All else being equal, the further away valuations are from their risk-return "CAPM equilibrium," the greater the gravitational pull of mean reversion.

But there's another issue I should emphasize: the betas are just statistical estimates produced by a risk model. They're not very forward-looking. In Table 1.1, non-US small caps have a lower beta than non-US large caps. I did not expect this result. It could be due to idiosyncratic factors that prevailed from February 2002 to January 2017. Over that same period, growth stocks dominated market returns, which could explain why they have a higher beta than value stocks. However, in the current environment, value stocks are more levered to economic growth and cyclical factors in general. Hence, their forward-looking beta to the economy and to the world portfolio should be higher, perhaps even higher than growth stocks' beta.

There are many extensions to the CAPM. Perhaps the most important extensions are Fama and French's 2012 three-factor model (market beta, value, and size), as well as Carhart's 1997 four-factor model (market beta, value, size, and momentum). I'll discuss these and other factor models in Chapters 9, 11, and 12. Most of them focus on the cross section of equity returns; they are more appropriate for equity risk models and stock-picking strategies than for cross-asset expected returns.

The CAPM *Is* Useful

One of my finance professors used to say that "there's nothing more practical than a good theory" and then chuckle to himself. It takes a high level of nerdiness to find that funny, especially toward the end of a three-hour lecture on asset pricing. I never heard any student laugh at that one. Yet there's something profound about the statement. Peter Bernstein (2007) recognizes the issues with the CAPM, but he also points out that it has influenced how we think about indexing, how we evaluate managers, and how we separate alpha from beta. In his words, "It frames the marching orders and responsibilities involved in the whole investment process." He concludes that the "CAPM is no longer a toy or theoretical curiosity with dubious empirical credentials. It has become a centerpiece of sophisticated institutional portfolio management." It's also one of the theoretical building blocks of a popular portfolio optimization technique used to avoid counterintuitive optimal weights, called the Black-Litterman model. I'll discuss this model in Chapter 14.

For multi-asset investors, the CAPM is one tool in the return forecasting toolset. Based on a risk model, it gives us an estimate of risk-proportional expected returns, where the only risk that matters is the asset's contribution to a broadly diversified portfolio's volatility. At equilibrium, these agnostic estimates make sense, provided we use a good risk model and calibrate the risk-free rate and market risk premium carefully.

Still, like a financial law of motion, the model only works in a world without friction. In the real world, markets deviate from equilibrium, sometimes over long periods of time. The effect of central bank policy on global bond yields provides a good example. As I showed earlier, in the current environment, many central banks have pushed rates down toward zero, such that non-US bond yields are much lower than would be expected given their beta risk. Ultimately, investors should use the CAPM as a reference, a first step toward return forecasting that we can use to test our assumptions about fundamentals and valuations.

Notes

1. See Jack Treynor (1961), Bill Sharpe (1964), John Lintner (1965), and Jan Mossin (1966).
2. "Professor William Sharpe Shares Nobel Prize for Economics," gsb.stanford .edu.
3. As I finalize this book at the end of March 2020, equity markets have suffered one of their worst and fastest sell-offs in history due to the coronavirus pandemic, combined with a major oil shock. The Federal Reserve has aggressively lowered rates, and the three-month US Treasury bill is at zero. These are unusual circumstances. In this context, expected returns across asset classes should be about 1–2% lower due to lower rates, compared with those of 2018. But on the other hand, valuations are more attractive than they were back in 2018, in a way that may offset lower rates.
4. For the nine years ending March 23, 2018.
5. Robert Huebscher, "Jeremy Siegel's Predictions for 2018," Advisor Perspectives, February 5, 2018.
6. Robert Huebscher, "Jeremy Siegel Versus Robert Shiller on Equity Valuations," Advisor Perspectives, February 23, 2017. As of Q1 2018, the CAPE ratio was still relatively close to where it was when this article was

published, hovering around 30. With the CAPE at 30, a simple earnings yield calculation would imply a 3.3% real return. It's not clear how Shiller arrives at 1%, but I suspect he's using a regression between the CAPE and subsequent returns to account for the fact that the relationship is not one-to-one.

7. http://shiller.barclays.com/SM/12/en/indices/welcome.app. The average of 24 major countries, excluding the United States, as of February 28, 2018, was 20.01.
8. https://www.pimco.com/en-us/insights/economic-and-market-commentary/global-markets/asset-allocation-outlook/singles-and-doubles.
9. https://www.blackrockblog.com/blackrock-capital-markets-assumptions/.
10. https://www.aqr.com/Insights/Research/Alternative-Thinking/2018-Capital-Market-Assumptions-for-Major-Asset-Classes; https://www.northerntrust.com/documents/white-papers/asset-management/cma-five-year-outlook-2017.pdf; http://www.aon.com/attachments/human-capital-consulting/capital-market-assumptions-2017-q1.pdf; https://www.bnymellonwealth.com/assets/pdfs-strategy/thought_capital-market-return-assumptions.pdf. All forecasts are for US equities, except for Northern Trust's forecast, which is for developed markets equities. In general, non-US equities forecasts are similar, or slightly higher in some cases.
11. This yield was 1.06% as of May 12, 2020, as monetary authorities lowered rates even further to respond to the COVID-19 crisis. Using data from Bloomberg Finance L.P.
12. Using data from Bloomberg Finance L.P., on the Barclays Global Aggregate and the MSCI ACWI (total return indexes).
13. https://www.telegraph.co.uk/business/2018/01/30/qe-set-27-trillion-last-hurrah/.
14. https://www.forbes.com/sites/phildemuth/2014/07/30/meet-the-global-market-portfolio-the-optimal-portfolio-for-the-average-investor/#5956a39970d1. This comment was made in reference to Roll's critique (1977).
15. As of 2012, which is the last year in their study.
16. Windham Portfolio Advisor.
17. Again, with the exception that the market risk premium can be calibrated with valuation models, as I've shown in my example.

2
Valuation and Something About Kool-Aid

To which earnings (E) should we apply the P/E ratio?
Valuation should be based on future earnings, not current earnings.
—JPP

FOR STOCKS, THE NEXT STEP IS TO REFINE OUR EARNINGS forecasts. Then we can decompose expected returns into more detailed building blocks. When I estimated the equity market risk premium as an input to the CAPM, I showed that the simplest way to forecast equity returns based on valuation is to invert the price-to-earnings ratio. We divide 1 by the quoted P/E number, *et voilà*, we have a reasonable long-term return forecast. But in finance, especially when we try to forecast returns, nothing is ever that simple. I introduced the battle of the professors between Siegel and Shiller, two equally credible academics. The choice of which ratio to use seems to be at the center of their debate. As mentioned, Shiller uses a ratio that's adjusted for cycles and inflation (the CAPE), while Siegel uses a more current P/E ratio. Also, Shiller doesn't simply invert the ratio. Instead, he models the relationship between initial CAPE and subsequent returns, based on a regression model.

Since its publication, the CAPE approach has received a lot of attention. As many as 204 research papers have cited the original article by Campbell and Shiller (1998).[1] In a recent paper, published in May/June 2016 in the *Financial Analysts Journal*, titled "The Shiller CAPE Ratio: A New Look," even Siegel admits that "the CAPE ratio is a very powerful predictor on long-term stock returns." He shows that, based on data from 1881 to 2014, CAPE forecasts have a 60% correlation with subsequent 10-year returns (35% r-squared). Although they don't always agree with each other, industry thought leaders and leading investors Cliff Asness, founder and CIO of AQR, and Rob Arnott, chairman and CEO of Research Affiliates, have both come to the defense of the CAPE against naysayers.[2]

Nonetheless, the naysayers make some good points. Siegel (2016) argues that accounting standards have changed over time, which biases current 10-year average earnings down and produces overly pessimistic CAPE forecasts. Rob Arnott, Vitali Kalesnik, and Jim Masturzo (2018) point out that:

> Since 1996, the U.S. CAPE ratio has been above its long-term average (16.6) 96% of the time, and above 24, roughly one standard deviation above its historical norm, more than two-thirds of the time. This dislocation is long enough to make even the most ardent fans of the CAPE take pause.

Siegel shows that if you use more consistent earnings measures, you can increase the model's predictive power and reduce the pessimistic bias. But even with a more consistent earnings methodology, data from 2008–2009 may still bias 10-year earnings down. As soon as these data roll out of the trailing 10-year sample, the CAPE automatically drops (as average earnings jump), even if nothing changes in investors' expectations. For example, the CAPE's drop could occur while the one-year P/E doesn't move. This cliff effect is a function of which 10-year smoothing methodology we choose. For that matter, 10 is a nice round number, but why not use a different window? As Asness (2012) puts it: "Ten years is, of course, arbitrary. You would be hard-pressed to find a theoretical argument favoring it over, say, nine or 12 years." The choice of time window matters because it drives significant differences in return forecasts.

Jeremy Grantham, founder and chief investment officer of GMO, also argues that recent earnings growth is sustainable, a regime change of sorts, due to "increased monopoly, political, and brand power."[3] Grantham says, "This time is different." He explains that if we believe recent earnings growth will continue for the next 10 years, we also believe the CAPE isn't as bearish a signal as it currently looks. This mental adjustment is equivalent to using a P/E based on recent earnings. The trailing 12-month P/E is still high, but it's not as extreme as the CAPE. Ultimately, we must keep in mind that the CAPE is not perfect, and there are decades in history during which it failed as a predictor of forward returns. The next decade could be one of these outliers.

I don't find that argument particularly convincing. My colleague David Giroux, portfolio manager and CIO at T. Rowe Price and one of the most talented investors I've ever worked with, recently pointed out in an internal memo (Q1 2018) that recent earnings on the S&P 500 have been inflated by a recovery in the energy sector and a weak US dollar, two factors that may not prevail going forward.

Moreover, I spent five years at PIMCO, where I drank the Kool-Aid of the new normal/new neutral narrative—a pessimistic view of the future that's typical of bond managers. If the economy continues to grow at a sluggish 2–3% rate due to long-term, persistent trends such as high levels of global debt (close to an all-time high at more than 300% of global GDP),[4] demographics (percentage of the world population age 65 and over to double by 2050),[5] and technology disruption (automation could replace 800 million jobs by 2030),[6] how can earnings continue to grow in the 10–15% range, especially when profit margins are already high? It's theoretically possible, but unlikely. I suppose the new normal Kool-Aid is not yet completely out of my system.

Then there's the relative valuation between stocks and bonds. Relative to global bond yields, stocks are much cheaper than they appear on the basis of the CAPE alone. Should we expect rates to remain low by historical standards for the next 10 years? Lower growth for longer (new normal) and lower volatility in macroeconomic variables such as GDP growth and inflation should, at least theoretically, lead to lower rates for longer. If so, the CAPE could remain elevated. It's simple math: lower discount rates mean higher valuations. But there's no doubt that unwinding global monetary stimulus poses risks (and even more risks in a post-COVID-19 world). Investors have priced markets for a perfect, beautiful landing. In an Asset Allocation Committee meeting in 2018, we discussed the risk of an inflation shock in the context of our tactical positions, when I asked, "Since when is 2% or even 3% inflation 'bad'?" One of our superstar investors responded wisely, "It's bad when the market doesn't expect it."

If we put it all together, the CAPE gives us a back-of-the-envelope signal that we shouldn't ignore, and it's on the pessimistic side. Despite its good track record, the CAPE doesn't tell the whole story. Other simple ratio-based forecasts, such as Siegel's, give more optimistic numbers. To improve our forecasts, we must get more specific about the components of our forward-looking views. What do we expect to receive as dividends? What's our earnings growth forecast? Do we expect significant valuation changes? To answer these questions, we must throw away our envelope and fire up a spreadsheet.

The Simplest Valuation-Based Model: Building Blocks

The building block model decomposes equity returns into three components: income, growth, and valuation change. I'm partial to it because my first research project in the industry was to backtest it on data for more than 20 countries. In this, I had help from Mark Kritzman, president and CEO of Windham Capital Management and senior partner at State Street Associates.

At the onset of the project, he handed me a 1984 paper by Jarrod Wilcox, titled "The P/B-ROE Valuation Model." This paper explains the theory behind the building block model. Wilcox first states that

Realized return = dividend yield + price change

Then, he splits the "price change" term into "growth" and "valuation change," such that

Realized return = dividend yield + growth + valuation change

For "growth," he uses growth in book value. For the "valuation change" term, he calculates the change in the price-to-book ratio.

Nowadays, investors use several variations of this model. For example, there are versions that use the P/E ratio, as well as different definitions for growth, such as growth in earnings, GDP, etc. There are many ways to forecast each of the components. In fact, this building block model has become a standard approach across the industry. Think of it as the valuation-focused equivalent of the CAPM: it's as simple as it gets, and it's ubiquitous. But as with the CAPM, the devil is in the details.

Wilcox points out that if you add a small (negligible) cross-term, you can perfectly explain realized returns. As he puts it, "The relationship is not causal; it is an inevitable consequence of the algebra." In other words, it's an accounting identity, just like $1 + 1 = 2$. In contrast, with the CAPM, we can't even explain realized return. Stocks (or asset classes) with high betas can underperform stocks with low betas over very long periods of time, even when we calculate the betas in-sample (Fama and French, 2004). With the building block model, we can explain 100% of past returns. And we can specify the time horizon over which we decompose realized or expected returns—another advantage of this model over the CAPM.

Once we understand how past returns were divided among income, growth, and valuation change, we can forecast each of these components.

For income, there's good news. Even though the price component of dividend yield is quite unpredictable, companies tend to adjust their payout ratio to smooth dividend yields over time. (Dividend yield = dividend/price, and the payout ratio is the percentage of earnings paid out as dividends.) For the S&P 500, based on data going back to the 1970s, my estimate of the correlation between one year's dividend yield and the following year's is 92%.[7] In a world where markets are reasonably efficient, that's a remarkably high level of predictability.

Corporate finance fundamentals give us the "sustainable growth rate," defined as the return on equity (ROE) multiplied by the retention rate (the percentage of earnings that's not paid out as dividends).[8] My estimate of the year-over-year predictability/autocorrelation in the S&P 500's sustainable growth rate is 48%, based on data going back to the 1990s.[9] It's less persistent than the dividend yield, but it's still quite predictable relative to price changes, for example. Also, the idea is to estimate a long-term, stable growth rate rather than focus on year-over-year variations.

This definition of sustainable growth is as basic as it gets. CFA charterholders will remember it as an important part of the program. It's a good building block to forecast returns. Theory says that a company's ability to grow its dividends depends on how well it can generate earnings for a given set of resources (book value), as well as how much of these earnings are reinvested in the company, presumably to finance growth projects. It's finance 101, and again I suppose there's nothing more practical than a good theory. In my backtests, when I replaced the economic growth model estimates with the sustainable growth rate for each country, the strategy's performance jumped significantly.

I was young, starting my career, and I was quite excited to see the strategy beat the pants off the MSCI World Index, with very limited look-ahead bias. (In hindsight, exceptional backtest performance is never that exceptional. A client once told me that he had never seen a backtest that didn't work. He added that the only people who can consistently generate Sharpe ratios of 3.0 or above were quants running backtests, plus Bernie Madoff. Even without explicit look-ahead bias, researchers benefit from years of published research on what works and what doesn't, which is itself an implicit look-ahead bias.)

The last and hardest building block to forecast is valuation change. Because yearly price changes drive changes in price-to-earnings (or price-to-cash-flows, or price-to-book) ratios, it's not surprising that valuation changes aren't correlated from one year to the next. Based on quarterly data going back to 1990, the year-over-year predictability/autocorrelation in the S&P 500's price-to-earnings ratio is −3%, and it's statistically indistinguishable from zero.[10] Last year's change in P/E tells us nothing about next year's change in P/E.

In any given year, valuation changes can dominate realized returns. Based on calendar-year data from 1990 to 2016, I get a correlation of 75% between total returns for the S&P 500 and concurrent changes in P/E ratio.[11] However, over the long run, there's a powerful mean-reversion effect in valuation levels. Hence, a fair assumption is that valuation changes average out to zero over time. The problem is that it's hard to model the speed of mean reversion, and the path is never smooth. Most investors assume that current levels will revert to their long-term mean over five to ten years. The math is straightforward: First, you calculate the difference between current valuation (for example, the current P/E) and its long-term average. Second, you divide this valuation spread by the number of years you think it will take to get back to the average. *Voilà*, you have your valuation change forecast. Unfortunately, over short time periods, these forecasts aren't very accurate. But there are ways to improve the forecast.

For my project, I compared the effectiveness of two valuation change models: one that assumed mean reversion and another that used proprietary data on institutional investor flows. I set up the flow-based model as a cross-sectional regression. My goal was to explain a country's stock market performance relative to that of other markets, rather than predict each country's valuation changes over time (i.e., a time series regression). It sounds like a technical nuance, but the difference between cross-sectional and time series forecasts is important.

The intuition for this cross-sectional approach was that if a country receives significant inflows from institutional investors, its valuation level should increase more than that of other countries, especially those with significant outflows. We made the implicit assumption that institutional investor flows were persistent, i.e., that they move incrementally, in part due to their size— like supertankers rather than speedboats. Harvard professor Ken Froot and several coauthors over the years have published serious academic research on these data. In a 2001 paper titled "The Portfolio Flows of International Investors," Ken, Paul O'Connell, and Mark Seasholes concluded that "the flows are strongly persistent."

In contrast with this academic research, my model was not as statistically robust. A key advantage of my approach was that it was simple. Simple is good. I focused on valuation changes as opposed to total returns. I assumed that flows and year-over-year valuation changes were mostly driven by sentiment, so I removed long-run fundamentals (income and growth) from total returns and focused on what I called "transitory valuation spreads."

To do so, I measured a beta between flows and subsequent valuation changes across countries. Then I applied this beta to recent flows. It worked very well: the first time I ran the backtest with the full forecast of income, growth, and flow-based valuation change, the results improved drastically. They got even better when I introduced the ROE component for growth. When I first saw these results, I stood up at my desk and danced like a prospector who's just struck oil.

Mark set up the project as a horse race between models. First, he asked me to run a backtest without *any* return forecast. To run a backtest without return forecasts, I set up the optimizer to solve for the risk-minimizing weights every month. Surprisingly, this approach outperformed the benchmark. It seemed that portfolio optimization could add value without *any* information about forward returns. So much for the GIGO critique. My risk-minimizing approach relied on five-year historical volatilities and correlations as risk forecasts, which are fairly "naïve" inputs. These results proved that during the 1980s and 1990s, the MSCI World was a very inefficient benchmark (from the perspective of its underlying country weights). It was an easy opponent to beat—a slow horse.

Then results improved further when I added forecasts for income and growth. Last, as mentioned, the valuation change forecast boosted performance meaningfully. For this component, I tested the flow-based approach against a model that assumed mean reversion in valuation spreads. Both approaches performed well, but the flow-based forecast won. Our final recommendation was to use an approach that combined everything: a risk component (volatilities and correlations) and the forecasts for income, growth, and valuation change. Each building block was expected to add value incrementally. This example fits well within the framework I advocate throughout this book: for a complete asset allocation approach, each building block— ideas, processes, investment views, inputs, models—must build on the others. Otherwise, simple is better. No need to unnecessarily complicate our process.

Over the next several years, the approach became a commercial success. One European institutional client invested more than $2 billion in the strategy. The client earned positive alpha over several years, before the client decided to convert to a passive approach due to personnel turnover on its side.

My strategy was tactical, as it rebalanced monthly. But the building block approach can be applied to longer horizons. It provides a good reality check on CAPM expected returns. In Table 2.1, I show long-run building block expected returns for the same equity asset classes we used in Chapter 1 for the CAPM.[12] I've added the earlier CAPM numbers for comparison.

TABLE 2.1   Building Block Model Expected Returns*

	Dividend Yield	Growth	Valuation Change	Expected Return	CAPM
US Stocks					
Large cap	1.9%	6.6%	−1.5%	**7.1%**	4.3%
Small cap	1.3%	9.1%	−2.3%	**8.2%**	3.9%
Growth	1.3%	14.2%	−6.5%	**9.1%**	4.5%
Value	2.5%	4.3%	0.5%	**7.4%**	4.1%
Non-US Stocks					
Large cap	3.1%	5.5%	2.8%	**11.5%**	5.2%
Small cap	2.4%	5.2%	−0.3%	**7.2%**	4.9%
Growth	2.2%	9.3%	1.4%	**12.9%**	5.3%
Value	4.1%	3.7%	3.7%	**11.7%**	5.2%
Emerging Markets Stocks	2.4%	7.0%	−2.1%	**7.3%**	6.4%

*Dividend yields are trailing 12-month numbers; growth numbers are the index-level return on equity multiplied by 1 minus the payout ratio (with the exception of US small caps, where I used Bloomberg estimated long-term growth because ROE numbers are biased down, due to negative earners and other structural issues); and valuation changes are −1/5 of the spread between the current price-to-book ratio and its long-term average (January 1995 to April 2018).

As usual with any forecasted returns, we must address data issues, caveats, and points of debate. Compared with our CAPM estimates, and certainly Shiller's pessimistic forecast for the US stock market, these numbers are very high. On the other hand, with 7.1% expected return for US large caps, they seem in line with Siegel's forecast. Dividend yields are close to an all-time high relative to rates, which partially explains why these numbers are higher than our CAPM estimates. (As I've shown, CAPM estimates anchor around the level of interest rates.) Also, the sustainable growth rate approach generates optimistic growth forecasts because earnings have been very high recently ("peak earnings") due to a recovery in the energy sector, sustained and coordinated economic growth, monetary stimulus, and fiscal stimulus in the United States.

Last, the pandemic and economic crisis of 2020 will require us to reassess dividend yields, sustainable growth, and valuation change estimates. As I finalize this book, equities have just crashed, which means that each of these components could be higher, although the jury is still out on the potential hit to companies' long-term fundamentals.

Regarding dividend yields, it's common practice to add share buybacks to estimate "total payouts." Buybacks are an important building block for forecasting returns. When companies buy their own stock, existing shareholders get a larger percentage claim on earnings, which leads to share price appreciation. Hence, with buybacks, companies are essentially returning cash to existing shareholders, almost like a dividend.

But there's a debate about how to estimate the effect of share buybacks on expected returns. My view is that share buybacks matter, but their contribution to returns is overrated. For example, how should we adjust for IPOs and new share issuances? If we do make these adjustments, then net buybacks have very little impact. But also, various scholars have different opinions about whether net buybacks should be calculated at the total market level or at the index level. When calculated at the index level, the dilution effect is much less pronounced on existing shareholders. This intellectual boxing match has been interesting to follow. Recently, the debate has intensified in the "Letters to the Editor" section of the *Financial Analysts Journal* (arguably its most entertaining section).

In favor of a negative buyback effect, William Bernstein and Rob Arnott argue that share issuances and IPOs have consistently outpaced buybacks. In a 2003 paper titled "Earnings Growth: The Two Percent Dilution," they estimate that the expected return adjustment for *net* buybacks should be –2%. They take a clear stance against the idea that the net buyback yield is positive:

"The vast majority of the institutional investing community has believed these untruths (that buyback yield is positive) and has acted accordingly. Whether these tales are lies or merely errors, our implied indictment of these misconceptions is a serious one—demanding data."

In favor of a positive buyback effect, Philip Straehl and Roger Ibbotson's 2017 paper "The Long-Run Drivers of Stock Returns: Total Payouts and the Real Economy" estimates that the net buyback yield has been +1.48% from 1970 to 2014—a significant difference from Bernstein and Arnott's −2% estimate.

In response to Straehl and Ibbotson's paper, Arnott and Bernstein (2018) refer to an article published in 2015 by Chris Brightman, Vitali Kalesnik, and Mark Clements (Arnott's colleagues at Research Affiliates) and double down on their position:

In 2014, buybacks totaled $696 billion, or 2.9% of starting market value. This is a stupendous buyback yield. Yet the [total stock market] CRSP 1–10 Index rose by 1.8% less than its market capitalization. Did 4.7% of stock market return simply go missing? No. It turns out that $1.2 trillion in new share issuance occurred—and was largely unnoticed by those tallying buybacks—in a single year, a year with supposedly blockbuster buybacks.

These disagreements come down to differences in methodologies, and there is no industry consensus on how to resolve the question. As mentioned, my view is that buyback yield estimates are often too high because they don't account for harder-to-measure dilution effects. Antti Ilmanen, a practitioner I mentioned in Chapter 1, comments that "the debate on whether and how to include buybacks will not end soon." If no related adjustment is made to the expected growth term, he recommends adding +0.5% to +1.0% for buybacks net of dilution.[13] BlackRock uses +0.5% for US stocks and −1.0% for non-US stocks.[14] J.P. Morgan uses +0.3% for US stocks.[15] AQR's estimates vary from −1.4 to 0.1% across regions. Let's keep it simple and assume that buybacks will roughly equal share issuances plus or minus some noise.

In addition to the income component, this debate has implications for another one of our building blocks: our growth estimates. As shown in Table 2.1, in the current environment, ROE-based estimates appear optimistic due to elevated earnings. A more common approach to estimate the growth term—at least for the market as a whole—is to assume that earnings will grow at the same pace as the economy. Corporate profit margins can't grow forever. It doesn't make sense to assume that over the long run, the corporate slice of the pie (versus labor) can grow faster than the pie itself. But on a *per share basis*, if we expect a dilution effect, we must adjust earnings or dividend growth estimates down (more shareholder mouths to feed), while if we expect net positive buybacks, we should adjust them up (fewer shareholder mouths to feed).

One of the issues is that per capita GDP also depends on population growth. And there are other points of debate: what the impact is of productivity growth, whether debt and leverage should be considered, and if new capital is indeed dilutive, as it is used to purchase new assets that benefit existing shareholders. Let's extricate ourselves from this technical quicksand, and let's simply state that, from a practical perspective, if we make an adjustment to the growth term, we should not double-count net buybacks in the yield term. We should adjust one or the other.

In the absence of a strong view on margins, it's common practice to assume that total market earnings will grow at the same rate as GDP.[16] Currently, the IMF forecasts world GDP to grow around 3.5–4% per year for the next five years (in real terms).[17] This "new normal" growth rate, when combined with the income and valuation change components, gets us closer to our earlier CAPM estimates.

While expected GDP growth is available at the country level, it doesn't apply directly to equity sectors or style/size sub–asset classes (large caps, small caps, value, and growth). However, it provides a reality check on the ROE-based numbers. If we assume a very long horizon, GDP growth puts an upper-bound on our estimates. Moreover, we can use regression analysis between GDP growth and sector-level earnings to build more granular, sector-level forecasts. In practice, while they don't necessarily run regressions, fundamental analysts intuitively account for the broad economic environment when they forecast company-level earnings. These forecasts can then be aggregated at the sector and asset class levels for use by multi-asset investors.

Earnings Forecasts and the Role of Fundamental Analysis

There's an elephant in the room of this debate around how to best estimate our "growth" building block. Ultimately, to forecast earnings growth, we need fundamental analysis. Yet clients and novice quants often look for formulaic approaches, because there's comfort in replicable methodologies. Sovereign wealth funds, for example, often ask asset managers for formulaic insights and strategies. In exchange for large mandates, they want the asset manager's intellectual property. They'll even send trainees to work in the asset manager's offices for weeks. Their goal is to apply these approaches to the assets they manage in-house. (But if your process is to rely on the judgment of experienced analysts and portfolio managers, the intellectual property transfer idea becomes impractical unless the Sovereign Wealth Fund hires your portfolio managers.)

My view is that the ROE-based sustainable growth rate, calculated from public, precooked, index-level data, is as good as any other formulaic approach. But there's no magic formula that has been shown to consistently generate forecasts that would be more accurate than consensus.

My team at T. Rowe Price recently started a survey-based process to generate capital markets assumptions across asset classes. It's a hybrid approach that marries forward-looking investment judgment with some quantitative structure. We ask portfolio managers to forecast various components of returns, based on the building block model. To make it intuitive, we ask them to forecast annualized earnings growth for the next five years. Most of these portfolio managers are bottom-up stock pickers, but they have a good sense of what to expect for their sector. They talk to CEOs, comb through company balance sheets and income statements, and stay on top of important trends in technology, labor costs, consumer demand, etc. Some of them may use a formal decomposition for earnings growth that starts with a forecast of sales (perhaps tied to GDP growth), adjusts for margins (which tend to mean-revert over time), and so on. Others may express a gut feeling, which, given their investment experience and expertise, is often better than any quantitative approach we could think of.

In the same survey, we ask them to forecast the level of the P/E ratio in five years. Most quants probably look at this approach the way scientists look at astrology. (But implicitly, our fundamental investors account for historical patterns such as mean reversion. Such historical patterns are also used to build model-based, quantitative forecasts. Hence, fundamental and quantitative approaches aren't as different as most people think.)

As an aside, for those more focused on formulas, I recently set up a horse race between the following ratios: price to earnings (P/E), price to book (P/B), and price to cash flow (P/CF). I wanted to know which of these valuation measures would produce the highest correlation with subsequent valuation changes, which I defined as

Valuation change = realized return – (income + growth)

This is the same "transitory valuation spread" definition we used in the building block model we discussed earlier. Recall that we forecast the income and growth components at the beginning of the period. If I look at the current level of P/E, P/B, or P/CF, which is most predictive of the difference between realized returns and my initial income and growth forecasts?

I focused on one-year forecasts. I had to scrub the data for outliers, especially P/E ratios and payouts around the 2000 and 2008 sell-offs, and adjust small caps data due to negative earnings, but the results were clear: P/CF won. Its average correlation with subsequent valuation changes was over 10% stronger than for the second-best ratio (P/B), and it won across seven out of nine asset classes (exceptions were small caps and non-US growth stocks).[18] Cash flows are harder to "game," or manipulate, than earnings and book values, and they're more comparable across asset classes.

In our survey process, we combine responses into the building block model, and we make the necessary adjustments for expected inflation. To finalize the forecasts, a committee of multi-asset investors as well as our group CIO will review and adjust the results. We look at the dispersion in views, evaluate consistency across asset classes, and make top-down adjustments as necessary.

This process imposes structure on how we express investment views. In the end, to harness fundamental analysis sometimes seems more ad hoc than historical analysis, but it is the key building block to forecast return. Interestingly, while stock return forecasts require a heavy dose of judgment, bond return forecasts are bounded by fairly precise mathematical guardrails.

Back to Bonds

As I mentioned in Chapter 1, it's easier to forecast returns for bonds than for stocks. For most fixed income asset classes, if your time horizon is long enough (3–10 years), current yield to maturity is a reasonably accurate predictor of future return. Recently, my colleagues Justin Harvey and Aaron Stonacek (2018) tested this assertion across time horizons for several fixed income asset classes. They looked at the correlation between initial yield to worst and subsequent returns, as a function of the ratio of

Time elapsed/starting duration

A ratio of 1.0 means that time elapsed is exactly equal to the initial duration. Currently, the Bloomberg Barclays U.S. Aggregate has a duration of 6.34,[19] so a 1.0 implies a horizon of 6.34 years. In their analysis, which goes back to 1976, Harvey and Stonacek find that the correlation between initial yield and subsequent return is above 80% for ratios of 0.5 to 2.0 (2.0 is the maximum ratio they tested). Initial yield reaches maximum predictability (at 97% correlation) at 1.08 times duration, and it remains quite high (above 95%) for longer horizons. Importantly, the authors show that *predictability is equally strong whether rates are rising or falling.*

They find similar (albeit slightly weaker) results for international hedged bonds. But for other asset classes, initial yield is not as predictive. Correlation for high-yield bonds peaks at 78% at 0.98 duration and hovers around 70–75% for the 1.0 to 2.0 range. For emerging markets bonds, it peaks at 89% at 1.9 duration. For unhedged international bonds, correlation peaks at 57% at 0.5 duration (here the effect of currency risk muddies the water).

Harvey and Stonacek conclude that "current yields are most highly correlated with future returns for higher-quality and hedged bond indexes.

As these indexes follow stricter maturity, duration, and quality rules, they present a more stable risk/return profile than unhedged and lower quality indexes."

For equity asset classes, even a 57% correlation between a simple, publicly available indicator and subsequent returns would be remarkable. Yet some of the fiercest debates I've witnessed on expected returns have been between bond quants, on how to account for minute details that may or may not improve the forecast. I've seen normally shy and introverted colleagues get into near-religious debates on how to forecast carry, roll down, defaults, and other components of total return, down to the basis point.

The important question is this: Can we improve on initial yield as the predictor of bond returns? Can we improve this forecast, for example, if we have a view on the direction of yields? If we want to keep it simple, over a finite horizon of one year, a good starting point to proxy return is as follows:

Return = initial yield − initial duration × change in yield

We earn the carry (yield) plus or minus the change in price (− duration × change in yield). Ilmanen (2012) uses a similar proxy as a building block to introduce various ways to estimate the bond risk premium.

The in-sample fit for this simple model is quite good. Based on rolling annual data from March 1990 to June 2018, my estimate of the correlation between realized returns for the Bloomberg Barclays U.S. Aggregate and this proxy is 97%.[20] This result doesn't indicate that the model provides a good *forecast*, because I used realized changes in yields. It merely shows that the "approximation" error for *realized* returns is very low. But if I extend the horizon to five years, the fit degrades to 94% correlation. One of the issues is that initial yield becomes a less accurate representation of carry over longer horizons.

For the survey that my team uses to build capital markets assumptions, we have expanded this simple decomposition into a model that increases the in-sample fit from 94% to 96% and allows us to avoid large deviations between estimated and realized returns in volatile markets:

Return = average yield + roll down + interest rate duration × change in yield + spread duration × change in spread where:

> Average yield = (yield in 5 years per survey – current yield)/2
> Roll down = duration × current slope (9 – 10-year yield)
> Change in yield = (yield in 5 years per survey – current yield)/5
> Change in spread = (spread in 5 years per survey – current spread)/5

We use two definitions of duration: interest rate duration measures the sensitivity of the bond portfolio's return to changes in the risk-free interest rate, and spread duration measures its sensitivity to changes in spread. (We'll review these measures in more detail when we discuss factors in Chapters 11 and 12.) For our five-year forecasts, average yield, change in yield, and change in spread incorporate views from the survey on where respondents think yields and spreads will be five years from now.

There are many ways to further expand these components, but in our model, average yield and roll down refer to total yield to maturity and combine the risk-free rate and spread components. We assume that we'll earn the average yield over the period. As rates rise, the investor reinvests coupons and principals at higher yields, and vice versa when rates decline. Principal gets reinvested when maturity is reached, as well as within the investment horizon to maintain duration and/or earn the roll down.

The roll down component is measured based on the steepness of the curve, and we assume a one-year holding period. If the yield curve slopes upward (as it does most of the time), and nothing else changes (the level of yields remains constant, defaults remain constant, etc.), a bond will appreciate in price over time. The intuition is as follows: One year from now, the bond will be one year closer to maturity. Since a bond with shorter maturity is discounted at a lower rate, its price will go up.

We divide changes in yield and spread by 5 to annualize. Then we multiply these annual changes by their respective durations to estimate annual price changes. Overall, the fixed income return decomposition that we use in our survey makes it obvious that price changes and income (yield/carry) work in opposite directions. This "counterweight" effect explains why at longer time horizons, as mentioned, the path of rates matters a lot less than most investors think. As rates rise, we earn more carry over time (per the average

yield component), which is offset by the change in price (the duration ×
change in yield component). Similarly, if rates decline, we earn less carry,
but we gain on price. The same counterweight effect works for the spread
components of return.

Notes

1. I refer to Shiller's participation in this debate, but the model itself was
   first described in a paper he coauthored with John Campbell. (Shiller and
   Campbell, 1998). For some reason, Shiller's name is much more associated
   with the CAPE than is Campbell's. Scopus compiled the 204 citations for
   this paper, http://www.elsevier.com/solutions/scopus.
2. https://www.researchaffiliates.com/en_us/publications/articles/645-cape-fear
   -why-cape-naysayers-are-wrong.html; https://www.aqr.com/Insights/
   Research/White-Papers/An-Old-Friend-The-Stock-Markets-Shiller-PE.
3. http://fortune.com/2018/01/16/why-wall-street-is-ignoring-cape-fear/.
4. https://www.bloomberg.com/news/articles/2018-04-10/global-debt-jumped
   -to-record-237-trillion-last-year.
5. https://www.nih.gov/news-events/news-releases/worlds-older-popula-
   tion-grows-dramatically.
6. https://www.mckinsey.com/global-themes/future-of-organizations-and-work/
   what-the-future-of-work-will-mean-for-jobs-skills-and-wages.
7. Based on quarterly data from Bloomberg Finance L.P. for the time period
   December 31, 1970 to March 31, 2018. Data field is Dvd 12M Yld. I compare current dividend yield (current price divided by dividends over the *next*
   year) with the same measure a year later. To do so, first I make an adjustment
   to the price component (I subtract the last 12 months of price appreciation),
   because the unadjusted data give me current price divided by dividends over
   the previous year. This adjustment is a subtlety; it doesn't change the result
   meaningfully. My data sample includes 182 rolling 4-quarter periods.
8. See Robert C. Higgins (2016).
9. Based on quarterly data from Bloomberg Finance L.P. for the time period
   March 30, 1990, to March 31, 2018. The time period was selected based on
   data availability. Data fields are DVD_PAYOUT_RATIO and RETURN_
   COM_EQY.
10. Based on quarterly data from Bloomberg Finance L.P. for the time period
    March 30, 1990 to March 31, 2018. The time period was selected based on
    data availability. Data field is BEst_PE.
11. Bloomberg Finance L.P., using SPXT and Best_PE in the historical regression
    analysis tool.
12. Data for the building block method are as of April 30, 2018. The list of
    underlying indexes is provided in Table 1.1. Sources are Bloomberg Finance
    L.P. and my own calculations. Bloomberg Finance L.P. data fields: EQY_
    DVD_YLD_12M, RETURN_COM_EQY, DVD_PAYOUT_RATIO,

PX_TO_BOOK_RATIO, and BEST_LTG_EPS for US small cap growth estimates.
13. Expected returns on major asset classes.
14. https://www.blackrock.com/institutions/en-us/insights/portfolio-design/capital-market-assumptions.
15. https://am.jpmorgan.com/gi/getdoc/1383498247596.
16. See, for example, Blackrock (https://www.blackrock.com/institutions/en-us/insights/portfolio-design/capital-market-assumptions) and BNY Mellon (https://www.bnymellonwealth.com/assets/pdfs-strategy/thought_capital-market-return-assumptions.pdf).
17. http://www.imf.org.
18. Monthly data from January 31, 1996 to April 30, 2018. *Source:* Bloomberg Finance L.P. Data fields used: EQY_DVD_YLD_12M, RETURN_COM_EQY, DVD_PAYOUT_RATIO, PX_TO_BOOK_RATIO, INDX_ADJ_POSITIVE_PE, PX_TO_CASH_FLOW. Asset classes used were the same equity asset classes as in the previous tables.
19. Bloomberg Finance L.P. As of March 31, 2018.
20. Quarterly data from Bloomberg Finance L.P., using total return, yield to worst, and option-adjusted duration.

3

Shorter-Term Valuation Signals and Something About Coffee and Egg Yolks

Financial analysis relies mostly on historical data. But our goal is to make decisions that will have repercussions in the future.
—JPP

SO FAR, WE'VE FOCUSED ON RELATIVELY LONG-TERM return forecasts, or "capital markets assumptions." These types of forecasts are useful for *strategic* asset allocation. Also, we saw that we can apply the equity building block model at shorter horizons, as in the equity country allocation model we discussed.

Let us now focus on shorter-term return forecasts. What are the most relevant predictive factors of returns for *tactical* asset allocation (TAA)? There are many macroeconomic, fundamental, and valuation signals that we can use.

The key is to build a process that marries unbiased, quantitative analysis with judgment and investment experience. We must test which variables have the best forecasting power historically and put the results in the context of the current environment.

How the Tactical Process Works in Practice

To illustrate, I refer to our TAA process in the Global Multi-Asset Division at T. Rowe Price. My goal is not to advertise, but I believe in our approach. I don't think our process is perfect (we always try to improve), and many TAA investors have been as successful as us (some more successful) with different approaches.

I prefer to focus on our process, because too many academics and practitioners explain how to forecast returns or build TAA strategies with sophisticated statistical studies and backtests, yet barely account for real-world, practical considerations. For example, the editors of the *Financial Analysts Journal* now reject any empirical study that doesn't include transaction costs. The paper is not deemed worth the referees' time—it goes straight back to the author(s) with a request to add transaction costs.

In our case, we apply this process to tactically manage asset class exposures on more than $250 billion in assets. As practitioners, we sometimes sacrifice "rigor" for simplicity and transparency. We don't want to overfit historical data, and we obsess over whether factor models, backtests, and other useful statistical analyses are relevant *given the current environment and going forward.*

At its core, our TAA approach is discretionary—it's not systematic, rules-based, or "quant."[1] Investment judgment is key. But we rely on a wide range of quantitative inputs to frame our discussions, and our decision-making process is consistent over time. Again, I'm biased, but I believe our Asset Allocation Committee marries fundamental and quantitative investment management in a "best of both worlds" way.

There are 13 committee members from across T. Rowe's three investment divisions: the Equity, Fixed Income, and Global Multi-Asset Divisions. [Rob Sharps, T. Rowe's head of investments and group CIO (my boss), and I are the only two members who are not currently full-time portfolio managers, although Rob was a very successful growth equity portfolio manager before his current role. Rob cochairs the committee with Charles Shriver, portfolio manager of our Target Allocation Strategies. Charles has over 20 years of experience as a multi-asset portfolio manager and has a stellar track record.]

Our Asset Allocation Committee focuses on TAA, and nothing else. All other aspects of our business are governed by our Steering Committee, which I chair. The Steering Committee appoints members of the Asset Allocation Committee. I emphasize these details of our two-committee governance process because in my view, it's important for investment decisions to be made independently of issues such as product design, people management, marketing, business strategy, etc. This structure means that when we discuss TAA, we don't get bogged down with anything else that may be a waste of time for investors from other divisions. Also, it means that while I'm head of our division, I don't own our tactical investment decisions. I'm simply a member of the TAA committee. The cochairs own our TAA decisions, so we do not vote, but it's a collaborative process.

We meet monthly, and our time horizon is 6 to 18 months. We implement tactical changes almost every month, but rarely across all asset classes. We tend to move our portfolios incrementally, as we build overweight and underweight positions over time. The crux of our approach is to take advantage of relative valuation opportunities. We look for extreme valuation dislocations, and we like to lean against the wind—we overweight asset classes when they're cheap, and we underweight asset classes when they're expensive.

Importantly, we trade everything on a relative basis, and we almost always discuss asset class pairs. Our discussions often start with stocks versus bonds, or, broadly speaking, whether we want to position the portfolios "risk-on," in which case we add to risk assets (stocks, high-yield bonds, etc.), or "risk-off," in which case we add to more defensive asset classes (bonds, cash, etc.). Then we look for relative value opportunities at a more granular level. For example, we often ask: Are value stocks cheap relative to growth stocks? What about small versus large? Are European stocks cheap relative to US stocks? Do we like high-yield bonds relative to emerging markets bonds?

While valuation is the main driver for our decisions, we account for macro factors (growth, inflation, central bank policy, geopolitical factors, etc.), index-level fundamentals (sales, earnings, margins, leverage, etc.), and technicals (sentiment, positioning, flows, momentum, etc.). Before each meeting, every committee member pores through an up-to-date book of over 180 pages, full of all types of relevant data, return signals, and risk analytics. (I'll discuss risk models and risk management at length in Part Two of this book.) Nonvaluation factors are used to confirm our valuation-based assessment. For example, if an asset class is cheap and other factors are positive, then our conviction is higher.

To illustrate, in early 2017, we noticed that US small caps were getting quite cheap relative to large caps. Their valuation relative to large caps was in the bottom 20%, based on data from the last 15 years and across several valuation ratios. At the same time, we thought the USD was cheap and may begin to appreciate, which tends to favor small caps over large caps; momentum was positive; M&A activity was likely to pick up in the asset class; earnings expectations were getting better; and politics were leaning toward protectionism and trade issues. It was one of those cases when the valuation, macro, fundamentals, and technical stars align. So we incrementally started to build an overweight small caps position. We continued to monitor the relevant factors, and over the next few months we built an overweight position relative to our long-term strategic allocation, which paid off.

Only in some *rare* cases, nonvaluation factors may drive our decision, such that we go long an asset class even though it looks expensive or short an asset class even if it looks cheap. For example, from a secular perspective ("secular": a wonky way to say "long term" that sounds good on Bloomberg TV), we like US growth stocks, as companies such as Facebook, Apple, Netflix, and Google can make money even when the economy is sluggish. Hence, at times we overweight growth stocks even when they're not particularly cheap relative to value stocks.

Our process illustrates how, in practice, many (perhaps most) multi-asset investors don't forecast shorter-term returns explicitly. Rather, they evaluate a variety of factors, and they scale positions in a risk-aware framework. A return forecast doesn't have to be a precise number with three decimals that goes into an optimizer. In our case, as I mentioned, we rely heavily on relative valuation. Over time, there's evidence that to "buy low and sell high," from a valuation perspective, pays off across asset classes. There's also evidence that valuation works particularly well when momentum agrees. Hence, in addition to "buy low and sell high," there's something to be said for another finance bumper-sticker adage: "The trend is your friend." (See, for example, Asness, Moskowitz, and Pedersen, 2013. We'll discuss the combination of value and momentum in more detail in Chapter 12.)

Also, valuation tends to work better at relatively long horizons. Hence our Asset Allocation Committee's process is slower and more incremental than those of other, more tactical investors, or "macro-gunslingers." Our marketing department recently released a short video that shows a powerful analogy for our TAA process. In the video, an acrobat jumps about 15 feet in the air, lands on a flexible bar held by two acolytes, and rebounds again 15 feet in the air, over and over again.

A voice asks: "What makes a performance beautiful? . . . . The power lies in a series of dynamic adjustments."

The camera zooms in on the acrobat and shows how she continually adjusts angles and balances movements and countermovements. These adjustments aren't necessarily large.

The narrator continues: "The smallest tilt. The slightest shuffle."

But those moves are well-timed and skillful. There's no need for sudden and drastic moves, which could wreck the performance. This analogy represents our process well, as we often build positions over time. To take advantage of a relative valuation opportunity, we almost always move our portfolios by increments. And we're not required to change all our positions every month. In some rare cases, we'll even decide that we're comfortable with our current overweight and underweight positions and not make any change.

After each meeting, I send my notes to an email distribution list of over a hundred investors throughout the firm. To give a window into our process, here is a note ("Nothing") I sent around in late July 2018, after we decided not to make any changes to our positions. Notice how we rely on a wide range of signals, how we incorporate our views into the process, and how we focus on relative valuations. For our TAA decisions to be well-timed (to deliver a *beautiful performance*), we need a lot of building blocks for our process, each of which must be additive to the others.

"Nothing"

At the end of our Asset Allocation Committee meeting last Friday, as we were discussing our tactical decisions, I turned to Charles Shriver, our cochair, and asked:

"So . . . nothing?"

Before Charles could respond, one committee member turned to me and said:

"That's probably a good title for your notes: 'Nothing.'"

This month we will not implement any changes to our positions. But this decision (or lack thereof) masks a lively discussion on our views regarding risk assets—the perennial risk-on vs. risk-off discussion.

First, we reviewed an analysis prepared by Chris Faulkner-MacDonagh on the impact of macro factors on stocks vs. bonds. While the committee focuses on relative valuations, we also consider macro factors. We know that markets anticipate, or price in, growth and inflation consensus forecasts. Therefore, **we always compare our views with what's priced in**.

To estimate market consensus, we used the Survey of Professional Forecasters. To measure realized growth and inflation, we used proprietary data published by DeepMacro. These data provide "live" estimates of growth and inflation. DeepMacro scans over 3,000 series, narrows the set to the most 127 most predictive variables, and keeps track of all releases **daily**. In backtests, DeepMacro data seem more predictive than official GDP and inflation numbers.

As of Wednesday last week, the DeepMacro signal is bullish (long stocks). This observation led to a broad discussion on whether we had de-risked our portfolios enough for now. There's a range of views on the committee. We currently have our most extreme underweight position in stocks (vs. bonds) since the late 1990s.

Simultaneously, while most fixed income portfolio managers remain slightly overweight spread risk, **equity portfolio managers across the firm have been de-risking their portfolios (which leads to a** "doubling-up" effect of sorts: underweight stocks in Tactical Asset Allocation, and underweight equity beta in security selection).

"This is the best environment we've seen in the U.S. in this economic expansion," said one committee member, playing devil's advocate to our generally bearish view. From a fundamentals perspective, this statement is quite defensible: earnings are growing at 20%+, and only 6–7% of this growth is attributable to tax reform. Inflation remains low, while consumer, CEO, and small business confidence indicators remain close to all-time highs. Moreover, we expect that the cash flow impact of tax cuts will be more pronounced in the second half of this year.

Another related controversial question was: *"Are we in 1994, in which case, the Fed hikes are just a temporary phenomenon, a pause in a long expansionary cycle?"* Due to the depth and structural damage of the 2008–2009 crisis, GDP growth in this recovery has been quite shallow. We've only reached about 20% on a cumulative basis, compared to 40% during the expansion of the 1990s. Is there room for more? A committee member cited a paper by Reinhart and Rogoff that suggests that following major economic blow-ups, countries take 10–12 years to get back to normal economic growth. We're approaching the 10-year mark.

The caveats are well known: we're late in the cycle; growth may be slowing outside the US; QE is unwinding; high expectations are priced in; 20% earnings growth is not sustainable; etc. Also, many relative valuations across financial markets are at extremes (non-US growth vs. value, non-US small vs. large, for example, sit at their 95–100th percentiles). *"And things feel much worse in Europe,"* added one committee member.

The bottom line, however, is that we're already positioned defensively, and this bull could continue to run. It's not uncommon to see strong risk asset returns late in the cycle. So, we don't see the need to de-risk further this month.

On US Value vs. Growth, the conundrum remains the same: value stocks look cheap, but we hesitate to load up on cyclicals at this point in the cycle, especially since our secular view on growth companies remains quite positive. We'll remain neutral.

We'll also remain neutral on EM equities (vs. developed markets). Headwinds for EM are significant, for example: rising US rates, a stronger dollar, and trade wars. But are all these risks already priced in? EM is down –8% YTD, has a P/E of 11, compared to 13 for non-US developed stocks, and 16 for US stocks. Earnings expectations for EM remain around 10% for the next three years. An interesting development this week has been that China seems to have taken its foot off the brake in terms of tightening. We'll continue to watch the asset class.

The fixed income team remains neutral on duration, and slightly overweight on spread. Some fixed income investors view inflation and rising US rates as key risks. At the Asset Allocation Committee level, we've taken a large underweight position in High Yield, a position that we're not looking to press further at this point, in line with our aversion to de-risking further this month.

We made no changes to investments this month, but we had a lively discussion, and we've moderated our appetite for further de-risking.

Which Valuation Signal Works Best for Tactical Asset Allocation?

In 2018, I tested the effectiveness of three valuation metrics as predictors of stock returns: price to earnings (P/E), price to book (P/B), and price to cash flow (P/CF). This test was similar to the project I mentioned in Chapter 2, when I evaluated which ratio best predicted valuation changes. To make it simpler, this time I focused on total returns. I also expanded the analysis to various time horizons and compared the effectiveness of valuation ratios as predictors of absolute *and* relative performance between asset class pairs.

I used the equity asset classes, shown in Table 3.1, that we've used so far in this book when we discussed the CAPM and other long-term return forecasts. I estimated the relationship between initial valuation levels and subsequent returns at the six-month, one-year, two-year, and three-year horizons for 10 equity asset classes and 6 relative bets between them. My monthly data sample started in January 1995 and ended in May 2018.[2] In total, I ran 192 out-of-sample correlations between signal and forward returns.

TABLE 3.1   List of Equity Asset Classes and Relative Bets

Absolute Returns		
US large cap	EAFE large cap	World ex-US
US small cap	EAFE small cap	Emerging markets
US growth	EAFE growth	
US value	EAFE value	
Relative Bets		
US large vs. small	World ex-US vs. US	
US value vs. growth	Emerging markets vs. US	
EAFE large vs. small		
EAFE value vs. growth		

Normally I would code such a repetitive empirical analysis in Matlab (a technical engineering and finance software program) and use Microsoft Excel to visualize the data and test pieces of my code. But I'm an inefficient and out-of-practice programmer, so I used Bloomberg as my source of historical data and ran everything in Excel. It made for a fun afternoon.

Some of the results surprised me. Valuation seemed to work consistently across equity asset classes and time horizons. Out of 192 correlations, across absolute and relative return forecasts, 187 had the expected sign, consistent with the "buy cheap (valuations), sell high (valuations)" intuition—a remarkable hit rate of 97%. And some of the failed signals seemed to be driven by outlier P/E data around the tech bubble. Also, it was surprising that the signals seemed to work well at shorter horizons (six months and one year).

But I should emphasize that there's a difference between a result that shows the expected sign on a correlation and the ability to make money with the signal. Average correlations were in the −20% range for six-month and one-year horizons and strengthened to −30 to −40% for two- and three-year horizons. (Valuation tends to work better at longer time horizons.) These numbers aren't very high: –40% corresponds to an R-square of 16%. (I used a convention whereby the expected sign on the correlation is negative, because high valuations lead to lower returns, and vice versa. In that context, the more negative the correlation, the more predictive the signal.) Plenty of times, the valuation signal will lead you astray. Over the last few years, for example, non-US equities have been consistently cheaper than US equities, but US markets have continued to outperform.

Consistent with my prior valuation horse race, to forecast *absolute* returns, P/CF worked better than P/B and P/E. At the one-year horizon, P/CF had an average correlation of over –43% with forward returns, compared with –26% for P/B and –22% for P/E.

However, when I ran the tests for *relative* returns, for example, large cap versus small cap stocks, the results surprised me. P/E worked better than P/CF at the six-month, one-year, and two-year horizons and worked about the same as P/CF at the three-year horizon. Why didn't P/CF win? What happened to my simple explanation that cash flows are harder to game and thereby more reliable?

When I struggle with a tricky question like this one, I usually walk out of my office, turn left, and find someone from our research team to help me think through the problem. As long as one member of this talented team is available to indulge my random questions, I know I'll get thoughtful answers, good hypotheses, and help thinking through the problem. Not every investor has access to such a team. Nonetheless, *when forecasting returns, I believe it's important to always run your assumptions by someone, even nonexperts, because verbalizing your thoughts to someone often leads to breakthroughs.*

This time Chris Faulkner-MacDonagh, who has a Yale doctorate and an impressive résumé, was happy to talk about my question: "Why would an indicator work well to forecast time series returns for individual assets, but not work well to forecast relative returns between those same assets?"

Off the cuff, he suggested two explanations. First, the obvious: "It might be an issue with autocorrelation. A variable may *seem* to work well as a time series forecast if it's highly autocorrelated (persistent), even if it's not particularly predictive. So if cash flows are more autocorrelated than other variables, perhaps your result for P/CF was spurious."

In other words, he suggested P/CF "cheated." He posited that cash flows may be more autocorrelated than earnings. However, a quick test revealed that this conclusion didn't apply to my asset classes. Chris was probably on to something, and there's a whole field of study in econometrics dedicated to these types of issues with autocorrelation, unit roots, cointegration, etc. But I was after the big picture, so I stepped away from this methodological rabbit hole.

His second suggestion was thoughtful as well: "If you use index-adjusted positive earnings, remember that negative earnings are removed from the aggregation, which makes asset class–level earnings less outlier-sensitive and more comparable across asset classes."

Good point. Adjusted positive earnings may be more comparable *across* asset classes, even though they're less predictive from a time series perspective, for a given asset class.

I also went to talk to Rob Panariello, portfolio manager and quantitative analyst. He's our expert on portfolio optimization and risk models. (Also, unlike many people with such an incredible intellect, Rob has a fantastic sense of humor and doesn't take himself too seriously. It's outside the scope of this book, but here are a few fun facts about Rob: he wears slippers to work; he grows strange plants in his office; he drinks 7–10 coffees every day; he used to be a power lifter; he regularly wins competitive taco-eating contests; and he owns an isolation tank where he likes to relax for hours at a time.)

I've coauthored papers with Rob. He has one of the most intuitive minds I've ever come across. He grasps issues quickly. When I asked him my question, he nailed the answer in two words: "Systemwide noise."

Of course! The time series forecasts may be completely off for two asset classes, but if the bias is systemwide—if it affects both asset classes the same way—then the comparison between the two can still be meaningful. It appears P/Es are more subject to systemwide noise than are P/CFs. So they perform better for relative return ("cross-sectional") forecasts than for time series forecasts.

In general, time series forecasts are useful for market timing. For over-weight and underweight decisions, *cross-sectional* forecasts are what matters. Good cross-sectional forecasts can be poor time series forecasts, and vice versa. The reason? Systemwide noise. Another way to think about this important distinction is that some investors may seek to predict when to invest in stocks (a time series question), while others may focus on whether value stocks will outperform growth stocks (a cross-sectional question).

Ultimately, whether the decision is about market timing or relative valuation (which is our focus in our own process), I don't think investors should rely on *one* signal, whether it's P/CF, P/E, or something else. In our tactical asset allocation process we use a variety of valuation ratios. We look for which ratios have been most predictive for each asset class pair, and we focus on them. We also build composite metrics across several indicators. Importantly, we always evaluate the data in the context of the current environment.

Relative Valuation Between Stocks and Bonds and Across Bond Markets

In Chapter 2, I mentioned a study by my colleagues Justin Harvey and Aaron Stonacek that showed that yield to maturity provides a simple and remarkably effective forecast for bond returns, especially when the investment horizon is close to the duration of the portfolio. What about *relative* returns between stocks and bonds and across fixed income asset classes?

For US stocks versus bonds, our research team's analysis shows a 35% correlation between the ratio of forward equity earnings yield (the inverse of the P/E ratio) to bond yield and the subsequent 12-month relative returns, based on monthly data from January 1990 to June 2018.[3] The intuition behind this signal is straightforward: when bond yield increases, bonds become cheaper; when earnings yield increases (P/E decreases), stocks become cheaper. So we keep track of the ratio between the two asset classes and try to "buy low and sell high." It's a decent signal, but it's far from perfect. It's mostly useful from a big-picture perspective. For example, rates have been so low in recent years that many investors have stayed in stocks despite high P/E ratios. We've had these discussions several times in our Asset Allocation Committee. One member would say: "Stocks are expensive. We've rarely seen P/Es this high."

Then another member would respond: "Yes, but have you looked at rates? Bonds are even more expensive."

Such is the plight of the tactical asset allocator. The important takeaway is that a P/E of say, 16, means different things if the 10-year yield is at 2% or 4%. One could argue that stocks are more "expensive" when the 10-year yield is at 4%, because they're less attractive *relative to bonds*—in other words, the equity risk premium is compressed. In an award-winning paper,[4] Arnott, Chaves, and Chow (2017) show that the Shiller P/E performs better as a short-term timing signal if we adjust it for inflation and real rates.

Yet we shouldn't push this intuition too far. The authors explain that the relationship is not linear. There's a goldilocks level of inflation and real rates that appear "just right" to justify high valuations. Ultimately, if the prediction horizon is one year, a 35% correlation indicates that many other factors matter: momentum, expected earnings, monetary policy, sentiment, etc. And the related, popular narrative that rising rates are bad for stocks can be misleading. The Fed often raises rates when growth accelerates and risk assets perform well. In fact, when rates have increased by 25 bps or more between January 1990 and February 2018, average stock returns have been *positive*.[5] At an Asset Allocation Committee meeting in April 2018, I titled my presentation, "What Do Rising Rates Have in Common with Coffee and Egg Yolks?" And I concluded with the following analogy:

> It's never been clear whether coffee and egg yolks are good or bad for your health, but everybody seems to have a black-or-white opinion on either side of the debate. The reality is probably more complex due to a variety of factors. Are rising rates bad for stocks? I don't think we should make such bold statements in the current environment. Rather, we should worry about softening economic growth and high valuations.

[Charles Shriver, cochair of the committee, then suggested that the same inconclusiveness applies to red wine: Is it good or bad for your health? In the same vein, at the end of my presentation, I added a reference to a study on running, which shows that running is *good* for your knees—clearly a controversial conclusion. (I'm diversified across these risks: I love red wine, I'm an avid coffee drinker, I eat a hard-boiled egg every day with my lunch salad, and I run about 20–30 miles per week.)]

Our chief US economist, Alan Levenson, offered a thoughtful response to my presentation. He provided some intuition for the relatively low power of the stocks versus bonds, yield-based valuation signal:

> The Fed's efforts to either cap inflation or stop the unemployment rate from falling eventually contribute to recessions. But I agree that in the early stages of Fed rate hikes, risk assets can rise alongside risk-free rates, because monetary policy is still simulative (right now, the real fed funds rate is roughly zero). If growth data stabilize/improve in the near term (and barring political/geopolitical disruption), rates and risk assets can rise together. The challenge is when policy becomes tighter (say, 100 bps from now on real fed funds) and economic fundamentals begin to roll over.

Moreover, it's not always clear whether the Fed leads the economy, or vice versa. Stefan Hubrich, portfolio manager, put it this way:

> Mistaken causality? The naïve interpretation is that rising rates cause the recession. Is it possible that instead, the oncoming recession caused the Fed to lower rates? "Recessions end tightening cycles" rather than "tightening cycles cause recessions"?

Therefore, the yield ratio for stocks versus bonds should be used with caution, and in the context of other factors. It's one piece of the puzzle.

In contrast, yield ratios across fixed income asset classes work quite well as stand-alone signals. In fact, some of these ratios may be the most predictive TAA signals we have in our arsenal. For example, the yield ratio between emerging markets bonds and US investment-grade bonds has a 70% correlation with 12-month forward relative returns; for US high yield versus US investment grade bonds, the correlation is 61%; and for US high yield versus emerging markets bonds, the correlation is 50%.[6]

This level of predictability doesn't seem attainable in equity markets. In the series of tests on P/E, P/B, and P/CF we discussed earlier, the average correlation across equity relative signals was −22% (a reminder that the sign was reversed simply by convention). Across 24 signals, only 2 had correlations stronger than −40%: P/E as a signal for US value versus growth stocks

(–48%) and P/E as a signal for world ex-US versus US equities (–43%). The lesson is that relative valuation signals work better in fixed income markets than in equity markets.

There might be ways to improve on simple yield ratio signals. In the monograph I coauthored with my former PIMCO colleagues Vasant Naik, Mukundan Devarajan, Andrew Nowobilski, and Niels Pedersen (2016), titled "Factor Investing and Asset Allocation: A Business Cycle Perspective," we use a definition of carry that includes roll down, based on the difference between spot and 12-month forward swap rates. My coauthors simulated a tactical strategy that ranks carry across six countries: United States, Germany, Japan, the United Kingdom, Australia, and Canada. The strategy goes long the top three carry markets and short the bottom three. It generates a Sharpe ratio of 0.73 between 2002 and 2015 (based on quarterly data).

Notes

1. Although our TAA process is broadly applied across almost all our portfolios, I don't want to discount systematic strategies, such as managed volatility, covered call writing, and dynamic risk premiums, which we also use in several portfolios and in our custom solutions. Such strategies have some advantages that discretionary approaches don't have—for example, they eliminate behavioral biases. I'll discuss these strategies in Part Two of this book. Also, one of our portfolio managers, Rick de los Reyes, runs a discretionary "best-ideas" portfolio that incorporates different multi-asset tactical approaches.
2. Bloomberg Finance L.P. Monthly data from January 31, 1995 to May 31, 2018. Data fields used are TOT_RETURN_INDEX_GROSS_DVDS, INDX_ADJ_POSITIVE_PE, PX_TO_BOOK_RATIO, and PX_TO_CASH_FLOW. Backtests involving EAFE small start on January 31, 1998, as data are not available going back to 1995.
3. Monthly data from January 1990 to June 2018, Russell 3000 Fwd. Earnings Yield versus Real YTW (YTW less Y/Y Core CPI) for the Bloomberg Barclays Aggregate. Sources are T. Rowe Price, Bloomberg Finance L.P., and BLS. Analysis by Chris Faulkner-MacDonagh and David Clewell. Unlike in the previous section, here I quote predictive correlations as a positive number, because the signal relies on yields. A high yield, ceteris paribus, means an asset class is cheap. For equities, yield is simply the inverse of the P/E ratio.
4. The article won the 19th Annual Bernstein Fabozzi/Jacobs Levy Award for best article appearing in the *Journal of Portfolio Management* during 2017.
5. Using monthly data from January 1990 to February 2018 on the Russell 3000.

6. Barclays US Aggregate for US investment grade (*Source:* Bloomberg Finance
    L.P., yield to worst and total return, time period based on other data series
    availabilities); JP Morgan EMBI Global for Emerging Market Bonds (*Source:*
    JP Morgan, yield to worst and total return from December 2001 to June
    2018); JP Morgan U.S. High Yield (*Source:* JP Morgan, yield to worst and
    total return from January 1999 to June 2018; start in December 2001 for
    correlation with EMBI).

4

Shorter-Term Macro Signals and Something About Driving a Truck

Finance has borrowed a lot from macroeconomics.
—JPP

WE'VE SEEN THAT ALMOST ALL VALUATION SIGNALS WORK reasonably well across markets, perhaps more than most investors realize. Correlations between equity valuation signals and forward returns almost always have the expected sign. In fixed income markets, yield ratios seem to be remarkably predictive.

I wouldn't make the statement that investors can make a lot of money if they mechanically follow simple valuation-based strategies, but as we'll see in Chapter 12, systematic strategies that combine valuation with momentum signals have worked well in backtests and in practice. As for nonsystematic processes, when I described our own approach to TAA, I explained that we look at a variety of factors, not just relative valuations. Again, it helps to think in terms of building blocks. Relative valuations are key building blocks, which we can add to other factors.

For example, there is a wide body of academic literature that suggests macro factors can be significant drivers of asset returns. And among practitioners, statements such as "Stocks make money in expansions and tend to lose money in recessions" are often held as self-evident. *My view is that short-term return forecasts and tactical asset allocation decisions must account for macro factors.* However, there is little published on how to use these factors to inform investment decisions. In a 2017 paper titled "Macroeconomic Dashboards for Tactical Asset Allocation," my colleagues David Clewell, Chris Faulkner-MacDonagh, David Giroux, Charles Shriver, and I take the practitioner's perspective. We show how to build dashboards to integrate macro factors into a broader, discretionary TAA process. Our goal is not to design stand-alone systematic trading strategies based on macro factors. Rather, we show how investors can build macro factor dashboards to introduce discipline into their asset allocation process (in combination with other inputs, such as relative valuations).

In Chapter 3, I showed that valuation signals don't always have very high correlation with forward returns. One of the reasons could be that valuation-based investment strategies tend to be more effective when valuations are at extreme levels. Importantly, strategies that focus *solely* on relative valuations can lead to disappointing outcomes when important macroeconomic shifts take place. There's ample evidence that macro factors also matter.

Academic Research on Macro Factors

Most of the academic literature focuses on whether macro factors get priced into markets. Chen, Roll, and Ross (1986) show that the sensitivities ("macro betas") of size-sorted stock portfolios to rates, industrial production, inflation, credit spreads, and consumption explain a significant portion of their relative performance over time. Fama and French (1989) use a different methodology that focuses on the broad stock and bond markets. They show that business conditions, as approximated by dividend yields, rates, and credit spreads, forecast broad market returns. Several other studies have confirmed the importance of macro factors in explaining a wide range of asset class and style premium returns. Factors covered in the literature include consumption, unemployment, inflation, GDP growth, and oil prices. I highlight some examples in Table 4.1.

TABLE 4.1 Prior Studies on the Influence of Macroeconomic Factors on Asset Returns

Jensen, Johnson, and Mercer (1997) show that the size and value effects depend largely on monetary conditions.
Booth and Booth (1997) emphasize the importance of monetary policy in explaining stock and bond returns.
Lettau and Ludvigson (2001) show how consumption patterns forecast excess equity market returns.
Dahlquist and Harvey (2001) show that movements in the yield curve are predictive of stock returns.
Zhang, Hopkins, Satchell, and Schwob (2009) find a link between macro variables and the size and style premiums.
Boyd, Hu, and Jagannathan (2005) find that the effect of unemployment on stocks depends on the economic cycle.
Ludvigson and Ng (2009) show that "real" and "inflation" factors have predictive power for bond returns.
Kritzman, Page, and Turkington (2012) show that GDP and inflation regime-switching models can be used for TAA.
Franz (2013) shows that macro factors can be used to dynamically optimize investors' stocks versus bonds allocations.
Page (2013) shows a significant link between GDP and inflation surprises and bond, stock, and commodity returns.
Naik et al. (2016) relate the business cycle to returns, risks, and correlations for a broad list of risk factors.
Bernanke (2016) shows that oil and stocks have a common exposure to aggregate demand.
Blair and Qiao (2017) build a stock market timing model with 20 factors, including oil, inflation, rates, and spreads.

Challenges with Practical Applications

While these studies provide credible evidence of the importance of macro factors, many practitioners still struggle to use these factors for tactical investment decisions at the 6- to 18-month horizons. Economists and investment teams often operate independently, and the question of what macro expectations are priced in markets is often left unanswered. Moreover, the sheer amount of macro data makes it difficult to separate noise from signal and anticipate which variables will drive returns.

Another challenge with prior studies in practice is that macro factors may influence asset class returns differently based on initial conditions. Boyd, Hu, and Jagannathan (2005), for example, show that a rise in unemployment has a different effect on stock returns if it occurs during an expansion or a recession. Similarly, we can expect that a decline in industrial production may have a different effect if starting business conditions are good or bad. In fact, in our paper we suggested that the same could be said of any macro factor—depending on the prevailing regime, the impact on asset returns will differ. Yet except for Boyd, Hu, and Jagannathan's study, previous research does not account for the relationship between current conditions and the subsequent impact of macro factors on asset returns.

To map macro factors to expected asset returns, we proposed using dashboards. We now use these dashboards in our Asset Allocation Committee. The approach is different from the econometric methods used in academic studies—it is meant to be simpler and more intuitive. In fact, one of my colleagues referred to these dashboards as "paintings by numbers." There's more that can be done to extract signals from macro data, and our research team continues to innovate in that area. But as I've mentioned a few times in this book, simple is good. Simple works.

Unlike historical regression analyses based on static data samples, our dashboards are meant to be dynamically updated such that investors can rely on them as a research tool or as a means to inform investment decisions on an ongoing basis. We focus on the relative returns between pairs of asset classes. We highlight which factors may have a significant impact on which pair trades, under various scenarios. Importantly, we incorporate current conditions, as reflected in the macro factors' levels. Our dataset covers a broad list of key macro factors: industrial production, inflation, oil prices, spreads, rates, gold prices, unemployment, etc. These factors are mapped to the pair trades we've discussed in this book so far (stocks versus bonds, value versus growth stocks, say small cap versus large cap, high yield versus investment-grade bonds, etc.).

For each pair trade, we partition historical asset returns to match a given scenario and current conditions. In total, we map 18 pair trades to 10 key macro factors, for a total of 180 "cells," produced for each of 4 scenarios (full sample, as well as stable, rising, and declining macro factors)—a grand total of 720 cells. We use color coding to make it easier to scan the data and mine for trade ideas.

Our entire framework is out-of-sample. Starting from each macro factor's current level, our dashboards answer the following question: If an investor has a one-year view on the direction of the macro factor, what is the corresponding forward one-year return?[1] For example, recently inflation has been low. Should we expect that value stocks outperform growth stocks if inflation rises from its current level? To answer these types of questions, we report historical hit rates, average returns, and confidence intervals across the 720 "cells." It's a lot of data, but we can easily spot some patterns.

In our paper, for example, we studied the link between US large cap versus small cap stock returns and the USD:

As of April 10, 2017, the U.S. dollar index stands at 100.6, which is in the top quartile of its history since January 1990. Suppose a tactical asset allocator expects the U.S. dollar to rise further. Starting from a top quartile level, when the U.S. dollar subsequently rose by 5% (or more) over the next year, U.S. small caps outperformed U.S. large caps 88% of the time, by an average of 8.2%, with the 10th to 90th percentile range between −2.3% and 15.9%. The outperformance of U.S. small caps in periods of rising USD may be attributed to their lower reliance on exports, compared to U.S. large caps.

This example seems significant, but we also explained that in general, statistical significance between macro variables and asset returns is low, *especially if we don't expect a significant move in the macro factors.* When I first presented this framework to our Asset Allocation Committee, I wanted to be clear that, despite all the academic literature in support of the significance of macro factors, most of these numbers should be ignored. You could have driven a truck through these confidence intervals with room on either side.

We should use the dashboards in context, not in isolation. Investors should think about what's already priced in, look for extremes—cases where we see real historical significance—and put the analysis in the context of current conditions (valuations and other nonmacro factors).

The bottom line is that these dashboards help identify relevant investment themes. Here are additional examples from our paper:

> Emerging markets currencies may be an important factor to watch. Stable or rising emerging markets currencies are supportive of emerging markets equities, real asset equities, and emerging markets bonds. Further, emerging markets currencies have depreciated significantly—the index currently sits at the bottom 5% of its historical range. If they move significantly up or down from their currently low level, they could correlate with meaningful directional volatility across assets. And the price of oil, if it remains stable or appreciates from its currently medium level (63rd percentile), could be a significant positive driver of emerging markets stocks, real asset equities, and emerging markets bonds. . . .
>
> Regarding style rotation, the direction of interest rates should matter in the current environment. Growth stocks have longer duration than value stocks. Therefore, even though dividend yield on value stocks is higher than on growth stocks, when rates decline, growth outperforms; and when rates rise, value outperforms. This effect occurs both in the United States and in EAFE markets. The large weight of negative-duration Financials in the value index partly explains this effect.

Overall, the results reported in our dashboards are in line with economic intuition, as well as with prior findings published in the literature. The contribution lies not in the dashboards' academic merit, but rather in their value to practitioners. The confidence intervals and hit rates help filter the continuous flood of macro data. Importantly, while the relationships among the macro factors and asset classes are reasonably persistent, the dashboards should be updated frequently, because as initial conditions change, some of the investment conclusions may change as well.

Caveats

With our macro dashboards, we don't claim to identify causation, which is almost always impossible to do given the complex and dynamic nature of how factors drive asset returns. Rather, we merely identify correlations that appear meaningful and leave it to the investor to assess causation. Investors shouldn't build systematic tactical asset allocation strategies based solely on these macro data.

Instead, macro factors are often used to confirm relative valuation signals. For example, if non-US equities are cheap relative to US equities based on valuation metrics (P/E and other such metrics) *and* if macro factors indicate non-US equities should outperform (weakening USD, non-US central bank stimulus, earlier stage in the business cycle versus that in the United States, potential GDP growth surprise, and so forth), then a tactical asset allocator may take a larger position in ACWI ex-US equities than if valuation and macro data don't agree.

Another caveat is that we don't model expectations directly. In theory, we should run our scenarios against the expectations that are priced into the market. The problem is that expectations are often difficult and, in many cases, impossible to measure. Survey data may be useful, but they rarely reveal what markets are truly pricing in, nor are survey results available in a timely—or broad enough—fashion going far enough back in time.

Regarding market-implied views, forward curves incorporate a risk premium, which makes it hard to disentangle an expectations component. Ultimately, Chen, Roll, and Ross (1986) conclude that spreads and interest rates series are noisy enough to be treated as unanticipated. The authors also find that econometric methods to extract the unanticipated component of industrial production do not offer any advantage over the unadjusted series.[2]

Last, we've selected investable asset class pairs. This list represents asset classes that asset allocators commonly use in practice. But in theory, it would be more elegant to isolate market factors and scale positions based on volatility. For example, we could hedge the equity risk factor common on both sides of the small versus large caps pair, or at least make sure the trade is equity-beta neutral. While statistical significance would likely increase (see Naik et al., 2016), the trades would not be easily implementable. Ultimately, our goal is to add discipline to the analysis of macro factors, and our framework is one piece of the puzzle, focused on idea generation. Portfolio managers can then combine macro with other factors, adjust broad market factor exposures, and risk-scale positions between the long and the short leg and across trades.

Notes

1. Here by "forward return," I mean the expected return if the macro factor scenario is realized over the next year.
2. However, they lead industrial production by one year. For tactical asset allocation, this obviously would be like cheating because it would assume perfect foresight.

5

Momentum and Something About Horoscopes

The frictions that prevent efficient markets are numerous.
—JPP

WE'VE SEEN THAT VALUATION IS A KEY BUILDING BLOCK TO forecast returns, but that we must account for other factors. Macro factors give us a lot more context to interpret valuation signals, i.e., what's priced into markets.

Sentiment also matters. One way to measure sentiment is to look at price momentum. There are many studies on asset price momentum. *These studies and my own experience suggest momentum is a useful building block for return forecasting in an asset allocation context, especially when combined with valuation and other signals.* However, there are many definitions of momentum. As for the other signals we've discussed thus far, we can analyze which definition of momentum works best and in which markets (as long as we don't overfit our data).

Quantitative investors have long used momentum in their models. In a 2014 *Forbes* magazine interview with Steve Forbes, Cliff Asness (one of the intellectual giants involved in the CAPE ratio debate we discussed in Chapter 2) talked about the value and momentum signals. When Asness first mentions that momentum works in practice, he says, "Sadly for pure efficient markets guys, good momentum tends to be a good thing in the short-term."

Asness simply means that "momentum works." Forbes responds with obvious skepticism: "Sort of the investing equivalent of horoscopes."

Similar skepticism prevails among many academics and value-oriented investors. For academics who believe in efficient markets, it's inconceivable that past returns should carry any information about the future. Efficient market theory is frustratingly circular, but the idea is that if its past returns had predictive power, it would be so easy to make money with momentum that investors would pile on these strategies, and opportunities would disappear. So momentum can't work, because everyone's doing it. Yet presumably if everyone's doing it, there must be money to be made; otherwise why do it? Apologies for the geeky spreadsheet analogy, but Excel would reject such a circular reference.

In the same vein, to manage client expectations and legal risks, all pitches for investment products include disclaimers that past returns aren't indicative of future returns. These disclaimers aren't only about lack of momentum in *asset* returns; they also speak to expectations about the persistence of "momentum" (or lack thereof) in investment managers' skills. (Meanwhile, I have yet to encounter an asset owner who *doesn't* consider past performance a major factor in manager selection.)

For value-oriented fundamental investors, the momentum pill is particularly hard to swallow. They tend to distrust momentum strategies. I know several investors who think that to buy something *just because* it has appreciated in price is perhaps the dumbest thing you can do in investment management: "Why would I buy something because it's gotten more expensive? It doesn't make sense!" is something I've heard many times. And the same logic applies with negative price momentum: "Why sell something that has gotten cheaper? Something I already thought was a good buy at a higher valuation? I should buy more!"

The key to momentum, however, is not to ignore valuation. It's to *combine* it with valuation, as Asness explains in his interview, and as we'll discuss further. Investors should look for opportunities when both signals agree. For example, buy a cheap asset when its momentum turns positive rather than on the way down, or sell an expensive asset with negative momentum.

Nonetheless, does momentum stand on its own two legs, without an assist from valuation? A lot of research has been published on this topic. In a recent working paper, titled "215 Years of Global Multi-Asset Momentum: 1800–2014," Christopher C. Geczy and Mikhail Samonov (2015) mention that in 2013, there were approximately 300 papers with the term "momentum" in the SSRN database. Based on their own study, the authors conclude that momentum works at the individual stock level and across asset classes:

> We utilize a large amount of historical asset classes to create an out-of-sample test of momentum back to 1800 in country equity indexes, bonds, currencies, commodities, and sectors and stocks. We find that the effect [works] in each asset class, across asset classes, and across momentum portfolios themselves.

They add that "momentum alphas are significant." The exception seems to be that commodities exhibit mean reversion, i.e., the opposite of momentum. They find that the correlations across momentum strategies have increased drastically in recent years. They suggest that this outcome is driven by the popularity of momentum as an investment style or factor. They warn of "increased strategy risk of overcrowding."

A Momentum Horse Race

In Chapter 3 we discussed the effectiveness of 3 valuation ratios (P/E, P/B, and P/CF) across 10 equity markets and 6 relative bets between them. We called it a horse race. I mentioned that P/CF won from a market timing perspective, but that P/E won from a relative returns perspective. Does momentum work even better than all three valuation ratios?

The Geczy and Samonov study suggests that positive-momentum assets ("winners") outperform negative-momentum assets ("losers") almost everywhere, quite significantly, and out-of-sample. But their study doesn't cover the same universe of assets and relative bets. My valuation analysis focused on tactical decisions across style, size, and regions, while their momentum study covered individual stocks, equity countries, and equity sectors.

Recently, I ran a study similar to my valuation analysis, but for momentum. My four horses were the trailing six-month, one-year, two-year, and three-year returns. I calculated the correlation between these signals and forward returns at various time horizons. I used the same start date of January 31, 1995, and extended the end date by two months to add recently available data (July 31, 2018).[1] Essentially, I replicated what I did in the valuation ratios analysis. Did the momentum signals beat the valuation signals? *No, not even close.*

For valuation, 97% of the 192 correlations had the expected sign. In contrast, momentum results were all over the place. I calculated correlations between the various trailing windows and one-month, six-month, one-year, two-year, and three-year forward returns. Across absolute and relative bets, I estimated 320 correlations. Only 122 (38%) of them had the expected sign (winners outperform losers). Hence, there was more evidence of mean reversion (losers outperform winners) than momentum.

The main issue appears to be that momentum works better at the one-month horizon than at longer horizons. At the one-month horizon, 66% of the correlations had the correct sign. If I focused on the six-month and one-year lookback windows, which are more commonly used for momentum signals than are two- or three-year windows, the number of correlations with the correct sign went up to 84% (only signals on US small cap stocks did not work in this case). Ultimately, momentum is a shorter-term signal than valuation.

Geczy and Samonov found similar results. They showed that the momentum signal is strongest at the one-month horizon and degrades gradually as the investment horizon gets longer. For stocks, the signal turns into mean reversion roughly around the one-year horizon.

But even at the one-month horizon, the momentum signal was relatively weak, despite high success rates across bets. Average correlation for the best-performing lookback (six months) was only 7% for absolute bets (market timing) and 6% for relative bets. As the lookback expanded, the results got progressively worse. In contrast, we saw in Chapter 3 that valuation signals generated correlations in the 20–40% range.[2]

Overreaction, or Valuation by Another Name?

An interesting paradox in finance is that as forecasting results get worse and worse, they become better. How does that work? The worst signal possible is one with zero predictability. Signals with strong *negative* predictability are *good*, because you can take the other side of the trades. Find the worst investor in the world, an investor who *consistently* gets it wrong and *always* loses money, do the opposite, and you'll be quite successful. (*A caveat:* The issue in quant finance, however, is that to reverse signals without a theory behind the decision amounts to overfitting/data mining.)

In my momentum study, I found the most predictability—in the form of significant mean reversion—for market timing with three-year lookbacks, applied to a three-year horizon. In other words, asset classes with *high* three-year returns tend to generate *low* forward three-year returns, and vice versa. This result could be explained by investor overreaction (De Bondt and Thaler, 1985) or another form of the valuation signal: High three-year momentum asset classes probably have high valuations, and vice versa.

Aside from the observation that a six-month lookback with a one-month forecast horizon worked best, I didn't find much consistency in my results across relative bets. I did notice that momentum worked consistently *at various lookbacks and horizons* for one relative bet: emerging markets versus developed markets stocks, a bet for which the valuation signal did not work well. In fact, compared with all other bets, it performed the *best* on momentum and the *worst* on valuation—an interesting signal diversification effect. In our tactical asset allocation, perhaps because we focus mostly on valuation, we've struggled with this emerging markets versus developed markets decision at times. On a few occasions, we've overweighted emerging markets based on valuation—because the asset class looked so cheap—only to get steamrolled by negative momentum. In general, over the last few years, US stocks have continued to outperform stocks in the rest of the world, despite high relative valuation of US stocks.

For absolute returns, however, I found a remarkably smooth pattern in my results, as shown in Figure 5.1. This chart shows the average correlation between trailing and forward returns, averaged across the 10 equity asset classes (US small, large, value, and growth; EAFE small, large, value, and growth; world ex-US and emerging markets).[3] Any number above the 0% line indicates momentum, while numbers below the line indicate mean reversion. The shorter the lookback window and the shorter the forecast horizon, the more momentum works. The longer the lookback window and the longer the horizon, the more mean reversion works. For these data, there was *no exception* to this rule of thumb, which I thought was interesting. Figure 5.1 also reiterates clearly that momentum signals were weak, relative to mean reversion/valuation.

FIGURE 5.1   Correlation between trailing returns and forward returns

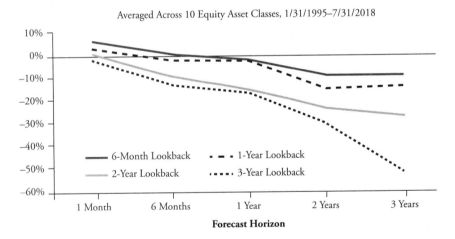

Some might argue that momentum works better if the most recent month is removed from the data. At the individual stock level, Geczy and Samonov showed that momentum only works if the most recent month is omitted, an adjustment supported by prior studies.[4] But to me, this adjustment smells

of data mining/overfitting. The authors didn't find any similar one-month reversal effects for other assets. Hence, I did not drop the most recent month in my momentum analysis. In light of Geczy and Samonov's results, I doubt it would have made a significant difference in my results.

Bond Momentum: Weak Evidence at Best

In Chapters 1 and 2, we discussed how yield to maturity is a good predictor of future bond returns. I referred to a study by my colleagues Justin Harvey and Aaron Stonacek on absolute bond returns that showed predictive correlations as high as 90%+, depending on the time horizon. Also, I ran a few examples for bond *relative* returns that revealed some of the best-performing signals I've ever found. In general, at the asset class level, valuation works better for bonds than for stocks. But what about bond momentum? Geczy and Samonov find that "although less than other asset classes, momentum is statistically present in government bonds." They certainly drink the momentum Kool-Aid. Based on my experiments, the evidence of momentum in bond returns is weak, at best.

For comparison purposes (and because my spreadsheets were already set up that way), I repeated the same horse race I ran for the equity asset classes, but for bond markets, shown in Table 5.1. I used the same period: January 1995 to May 2018.[5] I evaluated the effectiveness of time series momentum with six-month, one-year, two-year, and three-year lookback windows on 10 fixed income asset classes and 6 relative bets between them:

TABLE 5.1   List of Asset Classes and Relative Bets

Absolute Returns		
U.S. Aggregate	U.S. Credit Long	Global High Yield
U.S. Treasuries	High Yield	Emerging Markets
U.S. Long Treasuries	MBS	
U.S. Credit Credit/Corp	Global ex-U.S. Aggregate	
Relative Bets		
U.S. Agg vs. U.S. Treasuries	U.S. Agg vs. Global ex-U.S. Agg	U.S. Agg vs. Emerging Markets
U.S. Agg vs. High Yield	U.S. Agg vs. MBS	High Yield vs. Emerging Markets

From a time series/market timing perspective, results on one-month momentum were similar to that for equities: consistently positive across markets, but weak, with predictive correlations—averaged across markets—in the 2–8% range. Unlike for equities, one-month momentum worked well with longer lookback windows (two years and three years). In fact, I found the exact opposite pattern as I did for equities: momentum worked best with *long* lookback windows (two to three years) and for *long* predictive horizons (two to three years). With a three-year lookback window and across all predictive horizons, 43 out of the 50 correlations (86%) had the correct sign (compared with 4% for equities). Only high yield and global high yield showed mean reversion.

My take is that interest rates are linked to monetary policy and the business cycle, both of which tend to move incrementally over relatively long periods of time. Spreads also move in a long cycle, but to a lesser extent, with a shorter mean-reversion effect, as evidenced by my results for high yield.

As for relative fixed income bets, momentum did not work at all. It worked so consistently badly that I would qualify these results as "good": they show meaningful evidence of mean reversion in relative yields. Across bets, lookback windows, and horizons, only 21 out of 120 correlations showed momentum (17.5%), and there was no clear pattern.[6]

Another way to interpret the result that 17.5% of the correlations showed momentum is that 82.5% of the correlations showed mean reversion. This result agrees with my earlier observation that relative valuations (relative yields) are remarkably predictive in fixed income markets. For this momentum/mean-reversion study, my analysis showed that, as is often the case across markets, the longer the lookback window and the time horizon, the stronger the mean reversion.

To summarize some of the key takeaways on momentum, my view is that it works well when combined with valuation in equity markets. But in fixed income markets, if the objective is to invest across markets with a 6–18-month horizon, investors should focus on mean reversion.

Real-Life Example of Mean Reversion and Valuation and How We Put It All Together

In our Asset Allocation Committee, we use mean reversion in yields and spreads to guide several of our investment decisions. To illustrate with a real-life example, here I show my notes from a meeting in August 2018 when we decided to overweight emerging markets bonds based on valuation. These notes also offer a window into how we look at fundamentals such as aggregate profit margins, and how despite screaming "buy" valuation signals—in this example on US value versus growth—sometimes we hesitate to overweight an asset class if macro and fundamental signals disagree.

The bottom line is that, so far, we've discussed valuation, macro, and momentum factors mostly in isolation. But in practice, as these notes illustrate, investors must put it all together, with a heavy dose of experience, judgment, and intuition. (My old quant mindset just rolled over in its grave.)

"Extreme"

Sébastien Page, Notes from Asset Allocation Committee Meeting

The book we use to support our decisions in the Asset Allocation Committee is massive. It contains 180 pages of valuation data, macro signals, fundamentals, and risk analytics.

For each asset class, we get up-to-date levels and percentiles on important indicators. We also get estimates of each indicator's correlation with forward 12-month returns. If an indicator has high historical effectiveness, we pay more attention to it.

This month, I asked David Clewell and Chris Faulkner-MacDonagh, "Out of the 97 fundamental signals that are in the AAC book, what would be the top 3 trade ideas/signals?"

By trade "ideas" I didn't mean actual recommendations, because fundamental signals are only part of the puzzle. We explicitly excluded valuation and macro signals from this exercise.

To answer this question, we established the following criteria:

1. Identify the most "extreme" of all the fundamental signals from our AAC book.
2. Rank by R-squared (predictive correlation on forward 12M returns).
3. Pick top 3 most extreme signals with high predictive correlation.

The following top 3 signals surfaced:

Net bank tightening is <u>bullish</u> on <u>stocks vs. high yield bonds</u> (10th percentile over 10 years). Historically, net bank tightening has had a 44% correlation with the forward relative returns on stocks vs. <u>high yield</u>. Valuation metrics also indicate that stocks are cheap relative to <u>high yield</u> (39th percentile), and momentum has been positive for stocks over the last 12 months.

This trade has several risks. In general, in most market environments, it's a *net* risk-on position, despite the short high yield leg (unless we scale it to be risk-neutral).

Also:

1. A localized equity volatility shock as we saw in February, with limited spillover to <u>high yield</u>, would work against the trade.
2. There's a risk that earnings growth remains positive (limited change in <u>high yield</u> default risk) but misses expectations, which would be bad for stocks.
3. Regarding oil prices, energy companies tend to be priced on the long end of the curve, while spot/short-end oil prices affect cash flows and impact <u>high yield</u> spreads more directly. Hence, higher spot prices while the long end remains depressed would work against the trade.
4. Last, in a sideways market with limited risk appetite but no sell-off, <u>high yield</u> can outperform just on the basis of carry.

Verdict: At this point in the cycle, the committee will not add to stocks. And we already have a large underweight position to high yield.

The 7-year real yield differential between Treasuries and bonds is <u>bullish</u> on the USD. It's at an extreme (99th percentile over 10 years). This signal has a 48% correlation with forward USD appreciation. To benefit from potential USD appreciation, we could <u>move assets back from non-US into US equities</u> (as much as 40% of the risk in this bet is driven by currencies). However, while 12-month momentum is positive, US equity valuations are high relative to non-US equities (92nd percentile over 10 years).

The risks to USD appreciation and a long position in US vs. non-US equities include:

1. A change (toward a more dovish policy) in the path or rate hikes when the 2021 dots are published in September.
2. An unexpected shift in growth differentials, as earlier-cycle economies pick up relative to the US.
3. Earnings disappointments (in the face of high expectations) in the US despite global risk-on sentiment, which could lead to a narrowing of the valuation gap.
4. US debt and deficits lead to a loss of market confidence in the USD as reserve currency.

Verdict: Several committee members have a bullish view on the USD, but we decided not to add to richly valued US stocks.

EBIDTA margins for EAFE value are near an all-time low relative to EAFE growth (12th percentile over 10 years)—a <u>bullish</u> signal for EAFE value. Historically, relative margins revert to a mean—like trees, they don't grow to the sky. This signal has a 52% correlation with forward returns for EAFE value relative to EAFE growth. The <u>valuation</u> signal for EAFE value is also extremely bullish (first percentile over 10 years). However, momentum is negative, and this trade is perhaps the riskiest of the three, in particular because EAFE value loads heavily on European banks:

1. The European banking sector is at risk of continued low net interest margins, increasingly riskier loans, and a dollar funding squeeze.

2. The ECB could extend its policy of negative interest rates, which could lead to a Japan scenario for banks, according to which they would struggle to maintain profitability due to a flat yield curve.
3. A slowdown in global growth appears to be on the way, which would continue to favor growth stocks over cyclicals.
4. A small number of European banks have significant exposure to USD-denominated Turkey debt.

This analysis led to a broader discussion on extreme relative valuations. Throughout the world, value looks cheap relative to growth stocks. The spreads are at an extreme by historical standards. Similarly, international stocks look cheap relative to the US stocks.

But first, we started with the key question of the day in terms of extreme valuation: Turkey, and EM debt in general.

EM DEBT (USD) ATTRACTIVE ON VALUATION

"In fixed income markets, there's strong mean reversion (barring defaults). Unlike in equities, you get your money back—the terminal value is known!" said one committee member. Our dashboards in the AAC book support this statement: our strongest valuation signals are the relative YTMs on various fixed income asset classes. The terminology I often heard at my previous employer was that when the bonds are "money-good," you have "stored alpha."

The fixed income team has issued a high conviction rating on EM debt, on valuation. Relative to other risk assets in fixed income, EM debt looks cheap. For example, its ratio to high yield (on a spread basis) is near an all-time high.

The "house view," to the extent we have one, is that despite ugly headlines, it's not the first time Turkey has faced a crisis, and the current situation is unlikely to pose a systemic risk. Also, emerging markets have changed since the 1990s, with a stronger middle class, FX reserves, fewer cyclical companies, more technology companies, etc. **Therefore, we will evaluate liquidity conditions and move from an**

underweight −50-bps to an overweight +50-bps position in EM debt. We will fund this move from TIPS (we don't see major inflation pressure in the short run).

Doing so will increase our risk at the portfolio level, but as discussed before, we've already derisked our portfolios substantially.

To emphasize: We haven't changed our defensive, risk-off stance. This move is a valuation play, as we see this "extreme" valuation as a tactical opportunity.

GROWTH VS. VALUE AT AN EXTREME

Another extreme signal is how cheap value looks relative to growth. One committee member pointed to a dashboard from our book and asked the provocative question: "What will it take for us to decide to overweight value?" On the dashboard in question, 21 indicators flash bright red against growth and in favor of value. Eight of them are in the 99th percentile and above.

It's a puzzle to most committee members why value hasn't outperformed this year, in the face of cheap valuations, higher rates, a cyclical upswing in growth and earnings, and higher energy prices. The key issue might be that no one wants to overweight value this late in the cycle. Also, technology disruption plays a role. "A lot of value isn't value," said one committee member.

To which another member added: "18% of companies in the S&P 500 face secular risks. A majority of these companies are in the value sector."

Also, financials are the cheapest sector in the US market, but they could still take a hit in a mild recession. Meanwhile, it's hard to imagine Google's earnings going down −50%. A broader, related question, which will be discussed in an upcoming macro call, is the following: **Which sector would provide protection should we face a recession?** History might not be a good guide to answer this question—we must consider the current environment.

On the other hand, in favor of value, **growth feels concentrated.** Large technology platform companies have grown *at an accelerated* *pace*, which, mathematically, can't be sustainable, unless they eventually engulf the entire economy. And if we get a trade deal with China, we could see a value rally (energy, financials), perhaps of similar magnitude as when Trump got elected.

Takeaway: As in several of our previous meetings, we had a good debate on the value vs. growth question but **decided to stay at neutral**.

To conclude, this month we looked at extremes in fundamentals and relative valuations. We think EM debt presents a good opportunity. And we've derisked our portfolios enough that we feel comfortable playing some offense. Also, we recognize that value is extremely cheap relative to growth, but in the US market we will hold at neutral for now, given the late-cycle environment and our secular preference for growth.

Notes

1. EAFE large versus small tests start on January 31, 1998. Everything else, including EAFE large and EAFE small as individual assets, starts on January 31, 1995. *Data source:* Bloomberg Finance L.P. Field: TOT_RETURN_ INDEX_GROSS.
2. Here I'm reversing the sign for comparison with the momentum signal. Again, this is just a convention related to how the signals are interpreted.
3. EAFE large versus small tests start on January 31, 1998. Everything else, including EAFE large and EAFE small as individual assets, starts on January 31, 1995. *Data source:* Bloomberg Finance L.P. Field: TOT_RETURN_ INDEX_GROSS.
4. See Jegadeesh and Titman (1993), for example.
5. Bloomberg Barclays. Data series: U.S. Aggregate (LBUSTRUU Index), U.S. Corporate (LUACTRUU Index), U.S. High Yield (LF98TRUU Index), Emerging Markets (EMUSTRUU Index), Global ex-U.S. Aggregate (LG38TRUU Index), U.S. MBS (LUMSTRUU Index), U.S. Treasuries (LUATTRUU Index), U.S. Long Credit (LULCTRUU Index), U.S. Long Treasury (LUTLTRUU Index), Global High Yield (LG30TRUU Index).
6. Except that six-month and one-year lookbacks with one-month predictive horizon seemed to work with some consistency, albeit weakly—a result in line with equities and Geczy and Samonov's paper.

6

Thoughts on Return Forecasting and Something About the Feelings of Electrons

Some will find that finance is not easy. We don't know the outcomes
in advance. The information we use is always incomplete,
and we can't control the variables. Still, we must make decisions
because, often, the absence of decision is worse.
—JPP

A FEW YEARS AGO, I WAS IN A MEETING WITH SEVERAL senior investors when I put my foot in my mouth. I was the newbie in the room—I had just joined the firm. The topic of discussion was our long-term return forecasts. We wanted to build a new set of capital markets assumptions, to be used in solutions studies. The goal of these studies was to advise institutional investors on their strategic asset allocation decisions.

As the debate on one particular estimate intensified (I don't remember which estimate), a self-confident investor, who had such a successful career that he was clearly, enormously wealthy and didn't feel the need to sit in long meetings to build consensus, said, "Just use 2%."

I jumped in with a basic question: "How did you arrive at this estimate?"

With a smile, and a hint of sarcasm, he responded, "I made it up."

I was taken aback. I couldn't help it—I had to say: "But you can't make stuff up like that. We need a robust estimate."

In my introduction to this book I talked about the GIGO (garbage-in, garbage-out) critique. I explained that quants tend to get annoyed with the GIGO critique. Another critique, perhaps even more irritating and a favorite of academic journal referees, is to question an approach's "robustness."

He responded: "This firm has been 'making stuff up' for decades! In fact, we 'make stuff up' every day. And now, we're one of the world's leading asset managers."

The subtext was "Welcome newbie, you need to learn how we do things here. We use judgment." One of the reasons I was taken aback by his "I made it up" response was that he was a well-known quant investor. He used econometrics, statistics, and systematic strategies as core parts of his process. Had he become disillusioned with mathematical approaches?

Probably not. He simply recognized *when* and *how* to use judgment as part of a process that also relies on quantitative models. And importantly, he didn't think we should use just anybody's judgment—he recognized that some investors can forecast better than others. His main point, I suppose, was that *his* judgment, given his experience and track record, was probably better than any mathematically derived estimate.

One of the great misconceptions on portfolio theory is that it precludes the use of judgment and experience. It doesn't. It's right there in Markowitz's 1952 seminal paper, for everyone to see, in the first paragraph:

The process of selecting a portfolio may be divided into two stages. The first stage starts with observation and experience and ends with beliefs about the future performances of available securities. The second stage starts with the relevant beliefs about future performances and ends with the choice of a portfolio. This paper is concerned with the second stage.

With his "I made it up" comment, my new colleague meant that he had used "observation and experience" to form "beliefs about the future performance" of the asset class under debate. Nothing wrong with that. (Of course, it would have helped if he had walked us through his rationale, so that members of our Solutions team could explain the estimate to clients.)

In his recent book *Principles*, legendary investor Ray Dalio (2017) explains the evolution of his approach to marry quantitative analysis with judgment:

> Rather than blindly following the computer's recommendations, I would have the computer work in parallel with my own analysis and then compare the two. When the computer's decision was different from mine, I would examine why. Most of the time, it was because I had overlooked something. In those cases, the computer taught me. But sometimes I would think about some new criteria my system would've missed, so I would teach the computer. We helped each other.

From *PRINCIPLES: Life and Work* by Ray Dalio. Copyright © 2017 by Ray Dalio. Reprinted with the permission of Simon & Schuster, Inc. All rights reserved.

He adds that over time, the computer became more effective than he was, but the investor's role remained to evaluate the "decision-making criteria" used by the computer.

My view is that those who hope for a consistently effective return forecasting algorithm may suffer from what MIT professors Andrew Lo and Mark Mueller call "physics envy." In their 2010 paper titled "Warning: Physics Envy May Be Hazardous to Your Wealth," they warn that finance and physics are different:

> The quantitative aspirations of economists and financial analysts have for many years been based on the belief that it should be possible to build models of economic systems—and financial markets in particular—that are as predictive as those in physics. While this perspective has led to a number of important breakthroughs in economics, "physics envy" has also created a false sense of mathematical precision in some cases.

At the top of their paper, they picked a brilliant quote. It gets at the heart of the issue, which is that asset prices are set by humans. The quote is from the famous physicist and Nobel laureate Richard Feynman: "Imagine how much harder physics would be if electrons had feelings!"

I keep a related reminder on my office wall: a cartoon of two scientists in front of a blackboard full of complicated equations, with the following quote, spoken by one of the scientists: "Oh, if only it were so simple!" That cartoon has a bit of sentimental value for me. For the 10 years I worked with my mentor Mark Kritzman and learned most of what I know about quantitative investment research, he had the same cartoon on his office wall.

Rules of Thumb for Return Forecasting

Before we get to portfolio construction, in the next section of this book we will cover risk forecasting, an area where mathematical models are more prevalent and, I think, more useful than for return forecasting.

So far in this book, I hope I haven't shown "physics envy." To forecast returns, a key takeaway from everything we've discussed is that *it helps to keep it simple.* As a summary, here are my top 20 rules of thumb on how to build return forecasts. Ultimately, there are no precise cookbook instructions to forecast returns because the future is always uncertain.

Long-Term Forecasts:

1. When in doubt, assume that returns will be proportional to risk (beta). Free lunches are rare.
2. For stocks, check that your estimate is not too far from the inverse of the P/E ratio plus inflation.
3. For earnings (the "E" in P/E), don't rely on optimistic, short-run, or noisy sell-side estimates.
4. For more flexibility, break down returns into two building blocks: income and long-term growth.

5. Valuation changes are harder to model. When in doubt, assume valuation ratios revert to a mean.

6. For bonds, make sure your estimate is not too far from the asset class's yield to maturity.

7. Beware of large credit and currency risk exposures. Apply a default haircut when needed.

8. If possible, ask experienced investors for their forecasts of earnings growth, rates, spreads, etc.

9. Use these forecasts as the key inputs to transparent building block models that can be debated.

Tactical Forecasts:

1. For shorter-term equity forecasts, focus on valuation changes more than on income and growth.

2. Use valuation ratios (P/E, P/CF, P/B) to evaluate whether an asset class is cheap or expensive.

3. Pay close attention to P/CF for relative bets and to P/E for absolute (market timing) decisions.

4. Use 6- and 12-month momentum as secondary factors, to better time valuation-based trades.

5. With macro factors, account for current conditions and how macro factors affect asset prices.

6. Don't blindly assume that rising rates are bad for risk assets such as stocks and credit bonds.

7. When fundamentals (such as margins) reach extreme levels, assume they might revert to a mean.

8. For bonds, use yield-to-maturity ratios to forecast one-year relative returns between asset classes.

9. Don't expect return momentum to work in bond markets, except weakly in the very short run.

Two General Rules of Thumb:

1. *Use data and models* to estimate factor relationships, assess signal quality, and remove biases.
2. *Use judgment* to account for current conditions across monetary, fiscal, and geopolitical factors.

PART TWO

RISK FORECASTING

*To measure risk as the standard deviation of returns is fraught with
issues. But if we understand its limitations, this measure has the
advantage of simplicity.*

—JPP

Risk is easier to forecast than return. For example, based on a very large sample of daily US stock returns data from 1927 to 2018, the correlation in volatility from one month to the next is +69%.[1] This number is much higher than any of the one-month forward correlations we've discussed so far on the return side. That's without even trying: I just used the equal-weighted 21-day volatility as a predictor of volatility over the next 21 days. A caveat is that volatility is not always a good proxy for risk, especially if we define risk as exposure to loss. But ultimately, risk models are more deterministic than return models, which often require judgment calls, as I've argued in Part One of this book.

Therefore, many economists and financial analysts focus on risk models to satisfy their "physics envy." The ARCH model and its many extensions are an example of a class of models where advanced mathematics seems to add predictive value. Mark Kritzman, in a 1991 *Financial Analysts Journal* column titled "What Practitioners Need to Know . . . About Estimating Volatility, Part 2," demystifies the approach. His introduction is worth quoting directly:

Circle the correct answer:

Autoregressive Conditional Heteroscedasticity (ARCH) is:

1. a computer programming malfunction in which a variable is assigned more than one definition, causing the program to lock into an infinite loop;
2. a psychological disorder characterized by a reversion to earlier behavior patterns when confronted with unpleasant childhood memories;
3. in evolution, a reversion to a more primitive life form caused by inadequate diversity within a species;
4. a statistical procedure in which the dependent variable in a regression equation is modeled as a function of the time-varying properties of the error term.

To the uninitiated, all the above definitions might seem equally plausible. Moreover, the correct definition, (4.), may still not yield an intuitively satisfying description of ARCH.

This column is intended as a child's guide to ARCH, which is to say that it contains no equations. Our goal is to penetrate the cryptic jargon of ARCH so that at the very least you will feel comfortable attending social events hosted by members of the American Association of Statisticians. Of course, you should not expect that familiarity with ARCH will actually cause you to have fun at such events.

I suppose the *Financial Analysts Journal* was more relaxed back then. Before I interviewed with him for the first time, I read all Mark's papers. The last sentence made me spit out my coffee: "Of course, you should not expect that familiarity with ARCH will actually cause you to have fun at such events." For years I've tried to emulate his clever sense of humor, during conference presentations for example, with inconsistent success.

In a 2005 review of the literature on how to forecast risk, Ser-Huang Poon and Clive Granger summarize 93 published papers on the topic. Think of

Poon and Granger's article as the summary of a giant, multiyear, multiauthor horse race to find the best model. They compare the effectiveness of historical, ARCH, stochastic volatility, and option-implied models.

Historical models include the random walk model, which I used in my example on US stocks when I simply assumed that next month's volatility would be the same as this month's (plus or minus some unpredictable noise term). This model is perhaps the easiest to implement, and Poon and Granger conclude that it's very tough to beat. To clarify, this model doesn't assume volatility is random. It simply assumes that the most recent observation is the most relevant to forecast volatility over the following period—it assumes *persistence*. Other versions of the historical models use averages of past volatilities. These averages can be equal-weighted, they can be exponentially weighted (where more weight is put on recent observations), or they can be based on some form of fitted weights that maximize predictability. Historical models perform better than ARCH-type models in at least half the studies reviewed by Poon and Granger.

However, the ARCH models more explicitly fit the short-term persistence (predictability) in volatility, sometimes referred to as volatility clustering. [In 2003, the model's inventor, Robert F. Engle, won the Nobel Prize for "methods of analyzing economic time series with time-varying volatility (ARCH)."] Stephen Marra (2015) explains that conditional heteroscedasticity "refers to the notion that next period's volatility is conditional on the volatility in the current period as well as the time varying nature of volatility." Then he explains that the generalized autoregressive conditional heteroscedasticity, or GARCH version, "incorporates changes in the error term—or fluctuations in volatility—and tracks the persistence of volatility as it fluctuates around its long-term average." Several other versions of the ARCH model have been proposed to incorporate fat tails, asymmetries in volatility (the fact that volatility spikes *up* more than *down*), exponential weights, dynamic correlations, etc.

However, Marra shows that for US stocks, most sophisticated models, whether of the historical or ARCH classes, barely outperform the random walk model. The differences in model effectiveness don't look statistically significant. Other issues with sophisticated models include publication bias (only the good results get published), as well as a related, important issue: the possibility that these models may overfit the in-sample data.

It's hard to argue that one specific model should perform consistently better than to simply extrapolate recent volatility. Aside from a slight advantage for volatility estimates derived from options prices, Poon and Granger find that across 93 academic studies, there's no clear winner of the great risk forecasting horse race. And option-implied volatilities aren't a silver bullet either. Options don't trade for a wide range of assets anyway. In contrast with Poon and Granger's conclusion, Marra's results reveal that the option-implied approach performed the *worst* out of the eight models he backtested.

Of course, while no single model has surfaced as the most effective, some models perform better than others for specific asset classes and during specific time periods or market regimes. But in the end, the important takeaway remains that *short-term volatility, from one month to one year ahead, is quite predictable, even with simple models.* We'll discuss longer-term forecasts shortly, but for now, let us discuss how investors can take advantage of this short-term predictability.

Note

1. Fama-French data library (http://mba.tuck.dartmouth.edu/pages/faculty/ken.french/data_library.html). Time period: January 7, 1927 to June 29, 2018. Stock returns are net of the risk-free rate.

7

Risk-Based Investing and Something About Sailboats

Markets are only partially efficient.
—JPP

IN MAY 2016, I NEEDED IDEAS FOR A PRESENTATION AT THE 69th CFA Institute Annual Conference, held in Montreal. I'm French Canadian, so this was an especially exciting opportunity. My colleague Stefan Hubrich suggested research that he and colleagues (Bob Harlow, Anna Dreyer, and others) had done to capitalize on the short-term predictability in volatility. He mentioned that managed volatility and covered call writing are two of the few systematic investment approaches that have been shown to perform well across a variety of empirical studies. Moreover, they work well in practice (we manage such strategies as overlays or components of multi-asset portfolios). Stefan added: "So far, these two strategies have been studied separately, as stand-alone approaches. But it turns out that they're negatively correlated. When combined, they create a powerful toolset for portfolio enhancements."

Stefan, Bob, Anna, and other colleagues (David Clewell, Charles Shriver, and Toby Thompson) helped me prepare the presentation. Stefan, Bob, Anna, and I (2016) also published a paper for the conference proceedings, titled "Return of the Quants: Risk-Based Investing."

In Montreal, after a quick introduction in French, I switched to English. (While I speak French with family, I've lost track of how to translate technical finance terms from English to French.) I worried that terms like "fat tails" may sound odd in French.

I began my presentation with the observation that the financial services industry seems obsessed with return forecasting. Asset owners, investment managers, sell-side strategists, and financial media pundits all invest considerable time and resources to predict the direction of markets. Even so, I argued, risk-based investing may provide easier and more robust ways to improve portfolio performance, often without the need to forecast returns directly.

To emphasize the importance of risk-based investing, I showed that since 2000, volatility has increased significantly. In the 1940s, on average, there were four days per year during which stocks moved by three standard deviations or more ("three-sigma days"). The Second World War created a lot of this turbulence. In the six decades that followed, the average rose no higher than three days per year. But between 2000 and 2010, on average there were *nine* three-sigma days per year—more than any time in the preceding 80 years.[1]

Based on the normal distribution, a three-sigma day should occur only 0.6 time per year (on average). We often refer to extreme returns as "tail events" because they lie in the tails of the probability distribution. Clearly, the tails have gotten fatter in the markets, and the normal distribution may not be a reliable tool to measure investment risk.

I offered the audience several plausible explanations for this increase in market turbulence. Some of the usual suspects include central bank interventions, global market integration, high-frequency trading, and increased use of derivatives and structured products.

Whatever the root cause, I insisted that investors must manage exposure to large and sudden losses. And to do so, they must recognize that volatility—and thereby exposure to loss—is not stable through time. I showed that from 1994 to 2016, the rolling one-year standard deviation for a 60/40 portfolio (60% stocks, 40% bonds) ranged from a low of less than 5% to a high of 20%. This portfolio's rolling three-year standard deviation over the same period ranged from about 5% to about 15%.[2]

This example made it clear that a constant (fixed weight) asset allocation does not deliver a constant risk exposure. To a certain extent, it invalidates most financial planning advice. Is a 60/40 portfolio appropriate for a relatively risk-averse investor? The answer depends on the volatility regime. In some relatively calm environments, a 60/40 portfolio may deliver 5% volatility, which seems appropriate for a conservative investor. However, in turbulent markets, the same portfolio may deliver as much as 20% volatility, which seems more appropriate for an aggressive investor, with a thick skin and high risk tolerance. What's the solution? Is there a way to stabilize a portfolio's risk exposure over time?

Managed Volatility Backtests

The managed volatility strategy is designed for that purpose. It relies on the short-term predictability in volatility. In a nutshell, the strategy adjusts the asset mix over time to stabilize a portfolio's risk. For example, we may adjust a 60/40 portfolio's exposure to stocks all the way down to 20% when markets are volatile and all the way up to 75% when markets are stable. The asset mix becomes dynamic, but portfolio volatility is stabilized. As an analogy, think of how a sailor must dynamically adjust the sailboat's sails to adapt to wind conditions and keep a straight line. The strategy is portable and can easily be applied as a futures overlay to smooth the ride for almost any portfolio.[3] Importantly, it has been thoroughly backtested. In Table 7.1, I summarize a sample of 11 studies on the topic.[4]

To compare results across studies, I report alpha over volatility-matched, buy-and-hold benchmarks. Another way to think about these results is that for the same return, managed volatility portfolios delivered less volatility

TABLE 7.1 Prior Studies on Managed Volatility

Year	Authors	Backtest	Volatility Forecast	Universe	Period	Alpha (%)
2001	Fleming, Kirby, and Ostdiek	Daily, MVO	Nonparametric daily	4 asset classes	1983–1997	1.5
2003	Fleming, Kirby, and Ostdiek	Daily, MVO	Nonparametric intraday	4 asset classes	1984–2000	2.8
2011	Kritzman, Li, Page, and Rigobon	Daily	Absorption ratio	6 countries	1998–2010	4.5
2012	Kritzman, Page, and Turkington	Monthly, TAA	Regime switching	15 risk premiums	1978–2009	2.5
2012	Hallerbach	Daily	Trailing 6 months daily	Euro STOXX 50 vs. cash	2003–2011	2.2
2013	Kritzman	Daily, TAA	Absorption ratio	8 asset classes	1998–2013	4.9
2013	Dopfel and Ramkumar	Quarterly	Regime switching	S&P 500 vs. cash	1950–2011	2.0
2013	Hocquard, Ng, and Papageorgiou	Daily	GARCH	7 asset classes	1990–2011	2.6
2014	Perchet, Carvalho, and Moulin	Daily	GARCH	22 factors	1980–2013	3.0
2017	Moreira and Muir	Monthly	Trailing 1 month daily	10 factors, 20 countries	1926–2015	3.5
2019	Dreyer and Hubrich	Daily	Trailing daily	S&P 500 vs. cash	1929–2018	2.7

(and, it is hoped, less exposure to loss) than did their buy-and-hold benchmarks. When the authors did not report these results directly, I scaled Sharpe ratios to match the volatility of the static benchmark.

The results are encouraging, especially in a low-rate environment in which expected returns are depressed across stocks and bonds. Managed volatility seems to improve performance across studies. Indeed, the strategy appears to work well across risk forecast methodologies, asset classes (stocks, bonds, currencies), factors/risk premiums, regions, and time periods. These results suggest that any asset allocation process can be improved if we incorporate volatility forecasts.

But a few caveats apply. Cynics may argue that only backtests that generate interesting results get published (earlier I mentioned publication bias). Authors often make unrealistic assumptions about implementation. For example, they assume portfolio managers can rebalance everything at the closing price of the same day the signal is generated. Worse, some ignore transaction costs altogether. And a more subtle but key caveat is that some strategies do not use budget constraints, such that part of the alpha may come from a systematically long exposure to equity, duration, or other risk premiums versus the static benchmark.

Though these risk-adjusted alphas should be shaved to account for the inevitable implementation shortfall between backtests and reality, managed volatility has been shown in practice to reduce exposure to loss and smooth the ride for investors, at a very low—or even positive—cost in terms of returns. Dreyer and Hubrich (2019) treat cost and implementation carefully, because they are rooted in live portfolio experience.

Consider a backtest our team built specifically to represent real-world implementation, based on data from January 1996 to December 2014. For this example, we set a target of 11% volatility for a balanced portfolio of 65% stocks and 35% bonds. We scaled the overlay to avoid any systematically long equity or duration (i.e., bond) exposure versus the underlying portfolio—consequently, the strategy is expected to keep a risk profile similar to a 65/35 exposure *on average*. We allowed the managed volatility overlay to reduce equity exposure to as low as 20% and increase it as high as 75%.[5]

We then applied a band of 14% and 10% volatility around the target. As long as volatility remained within the band, no rebalancing was required. When volatility rose above or fell below the bands, the strategy rebalanced the overlay to meet the (expected) volatility target. We used a wider upper band because volatility tends to spike *up* more than it spikes *down*, so these asymmetrical bands were meant to reduce noise and minimize the intrusiveness of the algorithm.

Within the portfolio, we assumed that 95% of assets were invested directly in a balanced strategy composed of actively managed mandates (i.e., within each of the asset classes, managers selected securities).[6] The remaining 5% were set aside as the cash collateral for the volatility management overlay, which we assumed was invested in Treasury bills. When volatility was at target, the futures overlay was set to match the balanced portfolio at 65% stocks and 35% bonds. Equity futures were allocated 70% to the S&P 500 and 30% to the MSCI EAFE (Europe, Australasia, and the Far East) Index futures, to reflect the neutral US/non-US equity mix inside the balanced strategy. Last, we imposed a minimum daily trade size of 1% and maximum trade size of 10% of the portfolio's notional.

To forecast volatility, we used a DCC–EGARCH model (dynamic conditional correlation—exponentially weighted generalized autoregressive conditional heteroscedasticity) with fat-tailed distributions. This model closely replicates the implied volatility on traded options and thus how investors in general forecast volatility. DCC accounts for time-varying correlations. The ARCH model, as I mentioned, accounts for the time series properties of volatility, such as its persistence or tendency to cluster. We reestimated the model daily using 10 years of data ending the day prior to the forecast.[7] Volatility forecasts were updated daily using the most current parameter estimates. Importantly, we strictly used information known at the time to determine how to trade the overlay.

As expected, over the 18-year period studied, managed volatility consistently stabilized volatility compared with its static benchmark. The algorithm worked particularly well during the 2008–2009 financial crisis. The strategy was quite tactical. Although it did not trade more than 10% of the portfolio's notional value in futures in a given day, some of the shifts in equity allocations were meaningful and occurred over relatively short periods of time.

In this example, active managers added returns over passive benchmarks (after fees) in the underlying building blocks through security selection. They slightly increased exposure to loss. When we applied the managed volatility overlay to this portfolio, we sacrificed a few basis points of returns, but we reduced drawdown exposure. Because we avoided large equity exposures throughout the high-volatility regimes, the historical maximum drawdown was 10% lower than for a static benchmark.

Over the last two years, we have managed such strategies for an insurance company and other clients. As we manage through the equity sell-off of 2020, so far these strategies have performed well.

Why would managed volatility improve risk-adjusted returns? To explain this success, we must understand why volatility is persistent (and therefore predictable). Periods of low and high volatility—risk regimes—tend to persist for a while. This persistence is crucial to the success of the strategy, and it means that simple volatility forecasts can be used to adjust risk exposures. A fundamental argument could be made that shocks to the business cycle themselves tend to cluster. Bad news often follows bad news. The use of leverage—in financial markets and in the broader economy—may also contribute to volatility clustering. Leverage often takes time to unwind. Other explanations may be related to behavioral aspects of investing that are common to investors across markets, such as "fear contagion," extrapolation biases, and the financial media's overall negativity bias.

In terms of managing tail risk specifically, one way to explain how managed volatility works is to represent portfolio returns as a "mixture of distributions," which is related to the concept of risk regimes. When we mix high-volatility and low-volatility distributions and randomly draw from either, we get a fat-tailed distribution. By adjusting risk exposures, managed volatility essentially "normalizes" portfolio returns to one single distribution and thereby significantly reduces tail risk.

Short-term expected (or "forward") returns do not seem to increase after volatility spikes, which explains why managed volatility often outperforms buy and hold in terms of the Sharpe ratio (or risk-adjusted performance in general).

This phenomenon has been studied in academia (see the article published in the *Journal of Finance* titled "Volatility Managed Portfolios," by Alan Moreira and Tyler Muir, 2017). Most explanations focus on the time horizon mismatch between managed volatility and value investing. Moreira and Muir observe that expected returns adjust more slowly than volatility. Therefore, managed volatility strategies may re-risk the portfolio when market turbulence has subsided and still capture the upside from attractive valuations. The performance of managed volatility around the 2008 crisis is a good example. As Moreira and Muir put it:

> Our [managed volatility] portfolios reduce risk taking during these bad times—times when the common advice is to increase or hold risk taking constant. For example, in the aftermath of the sharp price declines in the fall of 2008, it was a widely held view that those that reduced positions in equities were missing a once-in-a-generation buying opportunity. Yet our strategy cashed out almost completely and returned to the market only as the spike in volatility receded. . . . Our simple strategy turned out to work well throughout several crisis episodes, including the Great Depression, the Great Recession, and the 1987 stock market crash.

Stefan Hubrich points out that there is another way to think about how managed volatility may increase Sharpe ratios in certain market environments: think of *time* diversification as similar to *cross-asset* diversification. Suppose we invest in five different stocks with the same Sharpe ratios but very different volatility levels. If we assume the stocks are uncorrelated, we should allocate equal risk (not equal value weights) to get the Sharpe ratio–maximizing portfolio. The same logic applies through time; the realized variance of the portfolio is basically the sum of the point-in-time variances. To get the highest Sharpe ratio through time, we should allocate equal risk to each period.

However, managed volatility does not always outperform static portfolios. For example, when spikes in volatility are followed by short-term return gains, managed volatility may miss out on those gains (versus a buy-and-hold portfolio). Also, it is possible for large market drawdowns to occur when volatility is very low. In those situations, managed volatility strategies that overweight stocks in quiet times (to a higher weight than the static portfolio) may underperform.

In sum, the empirical observations in support of managed volatility—volatility persistence and the lack of correlation between volatility spikes and short-term forward returns—hold on average, but not in all market environments. Ultimately, volatility is forecastable because it "clusters"; hence, managed volatility stabilizes realized volatility and reduces tail risk. It also improves risk-adjusted returns due to a "time diversification" between risk regimes, as well as the empirical reality that risk-adjusted equity market returns are *not* higher when volatility is high. (Absolute expected returns are higher in high-volatility periods, but not enough to compensate for the higher volatility.) It's possible that managed volatility can "sell low" into a bear market and lose ground, but it is also often "long risk" during expansions. Throughout the cycle, it may provide higher exposure to the equity risk premium than would a typical long-only fund without additional risk.

For more on this topic, as well as a robust empirical study and a fascinating discussion on how to think about managed volatility, see Dreyer and Hubrich (2019). To quote Stefan Hubrich, one of the authors of this paper:

> Managed volatility can have high tracking error to the underlying for extended (multi-year) periods, if it's scaled large enough so that it can make a difference. It's a fundamentally different strategic, very long-term asset allocation—rather than an "active" strategy benchmarked to the underlying that can be evaluated quarterly. Warren Buffet once said that if the internet had been invented first, we wouldn't have newspapers. I tend to believe that if managed volatility had been invented first, we might not have as many traditional balanced funds. It's really the more appropriate long term/unconditional way to invest, as the portfolio is always—each day—aligned with your risk tolerance.

Covered Call Writing (Volatility Risk Premium)

While managed volatility is used mostly to reduce exposure to loss, we can think of covered call writing as the other side of the coin for risk-based investing, in that investors use it mostly to generate excess returns. The basics of the strategy are simple: the investor sells a call option and simultaneously buys the underlying security or index. Covered call writing gives exposure to the volatility risk premium, one of the "alternative betas" that have risen in popularity recently.

The strategy relies on the predictability in the difference between implied volatility (embedded in options prices) and realized market volatility. Historically, implied volatility has almost always been higher than subsequent realized volatility. Hence, when appropriately hedged, the strategy *sells* implied volatility and *buys* realized volatility, without any (or with very little) direct market exposure. As mentioned by Roni Israelov and Lars N. Nielsen in "Covered Call Strategies: One Fact and Eight Myths" (2014), "The volatility risk premium, which is absent from most investors' portfolios, has had more than double the risk-adjusted returns (Sharpe ratio) of the equity risk premium."

In Table 7.2, I show results from several empirical studies on the performance of covered call writing.[8] The strategy has generated (simulated) alpha across markets and time periods and for several variations of the methodology. William Fallon, James Park, and Danny Yu, in their 2015 paper

TABLE 7.2   Prior Studies on the Volatility Risk Premium

Year	Authors	Analysis	Period	Alpha (%)
2002	Whaley	BXM with bid-ask costs	1988–2001	6.2
2005	Feldman and Roy	BXM	2003–2004	5.2
2006	Hill et al.	Dynamic strategies	1990–2005	7.0
2007	Kapadia and Szado	10 backtests	1996–2006	3.5
2008	Figelman	BXM	1988–2005	5.8
2015	Israelov and Nielsen	Delta-hedged BXM	1996–2014	1.7
2015	Fallon, Park, and Yu	34 asset classes	1995–2014	2.4

"Asset Allocation Implications of the Global Volatility Premium," backtest volatility risk premium strategies across 11 equity markets, 10 commodities, 9 currencies, and 4 government bond markets. They find that "the volatility risk premium is sizable and significant, both statistically and economically."

The same caveats apply as for the managed volatility studies—namely, that only backtests with good results tend to get published and that authors often ignore implementation shortfall between backtests and realized performance. Nonetheless, in practice, covered call writing has been shown to deliver good risk-adjusted performance, although perhaps not as high as 6–7% alpha across all market regimes.

As we did for managed volatility, we must ask why we should expect the volatility risk premium to continue to perform well going forward. What are the theoretical foundations behind the strategy? First, there's demand for hedging. For example, insurance companies need to hedge explicit liabilities they have written. Generally, investors in many countries are increasingly seeking drawdown protection. By selling options, investors should earn a risk premium. The magnitude of this premium is determined by the supply and demand imbalance for insurance.

Some observers may say that covered call writing does not sell protection. But if the puts are overpriced because of the demand for protection, calls should be overpriced as well, through put-call parity. Indeed, dealers can replicate the put with the call and a short forward position. As long as no arbitrage occurs, demand for protection will also drive up the call price.

The history of implied volatility for US stocks is consistent with the fact that investors crave protection. Historically, implied volatility was almost always higher than realized volatility. This spread loosely explains the performance of covered call writing.

Second, beyond the "demand for hedging" theory, a simpler explanation for the volatility risk premium has been proposed: it may simply represent compensation for its tail risk. Selling volatility generates long series of relatively small gains, followed by infrequent but large losses. (In statistical terms, returns are said to exhibit negative skewness and excess kurtosis. We'll define these terms in more detail in Chapter 8.) In 2008, for example, realized one-month volatility on the S&P 500 shot up significantly above implied volatility, and covered call writing strategies experienced significant losses. Fallon, Park, and Yu report similar tail risks in the volatility risk premium for 33 out of 34 of the asset classes they studied.

Both explanations—the demand for hedging and the compensation for tail risk—are, in fact, connected. Insurance providers should expect negatively skewed returns, by definition. The bottom line is that if long-term investors can accept negative skewness in their returns, they should get compensation through the volatility risk premium.

A Powerful Combo of Risk-Based Strategies

Investors can use managed volatility to reduce the tail-risk exposure in covered call writing. The idea is to think of risk-based strategies as a set of tools, rather than stand-alone approaches. Low or even negative correlations between risk-based strategies can add a lot of value to a portfolio, even when the individual strategies' Sharpe ratios are relatively low.

In my presentation at the CFA Institute Annual Conference, I used data from a study by my colleague Stefan Hubrich to show that the correlation of monthly returns above cash from January 1996 to December 2015 between covered call writing and managed volatility (overlay only, without the equity exposure) was −20%.[9] This result suggests that when investors incur a loss on covered call writing, they are likely to have already de-risked their portfolio with their managed volatility overlay, thus reducing the impact of the loss.

To further illustrate the power of diversification between covered call writing and managed volatility, Stefan estimated returns, volatilities, downside risk, and relative performance statistics for the stand-alone and combined strategies. Based on data from January 1996 to December 2015, the risk-return ratio of the S&P 500 is 0.41. When combined with the covered call writing strategy (with gross exposure capped at 125%), the S&P 500's risk-return ratio increases from 0.41 to 0.49, while downside risk is only marginally reduced. But when we add managed volatility, the risk-return ratio jumps from 0.49 to 0.69 (even though the stand-alone managed volatility strategy had a relatively low risk-return ratio of 0.17), and downside risk is reduced substantially.

Takeaways and Q&A

To summarize, volatility has been shown to be persistent, and in the short run, it has not been predictive of returns. Accordingly, managed volatility is one of the few systematic investment strategies that historically outperformed buy-and-hold benchmarks across a wide range of markets and data samples.

Covered call writing is another systematic strategy that has been shown to generate attractive risk-adjusted performance across many empirical studies and in practice. The strategy gives access to the volatility risk premium, which pays those who provide insurance and assume the associated tail risk.

Combining managed volatility and covered call writing can be extremely effective, because these two strategies are negatively correlated and can easily be added to conventional portfolios. And despite our industry's obsession with return forecasting, these two investment strategies focus on risk. They do not require bold predictions on the direction of markets.

Q&A

The large conference audience asked interesting questions, and I hope I offered insightful replies. What follows is an edited version of that conversation.

Q: *How is managed volatility different from risk parity?*
A: Risk parity seeks to equalize risk contributions from individual portfolio components. Usually, it is applied at the asset class level and assumes that Sharpe ratios are all the same across asset classes and that all correlations are identical. Low-volatility asset classes, such as bonds, are typically levered up to increase their risk contribution to the portfolio. On the surface, therefore, it is quite different. It is a way to allocate the portfolio that doesn't address risk disparity through time. (It's a fact that periods of high volatility with high exposure to loss alternate with periods of lower volatility.)

However, some risk parity strategies maintain a target volatility for the entire portfolio. In a sense, this means that there can be an implied managed volatility component to risk parity investing.

Still, to believe in risk parity investing, you must believe that Sharpe ratios are the same in all markets and under all market conditions, which I believe is not always the case.

Q: *Why not just focus on downside volatility?*
A: Downside volatility can be calculated in many ways. For example, you can isolate deviations below the mean to calculate semistandard deviation, or you can use conditional value at risk (average loss during extreme downside markets) and try to manage risk at that level. The volatility surface from option prices, for example, embeds implicit estimates of the tail of the distribution.

To focus on downside risk makes sense. Is there such a thing as upside risk? In general, though, it is more difficult to forecast the directionality of volatility than volatility itself. Doing so in managed volatility backtests may not change the forecast that much. We'll discuss downside risk forecasts in more detail in the next chapter.

Q: *The volatility risk premium has negatively skewed returns. Could you expand on the implications?*
A: Indeed, the volatility risk premium does not have a symmetrical payoff. The purpose of the strategy is to earn the premium from the difference between implied and realized volatility. Most of the time, you make a small gain. But when those volatilities cross, relatively large losses occur. That is one of the reasons for the risk premium. If you are a long-term investor and you accept this asymmetry, you should expect to be compensated for it.

Q: *Is there a risk of buying high and selling low with managed volatility? And how does managed volatility relate to a value-based approach?*
A: This question comes up often around managed volatility. The goal is to lower exposure to the market on the way down and get back in when volatility goes back down but when valuations are still attractive. Moreira and Muir (2017) have run a set of tests related to this question. They argue that time horizon matters. Across more than 20 different markets and risk premiums,

they show that the correlation between this month's volatility, calculated very simply on daily data, and next month's volatility is about 60%, which indicates persistence in volatility.[10]

Then they examined the correlation between volatility this month and returns next month. They found a 0% correlation. If it were negative, it would work even better, but the 0% correlation is good enough to substantially improve risk-adjusted returns through adjustments of risk exposures based on volatility.

The intuition is that value-focused investors try to buy low and sell high, but they typically do so with a longer time horizon. Often, they wait for market turbulence to subside before they buy low. In fact, valuation signals don't work very well below a 1-year horizon, and they tend to work best when the horizon is relatively long: 5 to 10 years.

The difference in time horizon between a managed volatility process with a one-month horizon and a longer-cycle valuation process often allows managed volatility investors to get back into risk assets at attractive valuations.

Moreira and Muir's study (2017) is particularly interesting because they tested several market crises, including the crash of 1987, and the strategy with a one-month volatility forecast outperformed buy and hold over all crisis periods.

Q: *Do liquidity issues arise when you implement managed volatility and covered call writing strategies for very big funds?*
A: You can run managed volatility with very liquid contracts, such as S&P 500 and Treasury futures. If the portfolio is not invested in such plain-vanilla asset classes, there might be a trade-off between basis risk (how well the futures overlay represents the underlying portfolio) and liquidity, but this trade-off can be managed with a risk factor model and a tracking error minimization optimization. Nonetheless, it's irrefutable that liquidity risk can create significant gaps in markets, and some investors—for example, insurance companies—buy S&P 500 put options in combination with managed volatility to explicitly hedge this gap risk.

As for covered call writing, index options on the S&P 500 are liquid. However, for other options markets, investors must assess the trade-off between illiquidity and the risk premium earned.

Q: *What are the costs of implementing these strategies?*
A: The trading costs for a managed volatility overlay are remarkably low because of the deep liquidity of futures markets, perhaps 10–18 bps. If the overlay is not implemented in-house, a management fee of 10–20 bps will be accrued. Accessing the volatility risk premium through options is probably on the order of 40–60 bps for transaction costs plus a management fee. Note that these are just estimates, and costs always depend on the size of the mandate and a variety of other factors.

Q: *Can you use managed volatility to inform currency hedging decisions?*
A: With currency hedging, investors must manage the trade-off between carry, which is driven by the interest rate differential, and the risk that currencies contribute to the portfolio. Importantly, the investor's base currency matters. When investors in a country with low interest rates hedge their currency exposures, they typically benefit from risk reduction, but it comes at the cost of negative carry. Japan, for example, has very low interest rates, which means currency hedging is a "negative carry trade." So it is very hard to convince Japanese investors to hedge, even though from a risk perspective, it may be the right decision.

In Australia, by contrast, currency hedging offers positive carry because local interest rates are relatively high. Australian investors love to hedge their foreign currency exposures back to the home currency. But the Australian dollar tends to be a risk-on currency. Ultimately, investors can use managed volatility to optimize this trade-off dynamically. As volatility goes up, they can adjust their hedge ratios to reduce exposure to carry (thereby reducing their risk-on exposures). To do so, they must recalculate the risk-return trade-offs on an ongoing basis and reexamine the correlations between currencies and the underlying portfolio's assets, as well as with their liabilities when applicable.

Q: *Is it better to do option writing when the Volatility Index (VIX) is high or low?*

A: It is generally better to sell options when implied volatility is overpriced relative to expected realized volatility. For example, when investors are nervous over a high-volatility event or a market drawdown, options may be overpriced. The determinant is not necessarily high or low volatility, but rather the effect investor behavior is having on option prices relative to the real economic volatility in the underlying investment. To get the timing right is not easy, of course, but active management may add value over a simple approach that keeps a constant exposure to the volatility risk premium.

Q: *With so much money chasing managed volatility, do you think the alpha is likely to become more elusive?*

A: It's true that managed volatility is harder to implement when everyone's rushing for the door at the same time. And the risk of overcrowding—and associated gap risk—is always there. But managed volatility still works well when we slow down the algorithm.

Also, over time, profit opportunities from "overreaction" should entice value or opportunistic investors to take the other side of managed volatility trades. I think of it as an equilibrium. As managed volatility starts causing "overreaction," the premium that value buyers can earn if they take the other side of the trade will become more and more attractive. That will entice them to provide liquidity.

Notes

1. Factset, Standard and Poor's, and T. Rowe Price. Standard deviation is measured over the full sample of data (1940–2015).
2. The balanced strategy is 60% S&P 500 and 40% Barclays U.S. Aggregate Index rebalanced monthly. *Sources:* Ibbotson Associates, Standard & Poor's, and Barclays.
3. With an overlay, we trade futures contracts to change broad market exposures in the portfolio. We typically don't transact in the underlying asset classes, which means the portfolio managers responsible for the various asset class–level mandates aren't affected. In other words, they are "undisturbed"; i.e., they can manage their portfolio as they normally do, without excessive inflows or outflows or changes to their process.

4. Readers should refer to the original papers for more information on the volatility forecast methodologies. I report the average of key results or the key results as reported by the authors. MVO refers to mean-variance optimization; TAA refers to tactical asset allocation, expressed as various multi-asset portfolio shifts; all other backtests involve timing exposure to a single market or risk premium. Countries refer to country equity markets, except for Perchet, Carvalho, and Moulin (2014), which includes value and momentum factors across 10 countries and 10 currencies. Some backtests in Fleming, Kirby, and Ostdiek (2001) and Perchet, Carvalho, and Moulin (2014) involve shorter time series because of the lack of available data. The backtest by Dopfel and Ramkumar (2013) is in-sample. The regime-switching model in Kritzman, Page, and Turkington (2012) combines turbulence, GDP, and inflation regimes. Regarding transaction costs, Fleming, Kirby, and Ostdiek (2001, 2003) assume execution via futures contracts and estimate transaction costs in the 10–20-bps range. Moreira and Muir (2017) report transaction costs in the 56–183-bps range for physicals. Dreyer and Hubrich (2019) use a 3-bps bid-ask spread for every futures trade, based on the actual trading pattern of the strategy. They show a 10–20% deterioration in results when adding these transaction costs to the simulation. However, they more than recover these costs when they also add caps on trading behavior: they only trade if the proposed trade is >10%, and they only implement up to 50% same day. All other studies do not report transaction costs.

5. The model allows for adding risk *above* the 65% strategic allocation when volatility is low. In fact, investors can calibrate managed volatility overlays to any desired risk level, including levels above the underlying portfolio's static exposure.

6. Note that we used an actual track record for an actively managed balanced fund. However, this example is for illustrative purposes only and does not represent performance that any investor actually attained. Model returns have inherent limitations, including assumptions, and may not reflect the impact that material economic and market factors may have had on the decision-making process if client funds were actually managed in the manner shown.

7. We used an expanding window, increasing from 3 years to 10 years, until 10 years of data became available.

8. The BXM Index refers to the CBOE S&P 500 BuyWrite Index. It is a benchmark index designed to track the performance of a hypothetical buy-write (covered call writing) strategy on the S&P 500. Fallon, Park, and Yu's start dates vary from January 1995 to February 2001 based on data availability, and alpha is averaged across all backtests.

9. All data sources and methodologies from this section are described in "Return of the Quants," *CFA Institute Conference Proceedings*, Third Quarter 2016.

10. These results are from a previous (2016) working paper version, not the version published in the *Journal of Finance*. I don't know why Moreira and Muir removed this section—perhaps because the working paper was quite long, and these were basic tests with little academic contribution (from a methodology perspective).

8

Longer-Term Risk Forecasting and Something About Dilequants

When we use standard deviation as our measure of risk, we assume
that returns are normally distributed, which is not always the case,
and we assume that investors follow a peculiar decision process.
—JPP

PREVIOUS RESEARCH ON MANAGED VOLATILITY AND covered call writing and Poon and Granger's review of 93 papers on risk forecasting—the mega, multiauthor horse race I mentioned in my introduction to this risk forecasting—all focus on short-term risk forecasts, mostly between one-hour and one-month horizons. For strategic asset allocation and many tactical asset allocation processes, these forecast horizons aren't long enough.

There also appears to be an unspoken assumption among the authors of these studies that the more complex the model, the better. Meanwhile, basic questions are left unanswered. For example, it's not always clear how to calibrate the models, let alone address questions on the lookback window (one month? one year? five years? more?) and data frequency (daily, weekly, or monthly?), irrespective of the volatility-forecasting model.

To address these issues, I asked my colleague Rob Panariello to set up our own study. Our goal was to help investors solve more mundane yet important questions on how to use the data available to them.

We wanted to directly study the persistence of other aspects of risk beyond volatility—the so-called higher moments. If we observe that losses tend to be greater than gains ("negative skewness"), should we expect the same going forward? And if we observe fat tails ("high kurtosis") in asset returns, should we expect fat tails going forward? In other words, while we know that volatility is persistent, are higher moments persistent (and therefore predictable) too? Or do they mean-revert? These higher moments matter because they can drastically change exposure to loss.

I prepared the data for Rob, using the same universe of asset classes and the same data sources as for the other similar analyses I've mentioned so far in this book. The dataset covers 33 data series: 20 asset classes (10 equity and 10 fixed income asset classes) and 12 relative bets (6 equity bets and 6 fixed income bets), as well as the stocks versus bonds relative bet. The list of equity asset classes and relative bets is on page 53, and the list for fixed income is on page 75. The start date for the daily and weekly dataset is August 30, 2000, and the end date is September 5, 2018. Monthly data start on February 28, 1993, and end on August 31, 2018. These dates are based on data availability.

I asked Rob if he could calculate the correlation between past and future volatility, skewness, and kurtosis for each of these 33 return series. I also asked him to vary the trailing windows as follows: one month (21 days), six months, one year, three years, and five years. I asked him to vary the forecast horizons in the same way and to repeat the entire experiment for daily, weekly, and monthly data.

For example, I asked Rob to calculate the correlation between (a) volatility as calculated over the last year based on weekly data and (b) volatility over the next month based on daily data. We then repeated the same experiment but looked at volatility over the next six months, one year, three years, and five years, looked at another asset class or relative bet, changed the look-back window, switched to monthly lagged data, and so on. The goal was to uncover what would have been the best way to forecast risk based on our data sample. We also wanted to uncover general rules of thumb (patterns in our results) about how to use data to build a risk forecast for asset allocation.

The number of experiments exploded. When all was said and done, we realized we wanted to look at the persistence in risk measures in 19,305 different ways: 195 lead-lag-data frequency combinations across three moments (volatility, skewness, and kurtosis) for 33 asset classes and bets. Rob's prodigious mathematical brain went into hyperdrive.

"I have to think about how to code this massive experiment and how to store and summarize the results," Rob said.

"Agreed. How long do you think it will take?" I asked.

"Let me get back to you," Rob answered.

The next day, he walked into my office. "It's done," he said, dropping the sample results on my desk. It only took him a few hours on Matlab. It would have taken me two or three weeks *full-time* to complete the project. I'm a "dilequant"—Mark Kritzman's term for those who dabble in quantitative analysis.

Results from Our Risk Forecasting Horse Race

It's difficult to summarize results for 19,305 risk predictability tests. This analysis revealed several important takeaways, supported by persistent patterns in our results. The conclusions differed depending on whether we looked at short-to-medium time horizons (one month to three years) or the longer horizon of five years.

First, persistence in volatility was highest at short horizons. It's easier to forecast volatility one month ahead than one year ahead, and so on. Across all combinations of data windows, forecast horizons, and data frequencies, *month-to-month volatility based on daily data showed the most persistence.* The average correlation between this month's daily volatility and next month's was +68%, with little variation across asset classes and bets. It was the highest positive correlation across all risk forecast permutations for 32 out of 33 asset classes or bets—a remarkably consistent result.

The only exception was Treasuries, for which the six-month estimation window of daily data produced slightly better (one month ahead) forecasts (+67% correlation) versus the one-month window (+65% correlation). These results seem to explain why managed volatility and actively managed covered call writing strategies rely on short-term volatility persistence.

A more surprising result was that *shorter* estimation windows also produced better forecasts at *longer* horizons. This result is important for asset allocation because it means we can also improve risk-adjusted returns without tactical volatility management. On average, across asset classes and bets, volatility measured over the most recent 21 days produced the best forecasts of medium horizon volatilities (six months, one year, and three years forward). Statisticians often claim that more data are better than less data and that we need long time periods to estimate something with "significance." Here the intuition is the opposite. Recent data carry more information about the future than older data. It's an oversimplification, but think of monetary policy, which often drives volatility in financial markets. Most of the time, the Fed's actions over the last few weeks should have more impact on market volatility going forward than what it did a year ago, for example.

In that context, suppose we want to produce a forecast of weekly volatility over the next year. Based on our results, we should use the last 21 days of data (+42% correlation with one-year forward weekly volatility), which gives a better forecast than the last six months (+38%), which in turn is more accurate than the last year (+30%). This result—that shorter estimation windows work better—held for forecasts of daily, weekly, and monthly forward volatilities. It was consistent across asset classes and bets. For horizons from six months to three years, we found a similar pattern for *all* 33 asset classes. This result means that investors should pay significant attention to recent volatility.

On the other hand, when it came to data frequency (daily, weekly, or monthly), our experiments revealed that *for the same estimation window,* more data were better than less data. We found that for short- and medium-term horizons, estimation windows based on daily data worked better than ones based on weekly data, which in turn worked better than ones based on monthly data. We didn't expect this result. We expected that it would be better to match data frequency between estimation and forecast. In other words, we expected that daily data would best forecast daily volatility, weekly data would best forecast weekly volatility, and so on. But we found that on average, daily data almost always produced the best forecasts, even for forward monthly volatility.

To summarize, the following patterns in short- and medium-term volatility held whether we looked at absolute or relative bets, and they held across equity and fixed income markets: *persistence works best at short horizons, shorter estimation windows work better even for longer horizons, and higher-frequency data work better than lower-frequency data.*

Mean Reversion at Longer Horizons

Another consistent pattern emerged at longer horizons: mean reversion. It started to appear when we used a three-year estimation window to forecast three-year volatility. It became strongest with the five-year estimation window for five-year forward realized volatility, across daily, weekly, and monthly frequencies.

When we look at longer time horizons, we must carefully interpret results because we automatically reduce the number of independent observations. In a 2019 article published in the *Financial Analysts Journal* titled "Long-Horizon Predictability: A Cautionary Tale," Boudoukh, Israel, and Richardson explain that long-horizon forecasts aren't always as accurate as they may seem. As we increase the time horizon, we reduce the number of non-overlapping data points, and the confidence intervals around our estimates widen.

Using overlapping data doesn't add much explanatory power, because the variables are autocorrelated. For example, suppose we use rolling monthly data for five-year forecasts. In this case, our February 2018 forecast covers 58 of the 60 months from our January 2018 forecast. Only the first and last month are different, so we haven't added much information to estimate the relationship. Therefore, in finance, all else being equal (particularly for the same time period), statistical estimates based on longer horizons—t-statistics, regression betas, or R-squares/correlations—are less reliable than shorter-horizon estimates and are more likely to show extreme values.

But the negative correlations in the five-year estimation—five-year realized "cells" in our results matrix—were remarkably strong. The averages (across asset classes and bets) in those cells ranged from –45% to –79%, depending on the data frequencies used for the estimation and realized volatilities. It was the strongest negative correlation—averaged across frequencies—for 32 out of 33 asset classes and bets.

This result has important implications for strategic asset allocation. Most institutional asset owners and individuals (or their advisors) use long windows of data to forecast risk when they establish their strategic asset mix. A five-year period of monthly data appears to be a popular estimation window. While it's probably better to use longer estimation windows, several asset classes and funds don't have long return histories. (The alternative space is one example.) There are ways to combine long and short histories—to "backfill" the missing data for the short series. For example, in 2013, I published an article in the *Financial Analysts Journal* titled "How to Combine Long and Short Return Histories Efficiently." But investors often just cut the entire dataset at the beginning of the shortest time series.

A key takeaway from our results is that while we found persistence at short horizons, especially one month ahead, the results were the *opposite* for long horizons. Five years of calm markets are more likely to be followed by five years of turbulence, and vice versa. Therefore, risk estimates for strategic asset allocation may be seriously flawed if they extrapolate the past. It would be better to model this mean reversion directly.[1]

However, there's an important caveat to these results on long-term mean reversion. In a follow-up experiment, we analyzed volatility persistence with a longer dataset (1926–2018, from Ken French's website[2]). Our results, again, revealed strong short-term volatility persistence. These findings were robust to the new dataset. But long-run mean reversion was not as strong as we observed on data from 1993 to 2018. In fact, in the long sample, mean reversion only appeared between the trailing 10-year and forward 10-year windows, and not across all asset classes. (We were able to add the 10-year windows due to the longer dataset.) Otherwise, in this longer dataset, we found mild *persistence* in long-run volatility.

What explains the difference in the two samples? I suspect that central banks played a role in the more recent mean reversion. The tech bubble and the 2008–2009 crisis were both followed by periods of data-dependent economic stabilization driven by central banks. Ultimately, my view is that the 1993–2018 sample may be more representative of the future. Central banks should continue to be more data-dependent than they were many decades ago. The business cycle should continue to dominate market volatility, compared with other factors that drove volatility in the longer sample, such as runaway inflation, world wars, etc. In general, I question the common assumption that the longer the dataset, the more reliable our estimate of financial markets behavior in the current environment. (Back in 1926, computers and televisions did not exist, and many people still used the horse and buggy for transportation.)

What About Higher Moments?

As mentioned earlier, we also wanted to look at features of risk beyond volatility. Our results were disappointing for "higher moments" (skewness and kurtosis). We didn't find much predictability. But first, the definitions of the terms "moments," "skewness," and "kurtosis" tell us something important about exposure to loss.

In finance, we try to predict the future. As Bernd Scherer said in response to the GIGO critique, if you can't formulate expectations about the future, "you shouldn't be in the investment business." But because we don't know the future with certainty, we must consider a range of future outcomes. To do so, we use probability distributions. The best way to represent a probability distribution graphically is to use histograms. The height of the bars in these histograms represents the likelihood of various outcomes, ordered from low to high on the x axis. The bars are usually high around the average outcome (say, for stocks, an expected return of 7%), and they get smaller and smaller as we move toward more extreme events (say, a return of –30% or +30%).

Moments are used to describe the shape of these probability distributions. The first moment is volatility, which we've discussed at length. The second moment, skewness, measures whether the distribution is symmetrical, as I've mentioned before. If large gains are more likely than large losses of the same magnitude, the distribution is positively skewed, which means that its "right tail" is longer than its "left tail." A call option, for example, is positively skewed. Unfortunately, in financial markets, *negatively* skewed distributions are much more frequent than positively skewed distributions, such that losses of −10% tend to be more frequent than gains of +10%, for example.

A cheesy but surprisingly reliable joke about skewness that I like to use at conferences goes as follows:

> Recently, I've been working on a paper on negative skewness and portfolio construction. We explain how naïve financial advisors tend to load up client portfolios with negatively skewed assets like credit and hedge funds, just because these assets have relatively low volatility and high returns. In doing so, they ignore the mismatch between volatility (which is low) and exposure loss (which is high). I thought I had a great title idea for the paper: "Skew You! Says Your Financial Advisor." *But my marketing compliance department didn't like it.*

Like many of my conference witticisms, I may have stolen this one from Mark Kritzman.

The third moment, kurtosis, measures whether the tails are "fat," i.e., whether the probabilities of large losses or gains are higher than we would expect from a normal distribution, irrespective of the symmetry or lack thereof in the distribution.

These so-called higher moments, skewness and kurtosis, matter a great deal when we try to forecast exposure to loss. In that context, our results were problematic. We found almost no predictability and no persistent pattern in either skewness or kurtosis, except for some mean reversion at the five-year horizon (similar to what we found for volatility, albeit weaker).

My intuition on this mean reversion is that following big crises, investors and monetary authorities become more careful, and the regulator puts measures in place to prevent excesses. Similarly, when markets have been quiet for a long time, investors become complacent, and asset price bubbles start to form. Nonetheless, some emerging markets (for example) have experienced crises in rapid succession, and sometimes there's a domino effect that can continue for several years.

In the end, we estimate higher moments based on very few, extreme data points, such as the tech bubble and the 2008 financial crisis. This lack of predictability and consistency across markets shouldn't be surprising. Yet for asset allocation decisions, we can't ignore higher moments. As we will see in Chapter 11, scenario analysis is a useful tool to address this problem. At the portfolio level, we can improve our estimation of higher moments if we account for how correlations change in down markets.

Notes

1. In general, our analysis raises this question: Would a model that includes both short-term persistence and long-term mean reversion work better than most other models?
2. mba.tuck.dartmouth.edu/pages/faculty/ken.french/data_library.html.

9

Correlations and Something About a Freezer and an Oven[1]

Let's not forget that the quality of a model must be
compared with another model. The best model is the one
that leads to better decisions.

—JPP

WHEN WE FORECAST RISK AT THE PORTFOLIO LEVEL, WE must estimate correlations, either directly or indirectly. The concept of diversification is at the core of every asset allocation decision. It's the key premise and goal of portfolio construction. The lower the correlations, the better the diversification, and if we hold everything else constant, the higher the risk-adjusted return.

Yet one of the most vexing problems in investment management is that diversification seems to disappear when investors need it the most. Of course, the statement that "all correlations go to 1 in a crisis" is both an oversimplification and an exaggeration. But it has been well documented that correlations tend to increase in down markets, especially during crashes (i.e., "left-tail events"). Studies have shown that this effect is pervasive for a large variety of financial assets, including individual stocks, country equity markets, global equity industries, hedge funds, currencies, and international bond markets.[2] Most of these studies were published before the 2008 global financial crisis. Yet the failure of diversification during the crisis, when left-tail correlations jumped significantly, seemed to surprise investors.

In a 2018 paper published in the *Financial Analysts Journal*, "When Diversification Fails," Rob Panariello and I encouraged investors to act on such findings. Full-sample (i.e., average) correlations are misleading. Prudent investors should not use them in risk models, at least not without adding other tools, such as downside risk measures and scenario analyses. To enhance risk management beyond naïve diversification, investors should reoptimize portfolios with a focus on downside risk, consider dynamic strategies, and, depending on aversion to losses, evaluate the value of downside protection as an alternative to asset class diversification.

The Myth of Diversification

Back in 2008, Charlie Henneman, Head of Educational Events and Programs at the CFA Institute, asked me to present at the Institute's Annual Risk Management Conference.

Charlie asked for my talk's title.

At the time, I had started to work on the instability of correlations. I suggested a wonky title: "Asymmetries in Cross-Asset Conditional Correlations."

Charlie didn't want a technical title. Who wants to attend a talk titled "Asymmetries in Cross-Asset Conditional Correlations"? Might as well call it "Another Obscure Academic Talk with Little Relevance to Investors."

I told him that essentially, I would show that diversification doesn't work when we need it the most. He then suggested a fantastic title: "The Myth of Diversification."

The talk was a success, as was a paper of the same title, written with David Chua and Mark Kritzman (2009), which won the 12th Annual Bernstein

Fabozzi/Jacobs Levy Outstanding Article Award. I'm convinced the title helped. The timing of the publication was fortuitous too: we used a precrisis data sample ending in February 2008 and documented significant "undesirable correlation asymmetries" for a broad range of asset classes. The events of the fall of 2008 reinforced our results.

We added another angle (as usual, Mark's idea): we showed that not only did correlations increase on the downside, but they also significantly *decreased* on the upside. This asymmetry is the opposite of what investors want. Indeed, who wants diversification on the upside? Upside unification (or antidiversification) would be preferable. During good times, we should seek to reduce the return drag from diversifiers.

In our more recent (2018) paper, Rob Panariello and I insist that despite the wide body of published research, many investors still do not fully appreciate the impact of correlation asymmetries on portfolio efficiency—in particular, on exposure to loss. During left-tail events, diversified portfolios may have greater exposure to loss than more concentrated portfolios. Marty Leibowitz and Anthony Bova (2009) show that during the 2008 global financial crisis, a portfolio diversified across US stocks, US bonds, international stocks, emerging markets stocks, and REITs saw its equity beta rise from 0.65 to 0.95, and the portfolio unexpectedly *underperformed* a simple 60% US stocks/40% US bonds portfolio by *9 percentage points*. Similar effects were just observed during the crisis of 2020.

Rob and I expanded the analysis of the original "Myth of Diversification" in several ways. We included post-2008 data, we covered a broader set of markets and factors, and we took an in-depth look at what drives correlations in numerous markets. As for methodology, we introduced a data-augmentation technique to improve the robustness of tail correlation estimates, and we analyzed the impact of return data frequency on private asset correlations.

How correlations change during extreme markets can be estimated in several ways. For example, we can identify months during which both assets moved (up or down) by at least a given percentage, which is called "double conditioning."[3] Rob and I used a similar approach, but we conditioned on a single asset. We wanted to measure differences in tail correlations based on which of the two markets sold off (or rallied). For some correlations, such as the stock-bond correlation, this difference can be substantial, and it adds information on the correlation structure.

We wanted to evaluate the effectiveness of bond diversification during US stock market sell-offs (the flight-to-safety effect). First, we isolated months in our data sample during which US stocks were down significantly: say, their worst 5% of all monthly returns in our sample. Next, we calculated a correlation between stocks and bonds in this subsample. Then we moved the percentile cutoff by a fixed increment to see how the correlation changes as a function of stock returns.

We also calculated the stock-bond correlation when bonds were in their bottom 5%. *We found that bonds diversify stocks when stocks sell off, but stocks do not diversify bonds when bonds sell off.* Double conditioning would fail to reveal this lack of symmetry in the diversification between the two assets.

Irrespective of how we partitioned the data, we expected subsample correlations to differ from full-sample estimates. To measure this "conditioning bias," we first simulated how correlations change when we move toward the left and right tails (from a standard "bivariate normal distribution") based on random data. For each asset pair, we simulated two normal distributions with the same full-sample correlations, means, and volatilities as those we observed empirically.

Then we compared the actual subsample correlations with their simulated normal counterparts. Differences indicated departures from normality. Also, under normality, downside and upside correlation profiles should be identical. Therefore, when we compared left-tail and right-tail correlations, the conditioning bias did not matter much because it "washed out." Any asymmetry we found indicated a departure from normality.

Another possible bias arises because extreme correlations rely on few data points, an issue similar to the estimation of higher moments I mentioned earlier. The further one goes into the tails, the smaller the sample. At the top or bottom 1 or 5% of the distribution, a single outlier may significantly bias correlations up or down. To increase robustness in our estimates, therefore, we augmented subsamples with data from the rest of the distribution.

We used an exponentially weighted approach. The closest the additional data points were to the cutoff of interest, the more weight they received in our estimation. These weights decreased exponentially as we moved further from the threshold. This approach, although simple and intuitive, had not been used in prior studies; hence, perhaps we made a modest methodological contribution to the measurement of conditional correlations. (To be more precise, we calibrated the model in such a way that observations further into the tails received exponentially larger weights, and we fixed the half-life at the percentile under consideration.[4])

For comparison, we also reported unadjusted conditional correlations. We found that the data-augmentation methodology generated estimates similar to those calculated conventionally, in terms of magnitude and directionality. But our estimates tended to be less noisy, and they were less sensitive to outliers.[5]

The Failure of Diversification Across Risk Assets

First, we looked at international equity diversion to illustrate our approach. Based on monthly data from January 1970 to June 2017, we calculated conditional correlations between US stocks (MSCI U.S. Total Return Index) and non-US stocks (MSCI EAFE Total Return Index). We conditioned correlations by percentile, based on the returns of US stocks. Our results showed how correlations changed from the worst sell-offs in US stocks (1st percentile) to their strongest rallies (99th percentile). For comparison, we showed the correlation profile that we would expect if both markets were normally distributed. In the normal case, we would expect perfect symmetry between upside and downside correlations. Conditional correlations would gradually decrease as we moved toward the tails.

Real-world correlations differed substantially from their normally distributed counterparts. When US stocks were rallying (in their 99th percentile), their correlation with non-US stocks dropped all the way to −17%. During the worst sell-offs, represented by the bottom 1% of all returns in US stocks, however, their correlation with non-US stocks rose to +87%. This asymmetry revealed that international diversification works only on the upside.[6]

We found similar results across risk assets. In Table 9.1, I show a comparison of left-tail and right-tail correlations for key asset classes, based on available data histories as of June 2017.[7] The focus is on US stocks versus other risk assets because the equity risk factor dominates the volatility factor (and exposure to loss) in most portfolios.[8] We used bond returns net of duration-matched US Treasuries (i.e., "excess returns") to isolate credit risk factors.

We also show results for style and size diversification within stocks. Most investors select equity funds—and thereby seek to diversify their portfolios—based on style/size characteristics. Across the board, left-tail correlations are much higher than right-tail correlations.

TABLE 9.1   Extreme Correlations

	Correlations (%)	
US Stocks Vs.	**Left Tail (Sell-Offs)**	**Right Tail (Rallies)**
Corporate bonds	54	7
Real estate	56	1
Hedge funds	73	−8
High-yield bonds	76	−3
MBS	77	−42
EM bonds	78	27
EM stocks	80	35
Non-US (EAFE) stocks	87	−16
Small vs. large stocks	91	28
Value vs. growth stocks	86	36

Studies on "tail dependence" (how crashes tend to happen at the same time across markets) corroborate these findings. Garcia-Feijoo, Jensen, and Johnson (2012) show that when US equity returns are in their bottom 5%, non-US equities, commodities, and REITs also experience significantly negative returns—beyond what would be expected from full-sample correlations. Hartmann, Straetmans, and de Vries (2010) show that currencies co-crash more often than would be predicted by a bivariate normal distribution. Hartmann, Straetmans, and de Vries (2004) estimate that stock markets in G5 countries are two times more likely to co-crash than bond markets.

Van Oordt and Zhou (2012) extend pairwise analysis to joint tail dependence across multiple markets and reach similar conclusions. They suggested a related approach to measure the systemic importance of financial institutions. These studies ignored asymmetries, however, between the left and right tails. They either focused on the left tail or used symmetrical measures of tail dependence, such as the joint t-distributions.

Regarding credit asset classes, the Merton (1974) model explains why credit and equity returns become more correlated in the left tail. Merton defined a corporate bond as a combination of:

- A risk-free bond—in normal times, the bondholders' upside risk is limited to the regular coupon payments and return of principal.
- A short put position on the company's assets. If the company's asset value depreciates below its debt, bondholders become long the company's assets and receive what's left through bankruptcy proceedings. (Meanwhile, as the stock price goes to zero, stockholders are wiped out.)

Hence, as a company approaches default, the market starts to expect that bondholders will be left holding the bag (of the company's remaining assets). Merton explained that "as the probability of eventual default becomes large, . . . the risk characteristics of the debt approach that of (unlevered) equity." In this context, it was not a surprise that during the 2008 crisis, credit and equity returns became highly correlated.[9]

Diversification fails across styles, sizes, geographies, and alternative assets. Essentially, all the return-seeking building blocks that asset allocators typically use for portfolio construction are affected. The asymmetry for the stock-MBS (mortgage-backed securities) correlation is notable. In "The Myth of Diversification" paper (2009), we had used precrisis data, and at the time of the study, MBS was one of the few asset classes that seemed to decouple from stocks in down markets. During the fourth quarter of 2008, however, which is included in this data sample, MBS clearly joined the ranks of risk-on assets.

Alternative assets are not immune to the failure of diversification. Beyond traditional asset classes, investors have increasingly looked to alternatives for new or specialized sources of diversification. In Table 9.1, Rob and I used a broad hedge fund index, but one could argue that hedge fund styles are so different from each other that they should be treated as separate asset classes. We decided to compare left-tail and right-tail correlations (versus US stocks) for seven hedge fund styles: equity market neutral, merger arbitrage, event driven, macro, equity hedge, relative value convertible, and relative value. Unfortunately, we found that all these types of hedge funds, including the market-neutral funds, exhibited significantly higher left-tail than right-tail correlations. While the average right-tail correlation was –7%, the average left-tail correlation jumped to +63%.[10]

A simple explanation could be that most hedge fund strategies are short volatility. Some are also short liquidity risk, which is akin to selling an option, as explained by my former PIMCO colleague Vineer Bhansali (2010) in his book *Bond Portfolio Investing and Risk Management*. Agarwal and Naik (2004) explain jumps in hedge fund left-tail equity betas through the Merton (1974) lens. They observed that "a wide range of hedge fund strategies exhibit returns similar to those from writing a put option on the equity index." In a related study, Billio, Getmansky, and Pelizzon (2012) use a regime-switching model to measure hedge fund correlations and market betas over time. They show that the average jump in correlations for hedge fund strategies in financial crises was +33%.

What about private assets? Over the past few years, institutional investors have significantly increased their allocations to private assets. Although many investors have become skeptical of the diversification benefits of hedge funds, the belief in the benefits of direct real estate and private equity diversification has been persistent. The advisory firm Willis Towers Watson reports that as of the end of 2016, pension funds, wealth managers, and sovereign wealth funds held more than $2 trillion in direct real estate and private equity investments.[11] Money has flowed into these asset classes partly because of their perceived diversification benefits. Consultants have used mean-variance optimization in asset allocation or asset liability studies to make a strong case for increased allocations. In the end, alternative assets are often sold as free lunches because they seem to offer high returns with low volatility and great diversification properties.

But there is more to these statistics than meets the eye. Private assets' reported returns suffer from the smoothing bias. In fact, in a paper my former colleagues Niels Pedersen, Fei He, and I published in the *Financial*

Analysts Journal in 2014, titled "Asset Allocation: Risk Models for Alternative Investments" (which won a Graham and Dodd Award for Excellence in Research), we show that private assets' diversification advantage is almost entirely illusory. We argue that reported quarterly returns for private assets represent a moving average of the true (unobserved) marked-to-market returns. On a marked-to-market basis, these asset classes are exposed to many of the same factors that drive stock and bond returns. For example, and as we've shown, after their smoothing bias is removed, private assets have exposure to credit risk, which does not truly diversify equity risk in times of market stress.

Even David Swensen, chief investment officer of Yale University's Endowment (which has a large proportion of its assets invested in private markets), acknowledges the issue in his 2009 book, *Pioneering Portfolio Management*:

> The low risk evident in data describing past returns from private investing constitutes a statistical artifact. . . . If two otherwise identical companies differ only in the form of organization—one private, the other public—the infrequently valued private company appears much more stable than the frequently valued publicly traded company.[12]

From *Pioneering Portfolio Management* by David F. Swensen. Copyright © 2000 by David F. Swensen. Reprinted with the permission of The Free Press, a division of Simon & Schuster, Inc. All rights reserved.

Not only is the true equity risk exposure of private assets higher than implied by their reported returns on average, but their left-tail exposures are much higher. To illustrate, in "When Diversification Fails," Rob and I showed results from a test that any investor can easily replicate. For direct real estate and private equity, we compared quarterly to rolling annual (four quarters) left-tail correlations with equity. (Rolling annual correlations are less sensitive to the smoothing bias than those calculated on quarterly returns.)

This remarkably simple adjustment revealed that private real estate and private equity don't diversify equity risk as much as most investors assume. Although the quarterly correlation between real estate and US stocks was +29%, it jumped to +67% on a rolling annual basis. For private equity, the quarterly correlation was $+13\%$, compared with $+85\%$ on a rolling annual basis.[13]

In addition to the smoothing bias, we surmised that liquidity risk contributed to the failure of private asset diversification. Because they don't trade as frequently, private assets are exposed to significant liquidity risk, perhaps even more than hedge funds. Systemic liquidity risk tends to manifest itself during stock market crashes.[14] A systemic liquidity crisis can be compared with a burning building, in which everyone is rushing for the door, with one exception: In financial markets, to get out (sell), investors must find someone to take their place in the building (a buyer). When no buyers are present, prices crash instantaneously, and correlations across risk assets jump.

What about risk factors? The failure of diversification across public and private return-seeking asset classes has led, in part, to the popularity of risk factors. Many authors have argued that risk factor diversification is more effective than asset class diversification.[15] Our results indeed revealed that several risk factors (equity value, cross-asset value, equity momentum, currency value, and currency momentum) appear to be more immune to the failure of diversification than are asset classes.

Others have pointed out, however, that risk factors aren't *inherently* superior building blocks.[16] They deliver better diversification than traditional asset classes simply because they allow short positions and often encompass a broader universe of assets. For example, the size and value factors in equities are often defined as long-short, security-level portfolios. But if factor definitions are restricted to linear combinations of asset classes, and short positions are allowed across asset classes as well as risk factors, then risk factors do not deliver any efficiency gains over asset classes. In a sense, the argument in favor of risk factor diversification is more about the removal of the long-only constraint and the expansion of the investment universe than anything else.

In addition, momentum strategies that sell risk assets in down markets provide left-tail diversification, almost by definition. Portfolio insurance strategies, for example, can explicitly replicate a put option (minus the gap-risk protection). Hence, as expected, we found that risk factors such as currency and cross-asset momentum had much *lower* left-tail than right-tail correlations with US stocks.

However, our results also showed that risk-on factors, such as size (i.e., small minus big stocks) and currency carry, may fail to diversify stocks when needed. Small cap stocks tend to have higher equity betas than large cap stocks, and this difference in market beta exposure is often expressed during stock market drawdowns. Similarly, the currency carry trade has an indirect equity beta exposure that remains dormant until risk assets sell off. The strategy is to buy high-interest-rate currencies (the Australian dollar, emerging markets currencies, etc.) and to fund these positions by shorting low-interest-rate currencies (for example, the Japanese yen).

In normal markets, the investor earns a risk premium because forward rates typically do not appreciate or depreciate enough to offset profits (the carry) from the interest rate differential embedded in currency forward contracts. But when risk assets sell off, the carry trade unwinds as investors sell the higher-risk currencies and buy the safe havens. In a sense, many carry strategies behave like the credit risk premium. These strategies are short an option, and investors sometimes refer to the adage "Picking up pennies in front of a steamroller" to describe them.

The example of the currency carry trade illustrates the impact of regime shifts on correlations, which may explain the widespread risk-on/risk-off characteristic of return-seeking asset classes and risk factors. Financial markets tend to fluctuate between a low-volatility state and a panic-driven, high-volatility state (see, for example, Kritzman, Page, and Turkington, 2012). In fact, Ang and Bekaert (2002) directly link the concept of regime shifts to rising left-tail correlations. But what causes regime shifts? A partial answer is that macroeconomic fundamentals themselves exhibit regime shifts, as documented for inflation and growth data.[17]

I think investor sentiment also plays a large role. In normal markets, differences in fundamentals drive diversification across risk assets. During panics, however, investors often "sell risk" irrespective of differences in fundamentals. Huang, Rossi, and Wang (2015), for example, show that sentiment is a common factor that drives both equity and credit-spread returns—beyond the effects of default risk, liquidity, and macro variables—and suggest that sentiment often spills over from equities to the credit markets.

In financial markets, fear is more contagious than optimism. Related studies in the field of psychology suggest that to react more strongly to bad news than good news is human nature. In their paper "Bad Is Stronger Than Good," Baumeister, Bratslavsky, Finkenauer, and Vohs (2001) explain:

> The greater power of bad events over good ones is found in everyday events, major life events, close relationship outcomes, social network patterns, interpersonal interactions, and learning processes. . . . Bad information is processed more thoroughly than good. . . . From our perspective, it is evolutionarily adaptive for bad to be stronger than good.

Is the Stock-Bond Correlation the Only True Source of Diversification?

When market sentiment suddenly turns negative and fear grips markets, government bonds almost always rally because of the flight-to-safety effect.[18] In a sense, duration risk may be the only true source of diversification in multi-asset portfolios. Therefore, the stock-bond correlation is one of the most important inputs to asset allocation.

In our study, we compared the empirical stock-bond conditional correlation profile with its normally distributed benchmark. Unlike results for other correlations, this profile was highly desirable. Treasuries decouple from stocks in bad times and become positively correlated with stocks in good times. The stock-bond correlation is difficult to estimate, however, and can change drastically with macroeconomic conditions (Johnson, Naik, Page, Pedersen, and Sapra, 2014).

In a 2014 *Journal of Investment Strategies* paper titled "The Stock-Bond Correlation," which I coauthored with my former PIMCO colleagues Nic Johnson, Vasant Naik, Niels Pedersen, and Steve Sapra, we demonstrate that when inflation and interest rates drive market volatility, the stock-bond correlation often turns positive. For example, we show that the 12-month stock-bond correlation was mostly positive during the 1970s and 1980s. Since 2008, central bank stimulus and declining rates have artificially pushed valuations higher in both the stock and bond markets. This type of "sugar high" can unwind quickly if policy normalizes unexpectedly. The "taper tantrum" of 2013, when Ben Bernanke first mentioned the idea of tapering the Fed's stimulus, provides a good example. It affected stocks and bonds negatively at the same time.

More recently, in 2018, when the Federal Reserve hiked its target rate from 2% to 2.5% and signaled further hikes in 2019, both stocks and bonds suffered negative returns over the entire calendar year, which is rare. In fact, *all* the 17 major asset classes that Morgan Stanley tracks were down in 2018, an unprecedented outcome.[19] So much for asset class diversification. Investors should remember that starting valuations can compound the effect. The higher the valuations in both stocks and bonds, the more fragile their correlation.

To illustrate how bond sell-offs can lead to a positive stock-bond correlation, we estimated the stock-bond correlation as a function of percentiles in *bond* returns instead of stock returns. This change in methodology revealed an interesting pattern. The correlation profile was not as desirable as when we conditioned on stock returns. Although the correlations were generally low, when bonds sell off, stocks tend to sell off at the same time. Ultimately, investors should remember that stocks and bonds both represent discounted cash flows. Unexpected changes in the discount rate or inflation expectations can push the stock-bond correlation into positive territory—especially when other conditions remain constant.

Despite consistent results across markets, there are caveats to our study. We showed that during crises, diversification across risk assets almost always fails, and even the stock-bond correlation may fail in certain market environments. But conditional correlations represent only one way to measure diversification. Conditional betas, for example, take into account changes in relative volatilities as well as correlations. In theory, it is possible for the correlation between two assets to increase while the volatility of the diversifier decreases relative to the main engine of portfolio growth. In this case, a correlation spike may be offset by decreasing relative volatilities, which could lead to a lowered stress beta and, perhaps, lower exposure to loss than expected. However, prior studies have shown that such outcomes are highly improbable.[20] Ultimately, we chose to study correlations. They measure diversification directly and have been used widely in earlier studies.

Another caveat is that we did not forecast left-tail events. Although we know that correlations are likely to increase if markets sell off, we do not necessarily know when this shift will take place. Equity sell-offs are unexpected, almost by definition. Investors can prepare for the failure of diversification, however, without the need to time markets. Consider as an analogy that although it is almost impossible for aircraft pilots to predict when they will encounter air turbulence, passengers can take comfort in the fact that airplanes are built to withstand it.

Recommendations for Asset Allocation and Tail-Risk-Aware Analytics

In light of our results, and as reinforced by the events of 2020, *I recommend that investors avoid the use of full-sample correlations in portfolio construction— or, at least, that they stress-test their correlation assumptions.* Scenario analysis, either historical or forward-looking, should take a bigger role in asset allocation than it does. A wide range of portfolio optimization methodologies directly address nonnormal left-tail risk and, ipso facto, the failure of diversification. The most flexible is full-scale optimization, which optimizes directly on the empirical distribution of returns, for any type of investor preferences and goals.[21] (We discuss full-scale optimization in Chapter 14.)

These analytics are commonly used, but almost always on a "posttrade" basis—that is, after portfolio construction has taken place. Investors should use such tail-aware tools as part of "pretrade" decisions. To do so will reveal that equity regions, styles, sizes, and sectors—as well as credit, alternative assets, and risk factors—do not diversify broad equity risk as much as average correlations suggest. To be clear, I'm not arguing against diversification across traditional asset classes, but investors should be aware that traditional measures of diversification may belie exposure to loss in times of stress. Investors should calibrate their risk tolerance accordingly against return opportunities.

In addition, beware the stock-bond correlation. Shocks to interest rates or inflation can turn it positive. In such situations, strategies that use leverage to increase the contribution to the risk of bonds—risk parity, for example— may experience unexpected drawdowns.

Finally, investors should look beyond diversification to manage portfolio risk. Tail-risk hedging (with equity put options or proxies), risk factors that embed short positions or defensive momentum strategies, and dynamic risk-based strategies all provide better left-tail protection than traditional diversification.

The strategy of managed volatility can be a particularly effective and low-cost approach to overcome the failure of diversification. As we discussed in Chapter 7, based on the empirical observation that risk is more predictable than return, this strategy adjusts the asset mix over time to stabilize a portfolio's volatility. It is portable and can easily be applied as an overlay to smooth the ride for almost any portfolio. Because managed volatility will scale down risk assets when volatility is high, it may offset left-tail correlation spikes and thereby reduce exposure to large losses without a significant reduction in returns on the upside.

As part of preparing to present this study at a conference for Canadian institutional investors, I formulated seven key recommendations for tail-risk-aware analytics and suggested six active management strategies. The tail-risk-aware analytics are necessary to evaluate the effectiveness of the active management strategies and to scale exposures to them. The items below sum up our earlier discussion in this chapter:

Recommendations for Tail-Risk-Aware Analytics

1. Don't blindly rely on full-sample correlations for portfolio construction.
2. Give scenario analysis a meaningful role in asset allocation decisions.
3. Estimate the end investors' risk tolerance accordingly against returns.
4. Use portfolio optimization tools that account directly for left-tail risks.
5. Beware of "diversification free lunches" in privately held asset classes.
6. Evaluate interest rate risk and its impact on stock-bond diversification.
7. Seek asset classes that provide upside "unification"/antidiversification.

We're not arguing *against* diversification. We're arguing for *better* diversification.

Active Management Strategies

1. Hedges with put options and proxies
2. Strategies that embed short positions
3. Momentum-based factors or strategies
4. Actively managed absolute return alts
5. Managed volatility overlays/strategies
6. Strategic or tactical cash allocations

These analytics and active management strategies are now widely available to help investors manage the failure of diversification.

To summarize the issue Rob and I highlighted in our paper, I often use the story of the statistician who had his head in the oven and his feet in the freezer. He suddenly exclaimed, "On average, I feel great!" (Straight from my repertoire of cheesy conference jokes. This one gets polite chuckles, at best.)

Similarly, as a measure of diversification, the full-sample correlation is an average of extremes. During market crises, diversification across risk assets almost completely disappears. Moreover, diversification seems to work remarkably well when investors do not need it: during market rallies. This undesirable asymmetry is pervasive across markets.

Notes

1. This section is largely taken from "When Diversification Fails," a recent paper Rob Panariello and I published in the *Financial Analysts Journal.* See Page and Panariello (2018).
2. See, for example, Ang, Chen, and Xing (2002), Ang and Chen (2002), and Hong, Tu, and Zhou (2007) on individual stocks; Longin and Solnik (2001) on country equity markets; Ferreira and Gama (2010) on global industries; Van Royen (2002b) and Agarwal and Naik (2004) on hedge funds; Hartmann, Straetmans, and de Vries (2010) on currencies; and Cappiello, Engle, and Sheppard (2006) on international equity and bond markets.
3. See, for example, Longin and Solnik (2001) and Chua, Kritzman, and Page (2009).
4. "Half-life," in this context, means the point at which the sum of the weights reaches 50% (out of 100%).
5. An important point regarding the conditioning bias is that we applied the same exponential adjustment to the corresponding simulated normal data.

Hence, in all cases, comparisons between empirical and normal correlations were apples to apples.

6. Longin and Solnik (2001), focusing on the correlations between the United States, France, Germany, the United Kingdom, and Japan, reported similar results for stocks at the country level.

7. In the table, EM is "emerging market." Monthly data, with start dates based on availability. See Appendix B from "When Diversification Fails" (Page and Panariello, 2018), available online at http://www.cfapubs.org/doi/ suppl/10.2469/faj.v74.n3.3, for start dates and data sources. Left-tail and right-tail correlations are at the 1st and 99th percentiles but were adjusted by the data-augmentation methodology. Full correlation profiles (adjusted, unadjusted, and normal) are shown in Appendix B.

8. See, for example, Page (2013).

9. See, for example, Naik, Devarajan, Nowobilski, Page, and Pedersen (2016).

10. See Page and Panariello (2018) for more details on the data and methodology.

11. As reported in the *Financial Times*, Chris Flood, "Global Shift into Alternatives Gathers Pace," July 16, 2017, http://www.ft.com.

12. David Foulke (2016) highlighted this quote on Alpha Architect.

13. Full correlation profiles available online at https://www.cfapubs.org/doi/ suppl/10.2469/faj.v74.n3.3.

14. See Page, Simonian, and He (2011).

15. See, for example, Bender, Briand, Nielsen, and Stefek (2010); Page and Taborsky (2011): and Ilmanen and Kizer (2012).

16. See Idzorek and Kowara (2013) and Cocoma, Czasonis, Kritzman, and Turkington (2017).

17. See, for example, Kim (1993) and Kumar and Okimoto (2007) on inflation and Hamilton (1989), Goodwin (1993), Luginbuhl and de Vos (1999), and Lam (2004) on GDP/GNP growth.

18. See, for example, Gulko (2002).

19. For the period during which data are available. *Source:* Morgan Stanley, monthly data pack, "Global in the Flow," 2018.

20. See, for example, Leibowitz and Bova (2009) on betas, Hartmann, Straetmans, and de Vries (2004, 2010) on co-crash probabilities, and Garcia-Feijoo, Jensen, and Johnson (2012) on tail dependence.

21. See, for example, Cremers, Kritzman, and Page (2005), Sharpe (2007), and Adler and Kritzman (2007).

10

Correlation Forecasts, Tail Risks, and Something About a Rug

When we estimate risk, we're not re-telling the past.
We're forecasting.
—JPP

THOUGH IT RECEIVED A LOT OF POSITIVE FEEDBACK FROM investors, our research on the failure of diversification skirted an important question: *Can we forecast correlations? The answer: sort of.* As we discussed in the previous chapter, the left-tail events that drive correlation shifts in the markets are basically impossible to predict. Perhaps all we can do is build the airplane to withstand the turbulence whenever it occurs. Nonetheless, if volatility is persistent, and if we can forecast *portfolio* volatility, which is in part driven by correlations among the underlying assets, shouldn't we observe some persistence in correlations as well?

Academic researchers have used ARCH-type models to address the question in a variety of ways. An early attempt, a model called the constant conditional correlation (CCC), blends *constant* correlations with *dynamic* volatilities (Bollerslev, 1990). Yet in the real world, correlations are as dynamic as volatilities because the two are linked by common factors such as investor sentiment. Hence, CCC has been used as a straw man, easily defeated by more realistic approaches in subsequent studies. For example, the DCC (dynamic conditional correlation) model we use in our managed volatility process assumes that correlations change every period (Engle, 2002). Another version incorporates a regime-switching model (the regime-switching dynamic correlation model; Pelletier, 2006).

But these studies suffer from the same issues as those on volatility forecasting, from the Poon and Granger (2003) review of the literature we discussed in Chapter 8. The models are built mostly for short horizons (typically, daily), and the mundane questions practitioners must address, on the frequency of the data and length of estimation windows, are left mostly unanswered.

To fill this gap, Rob Panariello and I decided to run yet another analysis, this time on correlations. We followed the same methodology I've used so far in this book to test the persistence of returns, volatilities, and higher moments: we looked at realized (trailing) correlations at one point in time and calculated the degree to which they matched up with future correlations. In other words, we tested whether correlations were persistent, just as we did for returns, volatilities, skewness, etc. Did the correlation between two asset classes, as observed over the *last year*, tell us anything about the correlation over the *following year*?

In a related study, Erb, Harvey, and Viskanta (1994) build a forecasting model for country-level equity market correlations, based on data from January 1970 to December 1993. They find that lagged correlations are an important predictor of the correlations of US stocks with four out of six major countries.

However, their analysis leaves several practical questions unanswered. Unlike our analysis, theirs assumes that the estimation window should match the forecast horizon: "The lag length, of course, depends on the forecasting horizon; for example, for five-year correlations, the lag is 60 months," they say. But empirically, to match the estimation window with the forecast horizon may not be the best approach. Windows shorter than the forecast horizon may provide a better forecast, as evidenced by our results on volatility, as well as the widespread use of exponentially weighted models, which emphasize recent data and provide further evidence that the more recent the data, the better the forecast.

Also, Erb, Harvey, and Viskanta use a multivariate model. In addition to lagged correlations, they add lagged country returns, lagged dividend yields, and lagged term spreads as predictors of future correlations. These additional variables improved the forecasts significantly—an important result, as it suggests a link between fundamentals (valuation and macro variables) and future correlations.

However, multivariate analysis merits its own strand of research because it muddies the waters on the simpler question of persistence. Indeed, the variables used are collinear (i.e., related to each other). While they improve the forecasts, they obfuscate the effect of individual predictors. Hence, we can't conclude whether correlations are persistent or mean-reverted on a stand-alone basis from this study. We can conclude, however, that *net of the effect of the fundamental variables*, correlations appear to mean-revert.

Last, Erb, Harvey, and Viskanta's dataset is too small: their sample ends 25 years ago, and it only covers monthly returns for seven country-level equity markets. It also excludes cross-asset correlations between stocks and various fixed income markets.

Our Analysis of Correlation Predictability

In our study, we evaluated the persistence of 3,211 correlations (19 asset class pairs multiplied by 169 lead/lag/data frequencies combinations). We used the same six equity asset class pairs listed as "relative bets" on page 53 and the same six fixed income pairs from page 75, as well as the stock-bond correlation. Our sample was the same as in our volatility study: August 30, 2000 to September 5, 2018, for daily and weekly data and February 28, 1993 to August 31, 2018, for monthly data.

To test the robustness of our results, we added six pairs from the longer Ken French data series, which cover factors and asset classes within US equities only: market versus small-minus-big; market versus high-minus-low (value factor); market versus big; market versus small; small versus big; and value versus growth. These data series go back to July 1, 1926, and end on December 31, 2018.

As we did for our volatility study, we mixed the frequencies between lookback and forecast data. By intuition, most investors match these frequencies. To forecast weekly correlations, they use past weekly correlations; to forecast monthly correlations, they use past monthly correlations; etc. Instead, we tested which of the daily, weekly, or monthly correlations best predicted future correlations at all frequencies. Our volatility study had revealed that higher frequencies led to better forecasts across the board. Would the same result hold for correlations?

Our results for correlations revealed similar patterns as for volatilities, with some nuances. Correlations appeared more predictable than higher moments, but slightly less predictable than volatilities. The month-to-month correlation in daily volatility was +68% (across asset classes and bets), compared with +4% for skewness, +2% for kurtosis, and +40% for correlations. Like volatilities, correlations were more persistent at short horizons than at long horizons, with some mean reversion observed at the three-year and five-year horizons (when we used three-year and five-year lookback windows). But as for volatilities, this mean reversion weakened and reversed in the longer data sample in many cases.

Unlike for volatilities, the observation that shorter (trailing 21 days) lookback windows are always the most accurate did not hold. Though we found that shorter windows generally worked better, the "sweet spot" for correlation predictability was between six months and one year. We found a similar pattern in the longer French data sample for US stocks.

However, we did find that holding everything else constant (for the same lookback and forecast windows), the higher the data frequency, the better the correlation forecast, especially at time horizons of one year or less. This rule of thumb was consistent with our results for volatilities. For example, suppose we forecast the correlation between two asset classes for the next 52 weeks. As with volatility estimates, many investors may be tempted to match the lookback with the forecast windows. Erb, Harvey, and Viskanta (1994) seem to consider this choice as self-evident. In this case, we would use the correlation observed over the last 52 weeks as our forecast for correlation over the next 52 weeks.

Yet when averaged across our asset class pairs, the best estimate of forward 52-week correlations would have been the trailing one-year *daily* correlations, with a +25% average correlation between trailing and forward correlations, compared with +22% for weekly and +14% for monthly data. Again, using a shorter window would have improved the forecast: the correlation between trailing 6-month daily correlations and forward 52-week correlations was +38%. These differences in forecasting power are relatively small, but we saw them on most of the correlations, across various time horizons, and for forecasts of daily, weekly, and monthly correlations. Moreover, our robustness study on the longer data sample validated these conclusions. *The rule of thumb for asset allocators is that correlations show some useful predictability when we use daily data from the last 6 to 12 months.*

Exposure to Loss Is What Matters

Volatility, skewness, kurtosis, and correlation are the key building blocks for risk forecasting. But ultimately, most investors care about exposure to loss. Conditional value at risk (CVaR), for example, is a popular risk measure. It provides an estimate of the average loss size during sell-offs, usually defined as the bottom 1, 5, or 10% of outcomes. For example, an annual CVaR of −10% at the 5% confidence level means that once every 20 years, we can expect to lose about 10% on our investment.

The literature on value-at-risk forecasting and other measures of exposure to loss is obviously related to—and as rich as—the literature on volatility forecasting. Based on equity factor data, Fortin, Simonato, and Dionne (2018) support the notion that more complex models aren't always the most predictive out-of-sample. They conclude that "univariate models, which are more parsimonious and simpler to implement than multivariate models, can be used to forecast the downside risk of equity portfolios without loss of precision."

To evaluate predictability in CVaRs, we used the same data as for volatilities, skewness, and kurtosis. Our results showed that volatility and correlations were remarkably predictable, while skewness and kurtosis were more difficult to model. But there are fundamental reasons that we can expect negative skewness and high kurtosis ("fat left tails") to prevail for a wide range of risk assets over time. Exposure to loss, here defined as CVaR, puts it all together. It is a function of volatility, skewness, kurtosis, and correlation. Perhaps the most important question for risk forecasting is whether CVaR itself is predictable. Is it persistent? Does it mean-revert? Or is it mostly random from one period to the next?

We found similar, albeit slightly weaker, patterns for CVaR as for volatility: persistence in the short run, mean reversion in the long run (in our main data sample), and better forecasting performance for higher-frequency and more recent data. It appears the lack of predictability in higher moments from one period to the next doesn't prevent reasonably good CVaR forecasts. This result could be explained by the (perhaps counterintuitive) fact that volatility drives exposure to loss more than higher moments do. A formal decomposition of the contributions to CVaR from volatility, skewness, kurtosis, and correlation could be informative, but remained outside the scope of our study.

Takeaways on the Importance of Basic Parameter Choices for Risk Forecasting

I don't dismiss the usefulness of complex models, especially when they are properly calibrated for specific applications such as managed volatility strategies. Even so, across all our analyses, Rob and I focused on the most basic of risk forecasts: equally-weighted, historical estimates. Based on a large sample of asset class returns, we answered questions that anyone who builds risk forecasts in the real world must answer, yet are almost always swept under the rug in the existing literature: Which lookback window is most predictive for various forecast horizons, and which data frequency should we use (daily, weekly, monthly)? We evaluated these choices for forecasting volatility, skewness, kurtosis, correlations, and, ultimately, value at risk.

Perhaps answers to these mundane questions don't bestow academic merit because they are deemed too basic and self-evident. Or maybe the hard truth is that the answers to these questions matter more than the choice of risk model itself. In any case, even when building the most advanced models, investors must choose a lookback window and a data frequency. In light of our result, I suspect most readers of the literature on risk forecasting (and perhaps some authors as well) underestimate the importance of these choices. Basic rules of thumb, such as the common practice of matching estimation and forecast parameters, do not perform best empirically. For example, Rob and I found that daily data produce better forecasts of monthly volatility than the monthly data, and that short data windows produce better forecasts than long data windows even when the forecast horizon is relatively long.

The key takeaway from all our risk forecasting studies is this: basic parameter choices matter a great deal. *A refrain I use in this book is that complexity is not always best. This rule applies to how we decide to spend time and energy to improve risk models.* Modeling details often considered too self-evident to be properly documented in the literature can drastically affect a forecast's accuracy. Moreover, investors should question adages such as "More data are always better than less data" and "Lookback and forecast horizons should match." I urge investors and academic authors to pay attention to these details. Too often, they aren't disclosed in published research. Yet I submit that they matter more than the fiftieth tweak on an ARCH-type model that marginally improves on the previous version and is likely to be overfitted to a specific data sample, and therefore deliver poor out-of-sample performance. (Moreover, this conclusion is convenient for me, because I'm not an econometrician. As a "dilequant," I don't have the skills to contribute to this strand of research on ARCH models.)

11

Fat Tails and Something About the Number of Particles in the Universe

We must accept that the normal distribution
is just an approximation of the true distribution.
−JPP

EARLIER I STATED THAT HIGHER MOMENTS MATTER, BUT they are more difficult to predict than volatility. This issue merits further discussion. If returns are normally distributed (or Gaussian, i.e., part of a family of bell-shaped probability distributions), we can approximate exposure to loss based on volatility. If not, we're likely to underestimate risk. *By how much* is the key question.

In our study, we estimated the persistence in risk measures, but we didn't estimate the *size* of measurement errors. Volatility is too crude a risk measure. Most investors and academics agree with this statement, and the events of 2020 have made it even more obvious. There are several analytical tools available to asset allocators to model fat tails, such as historical analysis, blended probability distributions, and scenario analysis.

Nassim Taleb (2010) argues that we can't predict higher moments. We don't know when extreme losses will occur, but we should build resilience to them. Black swans, like the pandemic and oil shock of 2020, are rare, but they do exist. Taleb notes, "The Black Swan idea is not to predict—it is to describe this phenomenon, and how to build systems that can resist Black Swan events."[1] And "Black Swans being unpredictable, we need to adjust to their existence (rather than naïvely try to predict them)."[2] There are many examples where we must build resilience to rare but consequential events that we can't predict, in all areas of life. Pick your analogy: skiers wear helmets; cars have air bags; houses are built to withstand hurricanes; boats are built to withstand rogue waves; planes are built to withstand lightning; etc.

However, a strict interpretation of Taleb's black swan theory seems impossible to implement with models and data, because, in his words (Taleb, 2010), a black swan "lies outside the realm of regular expectations, because nothing in the past can convincingly point to its possibility." If nothing in the past can convincingly point to the possibility of an event, we might as well throw our hands up and not even try to forecast risk. Or I suppose, we can imagine what *could* happen, even though it has *never* happened. Tomorrow, pigs could fly. There's something unsatisfying and defeatist about this interpretation of the theory.

For our purposes, let us define outliers as possible but rare events—the financial equivalents of the car crash, the hurricane, the rogue wave. We have little data for these events, but we do have evidence of their possibility. Our horse races showed we can't forecast the *timing* of these outliers (as evidenced by the lack of persistence or strong mean reversion in skewness and kurtosis). But we know they exist, and we know they matter. As Peter Bernstein (1996) wrote in his book *Against the Gods: The Remarkable Story of Risk*, "It is in those outliers and imperfections that the wildness lurks."

For example, suppose you invest $100,000 in a portfolio composed of 60% US stocks and 40% US bonds. What's the most you could lose in one year? We might not know *when* this loss will occur or *what* will cause the loss (like a pandemic), but we still want to know whether it *could* occur. Throughout history, we have enough evidence to hypothesize that financial crashes are always a possibility. Often, what causes them are "once-in-a-hundred-year" events or, sometimes, events that have never happened before.

Let us define this exposure as the minimum loss you could suffer 1% of the time—in other words, we want to estimate the one-year value at risk at the 99% confidence level. If we model the exposure based on the portfolio's volatility, without special consideration for fat tails, your "maximum" loss is $12,028.[3] But it's not too difficult to account for fat tails. If we have a representative data sample, we can simply use the data directly, instead of the volatility-based estimate. If we look back at monthly returns from February 1976 to January 2019 to measure your exposure directly, the estimate almost *doubles*, to $23,972.

As I've mentioned, fat tails matter, and volatility is a poor proxy for exposure to loss. *Financial advisors, investment managers, consultants, individual investors, and everybody else involved in investment management must at some point determine their (or their end investor's) risk tolerance and align the portfolio's risk accordingly.* If we ignore fat tails, we underestimate exposure to loss and take too much risk relative to the investor's risk tolerance.

Of course, risk tolerance itself is a fuzzy concept. Several years ago, a client asked Mark Kritzman and me how we calibrate risk tolerance. As usual, Mark had an interesting, tongue-in-cheek answer:

> There's some research that was done at MIT to estimate people's risk tolerance based on neurochemical science. For example, individuals with higher levels of specific enzymes may have higher risk tolerance. However, our clients have found the idea of a blood test a bit too invasive.

Less invasive approaches include survey methods. We ask investors questions such as "What's the most you could tolerate to lose in one year?" Robo-advisors rely on such questions to select portfolios for individuals without human intervention. This approach obviously requires the ability to estimate exposure to loss correctly, with consideration for fat tails. Otherwise, when we select the portfolio for the investor, we create a dangerous misalignment between exposure to loss and the investor's risk tolerance.

These issues about fat tails have been well known and discussed ad nauseam in academia and throughout our industry for decades. As MIT professor Andrew Lo explains in the 2001 article "Risk Management for Hedge Funds":

It is well known that financial data . . . are highly non-normal; i.e., they are asymmetrically distributed, highly skewed, often multimodal, and with fat tails that imply many more "rare" events than the normal distribution would predict.

Yet though I'm sure he would disagree with many of the concepts I present in this book, Nassim Taleb makes a valid point: too often fat tails are ignored, even by very smart people who should know better. *Fat tails matter because asset allocators must forecast exposure to loss when they construct portfolios.* For example, I'm always surprised at how many professional investors, who know the impact of fat tails on exposure to loss, still ignore them when they discuss Sharpe ratios (defined as excess return over cash, divided by *volatility*). Clearly, we should not use Sharpe ratios to compare strategies that sell optionality (like most alternative investments) with traditional asset classes, investment strategies, and products. But I continue to hear such comparisons everywhere.

In early 2019, I attended a conference on risk premiums in New York. On the stage, several investment pros discussed the role of risk premiums in investors' portfolios. The mood was somber, as 2018 was a tough year for these strategies. Aside from one panelist who clearly was a salesperson (disguised, as is often the case, as a "product manager"), all others were full-time investors. I recoiled at all the mentions of "high Sharpe ratios" for risk premiums that are long carry and/or short optionality.

In the same article from which I took the earlier quote on fat tails, Andrew Lo presents a fascinating case study on this issue. Based on monthly data from January 1992 to December 1999, he simulates a mystery investment strategy that requires no investment skill whatsoever: no analysis, no fore-sight, no judgment. When I mention this case study during conference pre-sentations, I usually say that "the strategy is so simple, a monkey could do it," which is only a slight overstatement.

Despite its simplicity, in Lo's backtest, the mystery strategy *doubles* the Sharpe ratio of the S&P 500, from 0.98 to 1.94. And from January 1992 to December 1999, it experienced only 6 negative months, compared with 36 for the S&P 500. "By all accounts, this is an enormously successful hedge fund with a track record that would be the envy of most managers," teases Lo.

Then Lo reveals the simulated strategy: he sold out-of-the-money put options on the S&P 500. Essentially, the strategy loaded up on tail risks. Like the currency carry strategy I mentioned in Chapter 9, it picked up pennies in front of a steamroller. Lo concludes:

> In the case of the strategy of shorting out-of-the-money put options on the S&P 500, returns are positive most of the time, and losses are infre-quent, but when they occur, they are extreme. This is a very specific type of risk signature that is not well summarized by static measures such as standard deviation.

He hints that many hedge funds, under the cloak of nontransparency that they enjoy compared with the transparency of mutual funds (many hedge funds operate as a "black box"), may use this type of strategy to juice their track records. As a caveat, he doesn't argue that selling insurance in financial markets is wrong per se, as evidenced by the significant need for insurance from institutional investors. Some entities must provide insurance, and there should be a premium to entice them. I made a similar risk premium argument in Chapter 7 when I discussed our covered call writing strategy. Lo worries about the risk management of such strategies for hedge funds themselves, and most importantly, on the part of institutional investors such as pension plans that use Sharpe ratios to select investments. As I mentioned earlier, when it comes to all aspects of risk forecasting, higher moments matter.

This fact of life became evident during 2007 and the subsequent financial crisis, as well as in 2020. In a wonderfully sarcastic article, "How Unlucky

Is 25-Sigma?," Kevin Dowd, John Cotter, Chris Humphrey, and Margaret Woods (2008) illustrate the limitations of risk forecasting models based on normal distributions. If we ignore nonnormal higher moments, some extreme losses should be virtually impossible. The authors quote executives at Goldman Sachs and Citigroup who seemed to imply that normal distribution probabilities explained how "unlucky" or unforecastable losses were. But clearly, the risk models themselves were wrong. Goldman's CFO was quoted as saying, "We were seeing things that were 25-standard deviation moves, several days in a row."

A 7-sigma event, let alone a 25-sigma event, should occur 1 day out of 3,105,395,365 years, Dowd and coauthors explain. They provide some intuition for such probabilities (for noncreationists):

> A 5-sigma event corresponds to an expected occurrence of less than just one day in the entire period since the end of the last Ice Age; a 6-sigma event corresponds to an expected occurrence of less than one day in the entire period since our species, Homo Sapiens, evolved from earlier primates; and a 7-sigma event corresponds to an expected occurrence of just once in a period approximately five times the length of time that has elapsed since multicellular life first evolved on this planet.

Then they help the reader understand the infinitesimal nature of 25-sigma probabilities:

> These numbers are on a truly cosmological scale so that a natural comparison is with the number of particles in the universe, which is believed to be between $1.0e+73$ and $1.0e+85$. Thus, a 20-sigma event corresponds to an expected-occurrence period measured in years that is 10 times larger than the high end of the estimated range for the number of particles in the universe. A 25-sigma event corresponds to an expected-occurrence period that is equal to the higher of these latter estimates, but with the decimal point moved 52 places to the left!

This analysis puts in perspective the statement that Goldman saw such events "several days in a row."

To be fair, I suspect the Goldman statement was made simply to illustrate the unlikely nature of the market moves, not to imply that fat tails don't exist or that we should use the normal distribution to assess the likelihood of these losses. The events of 2007, 2008, and the first quarter of 2009 were still very unusual. In hindsight, the speculative excesses in subprime mortgages and the fragile, house-of-cards derivatives edifice built on top of them explain a large part of the financial crisis. But at the time, most risk forecasting models were not built to incorporate such unobserved, latent risks. Perhaps that's what Taleb means when he writes that a black swan "lies outside the realm of regular expectations, because nothing in the past can convincingly point to its possibility." Except that in 2007, a lot of signs *in the present* pointed to a possible blowup. Credit spreads on structured products had never exploded in the past; yet unprecedented pressures were building in the entire system.

A decade later, as asset prices reached new highs across markets, in our Asset Allocation Committee we constantly asked ourselves, "Where's the excess speculation, the latent risk?" In other words, *where's the bubble?* The answer isn't obvious. The postcrisis rally in risk assets has been largely supported by fundamentals. Investors have become more cautious. Some refer to this rally as an unloved bull market. There was a bubble in cryptocurrencies, but it's been deflating somewhat slowly and, so far, without systemic consequences. However, we do worry about latent risks such as the unprecedented levels of government debt and 0% interest rates outside the United States.

As the events related to the coronavirus pandemic of 2020 continue to unfold, pundits like to compare this crisis with the 2008 financial crisis. Yet there are important differences. The 2008 crisis involved a speculative bubble in real estate. Systemic risk was high, in great part because banks owned structured products linked to this bubble. A shaky edifice composed of layers upon layers of complex, interconnected structured products and derivatives stood on the shoulders of risky subprime borrowers.

In 2020, financial institutions are not in the thick of the storm. However, the novel coronavirus will cause an economic shock of unprecedented size—an economic heart attack. Small businesses, countless levered companies, and the consumer are all at risk. Monetary and fiscal authorities have taken out their defibrillators, with rate cuts, asset purchases, and trillions of dollars in fiscal stimulus. As I hand over this manuscript to my editor, we have yet to determine the shock's full impact.

Asset allocators can use the concept of risk regimes to model, and perhaps forecast, latent risks. We discussed risk regimes in Chapter 9 in the context of tail correlations. If markets oscillate between high- and low-volatility regimes, we should expect fat tails. The idea is that the fat tails belong to another probability distribution altogether—the risk-off regime, which is characterized by investor panics, liquidity events, and flights to safety. And if we blend two normal distributions (risk-on versus risk-off or "quiet" versus "turbulent"), we can get a highly nonnormal distribution. In other words,

Normal distribution + normal distribution = nonnormal distribution

In that context, a "25-sigma event" could be a 1- or 2-sigma event generated from the risk-off distribution. For example, high-yield bonds have very different volatility when the S&P 500 sells off, compared with what happens in more normal times. They have an annualized volatility of 31% when the S&P 500 sells off 7% or more in a month. But on the rest of the dataset (i.e., on months during which the S&P 500 returns –7% or *better*), they have a volatility of only 9%.[4] Here I've defined the regimes based on an arbitrary cutoff for S&P 500 monthly returns (–7%), but there are several more advanced ways to parse out risk regimes. (For example, see Chow, Jacquier, Kritzman, and Lowry, 1999, on the Mahalanobis distance, which we will discuss further in Chapter 14, as well as in the context of Markov-switching models.) Also, I could have used a cutoff on high-yield returns, but I chose –7% the S&P 500 to make my regime definition more "systemic." US equities are a good indicator of risk-on versus risk-off sentiment across markets.

If we assume that the average annualized return for high-yield bonds is +7% in the normal regime and –10% in the risk-off regime, we can model two normal distributions:

1. Normal times: average of +7%, volatility of 9%
2. Risk-off regime: average of –10%, volatility of 31%

Both distributions have a skewness of zero and a kurtosis of 3, which are the values we should expect for normal distributions. (In other words, when skewness is zero and kurtosis is 3, there are no fat tails.) To define these regimes, I've used a filter on monthly returns and then expressed the averages and volatilities in annual terms. This conversion between monthly and annual return distributions requires some mental and mathematical gymnastics, but these technicalities are beside the example's point.

Suppose there is a 5% probability that we shift to the risk-off regime in any given year. Otherwise, 95% of the time, we remain in the "normal" regime. We can use these regime probabilities in a simulation. The goal is to add the two distributions and thereby simulate returns for high-yield bonds in a way that accounts for regime shifts. It's remarkably simple, and it's a fun exercise. It takes less than five minutes, so I would encourage even non-quants to try it to gain important intuition on risk regimes. Here's how it works in Excel, for example:

1. First, simulate a series of returns, say 10,000 observations, for each regime. In the first column, copy and paste the following formula 10,000 times, for a total of 10,000 rows:

   =NORMINV(RAND(), 7%, 9%)

   And do the same in the second column for the risk-off regime:

   =NORMINV(RAND(), –10%, 31%)

2. In a third column, use the RAND() function to draw a number from 0 to 1 randomly, also 10,000 times.
3. In a fourth column, use an IF function that selects a simulated return based on the outcome of the RAND() function. Select a return from the risk-off regime only when the random number draw is 0.05 or below. Otherwise, select a normal regime return.

Suppose normal regime returns are in column E, risk-off regime returns are in column F, and the RAND() is in column G. Also, suppose the simulation starts on row 4. Here is the formula:

   =IF(G4<0.05,F4,E4)

The simulated return distribution that includes regime shifts (fourth column) has a skewness of −1.65 and a kurtosis of 12.6. It's extremely fat tailed, even though it was generated from two normal distributions (again, normal + normal = nonnormal). In that context, extreme losses represented by 6-, 7-, or more sigma events aren't expected to be as rare as "once in the history of the universe" or other such claims. In light of the "25-sigma" paper, perhaps our industry has underestimated the power of this regime-based framework for risk forecasting.

Yet academics and quantitative practitioners have developed a wide range of models to define and forecast regimes. In the paper "Regime Shifts: Implications for Dynamic Strategies (Corrected)" that Mark Kritzman, David Turkington, and I (2012) wrote, we explain how to use so-called Markov models to define regimes. In my previous example with high-yield bonds, I use a threshold of −7% equity returns as the cutoff for the risk-off regime. But we can reduce noise if we define regimes based on "maximum likelihood." In our paper, we show that because they ignore regime persistence, thresholds give more false signals than advanced techniques.

As we saw in the discussion on risk forecasting, there is significant month-to-month persistence in volatility across asset classes. Suppose we observe a somewhat benign return, close to the long-term average of the normal regime. A threshold method would classify this return as part of the normal regime. But if the observation follows several extreme returns, it's more likely that it is part of the turbulent regime and that the next observation will be volatile. As an analogy, in the middle of turbulence, the airplane may glide quietly for a few seconds. If you're like me, a born worrier, you probably think, "This is not over." If the last few minutes have been rough, the probability that the plane will continue to experience turbulence is higher than it would be if the air had been smooth for a while. The advanced techniques we used in our paper account for the fact that asset returns (as well as fundamental and economic data) tend to cluster, like air turbulence.

Maximum likelihood models also better capture relative volatilities. Suppose regime 1 has a higher average return than regime 2, but with a higher volatility. In that case, it's possible that several large negative returns come from regime 1, even though it has a higher average return than regime 2.

In my view, regardless of how we define the regimes, the most interesting aspect of the approach is that we can specify regime probabilities to build a risk forecast. Historically, regimes are highly persistent month to month, like air turbulence. For example, in "Regime Shifts: Implications for Dynamic Strategies," we show that there's a 90% or more probability that we stay in the current equity turbulence regime from one month to another. Such transition probabilities form the basis of the Markov regime-switching model. (In the paper's appendix, we provide Matlab code to estimate this model.)

Still, these improvements are technical details, and the regime-based approach can be useful even to investors who don't want to deploy this heavy econometric artillery. As a simpler application, let us go back to my example with high-yield bonds. Suppose we form a view that there's a 10% probability of a recession over the next year, and we think the market hasn't priced in this risk. In that case, we would apply a 10% weight to the risk-off regime, instead of 5% as I did earlier. As a result, we would get a fatter-tailed mixture.

Investors should pay attention to this key idea for risk forecasting: we can parse historical data into regimes and then apply forward-looking probabilities to reweight them. These probabilities should depend on current conditions. Is monetary policy accommodative or restrictive? Are valuations particularly elevated? Are equity earnings likely to surprise on the upside or disappoint? This framework provides a rare opportunity to merge fundamental views with quantitative methods in a coherent and transparent way. Quants should use judgment and experience to determine forward-looking probabilities, and fundamental investors should be ready to rely on the data to define the regimes.

Scenario Analysis

Another approach to tail-risk estimation is scenario analysis, also referred to as stress testing. Like the risk regime framework, scenario analysis often marries quantitative and fundamental inputs. In the Global Multi-Asset Division at T. Rowe Price, we apply a wide range of historical scenarios and forward-looking shocks on our 200+ portfolios.

In its simplest form, historical scenario analysis is straightforward. We multiply current asset class weights by asset class returns from a historical episode:

Current asset class weights × asset class returns during a past crisis

Suppose your portfolio is invested 80% in stocks and 20% in bonds, and you would like to know how this portfolio would perform in another financial crisis such as the 2008–2009 meltdown. You could simply multiply 0.8 × the return of stocks during the crisis, plus 0.2 × the return of bonds during the crisis.

There are many applications for this framework: financial advisors can use it to help individual clients better assess their risk tolerance; asset allocators can stress-test their portfolio to determine whether they are properly diversified; plan sponsors can use it to manage expectations with their boards of trustees; and so on. We'll revisit scenarios in Chapter 14 when we discuss tail-aware portfolio construction, but as I mentioned in Chapter 9 when we discussed the failure of diversification, there is a need for our industry to move scenario analysis from the back office (after-the-fact reporting) to the front office, where investment decisions are made.

Examples of past crises include the crash of October 1987, the global financial crisis (June 2008 to February 2009), the US debt downgrade (August 2011 to September 2011), the taper tantrum (May 2013 to June 2013), and the current 2020 pandemic crisis. For strategies that are managed against a benchmark, investors should consider upside scenarios as well. If the active portfolio is under-risked relative to its benchmark, by how much could it underperform in a market rally ("melt-up") event? For example, a scenario dashboard could include a reflation scenario (March 2016 to December 2016).

Of course, to define the scenarios is not an exact science. We must make a judgment call on the start and end dates for each historical episode. I have found peak-to-trough scenarios to be useful, because they relate to the concept of maximum drawdown. When we use the market's peak as the start date and the trough as the end date, we ask, "How bad can it get?"

An important, and often underappreciated, drawback of this simple approach to historical scenarios is that asset classes change over time.

Fluctuations in sector weights within the S&P 500 provide a good example. The most unstable sector in the index has been technology. From 5% of the index, it reached a peak of 29% in 1999, during the dot-com mania. Then it declined back to a trough of 15% in 2005. With the recent rise of the tech giants (Amazon, Apple, Facebook), it now stands at 21%.

Over time, the S&P 500 index has become less exposed to cyclical sectors. In 2007, before the global financial crisis, the financials and energy sectors represented 31% of the index. These two sectors now represent only 19% of the index. Sector weights for industrials and materials have gone down over this period as well.[5] Therefore, not only will the next crisis be different (as crises always are), but the sensitivity of US stocks to that new crisis will be different as well. They should be more resilient to an economic downturn that affects mostly cyclicals. Recent market performance during the coronavirus pandemic proves this point. Large technology companies have protected the S&P 500 from the much larger drawdown it would have experienced if it still had a 31% weight in financials and energy.

These changes in sector weights also make time series analyses of valuation ratios on the S&P 500 less reliable. In 2019, a P/E ratio of 16x on a less cyclical, more tech-heavy S&P 500 means something different than does a P/E ratio of 16x from the early 1970s, for example. (To complicate things, even the nature of tech itself has changed, from a speculative bet on no-earning internet companies in 1999 to the solid cash flow growers that we know today.) In Chapter 1, when we discussed return forecasting and compared the Shiller and Siegel approaches, we didn't adjust for sector exposures when we made statements such as "Markets are expensive relative to history." But in practice, such adjustments can be helpful. They may reveal that markets aren't as expensive as they seem. For scenario analysis, valuations matter as well. High P/Es often indicate fragile markets with elevated probabilities of tail events.

Emerging markets stocks provide an even more pronounced example of how an asset class can drastically change under the hood. This asset class has changed substantially compared with how it was a few years ago. In fact, it doesn't even look like the same asset class. This change invalidates most unadjusted historical analyses (volatility and correlation estimation, scenario analysis, valuation, etc.) that involve emerging markets stocks. In a 2017 article published in the *Financial Times*, "Emerging Market Assets Are Trapped by an Outdated Cliché," Jonathan Wheatley says:

> [In] November 2014, . . . the weight of technology stocks in the benchmark MSCI EM equities index overtook the weight of energy and materials—the commodities stocks that many see as emblematic of emerging markets.
>
> This transformation has been dramatic. When the commodities supercycle was in full swing, in mid 2008, energy and materials accounted for more than a third of MSCI EM market capitalisation and tech companies just a tenth. Last month, the commodities group was barely an eighth of EM market cap, and tech companies more than a quarter.
>
> This should be no surprise. EM tech companies include the Chinese internet trio of Tencent, Alibaba and Baidu and longer-established names such as Hon Hai and TSMC of Taiwan and Samsung Electronics of South Korea.[6]

Emerging markets stocks have become more "high tech" and less commodity-dependent. Consumer sectors have also become more prominent. Like the S&P 500, all else being equal, the asset class should be more resilient to traditional economic downturns than in the past. Also, while political crises still occur (as evidenced by 2018 events in Turkey and Venezuela), most emerging markets countries now have stronger current account balances. The risk of contagion appears to have decreased. So far in the first half of 2020, emerging markets have been more resilient than during previous crises (on a relative basis).

In fixed income markets, changes in factor exposures within asset classes can affect the fundamental nature of how they react to macroeconomic shocks. This issue is problematic for index investors. Take the Barclays Aggregate, for example.[7] In early 2008, before the global financial crisis, Treasuries constituted less than 25% of the index. They now represent close to 40% of the index. Unlike in stock markets, where supply and demand regulate market capitalization weights, in fixed income markets, index weights are driven mainly by supply. The more an issuer borrows, the larger the issuer's weight in the index. This perverse effect has been an argument against passive/index approaches in bonds. (Ultimately, it's an oversimplification, but please bear with me, for the sake of argument.)

Postcrisis fiscal stimulus and accumulated budget deficits have forced the US government to borrow more and more. The debt-to-GDP ratio in the United States has reached 104%, from 63% in Q4 2007.[8] This increased borrowing explains the rise in the relative weight of Treasuries in the index. In theory, it makes the index more resilient to risk-off shocks.

On the other hand, there might be a scenario in which the government's excess borrowing degrades the credit quality of its debt to such an extent that US Treasuries cease to be the safe-haven asset class. It's unlikely now, but this never-before-seen scenario is perhaps an example of Taleb's black swans. US government debt was indeed downgraded in 2011. Stocks sold off while Treasuries, somewhat unexpectedly, remained the safe haven despite their lowered rating. Where else were investors supposed to hide?

Nonetheless, there might be a breaking point in the future. Treasuries could become a risk asset. Beyond their inflation risk, default risk could begin to drive part of their volatility, similarly to, say, Italian government debt. With over $2 trillion in fiscal measures to address the crisis of 2020, who knows?

Meanwhile, the duration of the Barclays Aggregate Index has increased, from an average of 4.5 years in 2005 to 6 years in 2019. Again, the inflection point was the global financial crisis. Before this crisis, duration had remained stable for over two decades, from the start of the data series. Since then, it has climbed steadily, which means that the index has become much more sensitive to interest rate shocks.

If we create a historical scenario analysis of the 1994 surprise rate shock when the Fed started tightening, we must adjust the historical asset class returns downward to account for the now longer duration of the index. With a 6-year duration, a +100-bps rise in rates roughly translates into a –6% price drop (–6 × 1%), compared with –4.5% with a duration of 4.5 (–4.5 × 1%). The rise in duration is attributable to corporate debt issuance. Corporations, especially in the industrials sector, have taken advantage of lower rates to issue long-term debt. When rates decline, duration increases mathematically due to convexity, but this effect is relatively minor.

There is another way in which passive exposures to US bonds have become riskier: a degradation in credit quality, *despite the rise in the index weight of Treasuries.* Based on data for the Barclays U.S. Aggregate from January 2008 to February 2020, if we exclude Treasuries and securitized bonds, the weight of high-quality bonds (rated AAA or AA) has decreased from 21 to 2% as a share of corporates. Hence, the weight of the riskier bonds (rated A or BAA) has increased from 89 to 98% of corporates and from 15 to 23% of the entire index.

Therefore, a risk-off scenario based on historical returns for the index would likely underestimate exposure to loss. As the coronavirus and oil shock events unfolded during the first half of 2020, this deterioration in credit became painfully evident.

There are many other such examples across asset classes. US small caps have deteriorated in quality; value stocks have become more cyclical; etc. The bottom line is that a simple scenario analysis based on historical asset class returns can lead to an underestimation or overestimation of exposure to loss, because asset classes change over time.

Factor analysis provides an easy solution to this issue. Factors and risk premiums have captured the attention of investors over the last decade, so we will cover these topics in Chapter 12. In the context of risk models, asset classes can be represented as a collection of underlying risk factors, such as equity beta, value, growth, momentum, interest rate duration, credit duration, and currencies. The risk factors cut across asset classes, which means that several asset classes may have exposure to the same risk factor. Non-US asset classes are exposed to the same currency factors; fixed income asset classes have common exposures to interest rate duration; equity asset classes have common exposures to sector and country factors; real estate, hedge funds, and almost all risk assets are exposed to equity market beta; and so on.

For factor-based scenario analysis, we can replace asset class weights with risk factor exposures, and we can replace asset class returns with risk factor returns. We used this model for asset class returns:

Current asset class weights $\times$ asset class returns during a past crisis

With the risk factor framework, we use:

Current risk factor exposures $\times$ risk factor returns during a past crisis

There is no industry consensus on how to convert asset classes into risk factor exposures. We'll review a few approaches shortly. For now, let me say that for scenario analysis at T. Rowe Price, our risk systems produce security-level factor mappings. These mappings are then aggregated at the asset class and portfolio levels.

Unlike asset class–based scenarios, factor-based scenarios rely on *current* exposures. For example, the Barclays Aggregate is modeled based on its *current* duration; emerging markets stocks are modeled based on their *current* sector exposures; etc. I've heard from clients that some risk system vendors market this approach as "forward-looking." It's an exaggeration, because factor-based scenarios rely on historical factor returns, but at least the framework circumvents the issue that factor exposures within asset classes change over time.

Suppose that as of January 31, 2019, you held the following typical 60% stocks/40% bonds asset mix, all invested in passive benchmarks: 42% in US equities (Russell 3000); 18% in non-US equities (MSCI AC World ex-U.S.); 32.5% in US bonds (Barclays Aggregate), and 7.5% in short-term inflation-protected bonds (Barclays U.S. TIPS 1-5).

Based on current factor exposures, Table 11.1 shows potential losses and gains under various historical episodes.[9]

TABLE 11.1   Scenario Analysis

Start Date	End Date	Scenario	Return
June 2008	February 2009	Global financial crisis	−29%
September 2008	October 2008	September–October 2008	−19%
May 2013	June 2013	Taper tantrum	−1%
March 2016	December 2016	Reflation	+11%

Our systems also account for active positions. For each scenario, we can apply an attribution model to produce a detailed, hypothetical attribution.

Our model decomposes returns into contributions from security selection, tactical asset allocation, and strategic asset allocation. It further decomposes these returns into asset class-, factor-, and security-level contributions.

The ability to zoom in and out of decision layers is remarkable. For example, we can make statements such as, "Given our current exposures, if we were to face another 2008-like scenario, we would lose X% from our security selection within US growth equities (of which Y% would come from our position in company XYZ, a large tech company), gain Z% from our tactical underweight to equities, and lose A% from our strategic overweight to high-yield bonds."

However, there are drawbacks to this factor-based approach. First, it's often difficult to map portfolios to risk factors. Some exposures contain a fair amount of unexplained volatility (so-called nonfactor-based, or "idiosyncratic," volatility). Absolute return strategies with small or unstable factor exposures are particularly difficult to model, for example. Suppose a hedge fund *currently* holds very little equity beta, while *over time* it often takes significant directional exposure to equities. The snapshot that we take when the fund happens to have minimal equity exposure may underestimate exposure to loss. In this case, we should probably use the longer-run average rather than the current exposure.

Another issue is that every crisis is different. It may be an obvious statement, but in the context of scenario analysis, it becomes particularly important. For many investors, in 2020 it became evident that portfolios built to be resilient to a past crisis may not be as resilient to the next one. For example, structured products were resilient to the tech bubble burst. From December 31, 1999 to December 31, 2002, the S&P 500 crashed, losing 38%. Over the same period, the Barclays Commercial Mortgage Backed Securities (CMBS) Index was up 44%. Hence, CMBS provided a remarkable hedge to the equity sell-off.

Now, let us fast-forward to the 2008–2009 crisis. The picture looks quite different. In three months, from September 19 to November 20, 2008, the S&P 500 crashed, losing 40%. Over the same period, the Barclays CMBS Index lost 37%. This move in the CMBS index was extreme on a risk-adjusted basis. It speaks to our earlier discussion on the article "How Unlucky

Is 25-Sigma?" The quarterly volatility in the CMBS index from the start of its history in Q1 1997 to before the sell-off in Q2 2008 was 2.4%. The 37% loss was, therefore, a 15-standard deviation event.[10]

After the 2008–2009 crisis, I met with a senior bank executive to discuss scenario analysis. He showed me a chart of structured credit spreads that spanned precrisis data. Before 2008, the line was almost flat. It showed barely *any* volatility. Banks held significant allocations to these products, for their risk-return free lunch, as well as a regulatory (capital charge) free lunch. He rhetorically asked, "That's the data we had at the time. Who could have predicted the types of moves we saw during the crisis?"

I don't know. Quantitative value-at-risk models rely on past data, and to the extent that a latent risk has not materialized yet, these models will give a false sense of security. A lot has been said about this crisis with the benefit of hindsight. I do remember some thought leaders raising alarm bells before the sell-off unraveled (Nouriel Roubini, Robert Shiller, and others).

My point is that robust scenario analysis requires forward-looking scenarios as well. Most quants are uncomfortable with "made-up" scenarios, but the risk factor approach provides a useful compromise between art/fundamental judgment and science. Instead of historical factor returns, we can specify hypothetical factor returns:

Current risk factor exposures × hypothetical factor returns

It is common practice to specify shocks to one or two factors and then propagate these shocks to the other factors. Essentially, we use the betas (sensitivities) between factors. Suppose we shock the equity risk factor by –20%. To propagate this shock to credit spreads, we multiply –20% × the beta between credit and equity. We can also adjust the propagated shocks for the differences in means (expected return) between factors.[11] This approach also allows shocks to nonfinancial factors, such as GDP and inflation, as long as we can estimate the betas between the nonfinancial and the financial factors.

If we don't propagate shocks, we assume, very mistakenly, that the other factors would remain stable under stress. For example, if we shock the equity factor in isolation, we assume credit spreads, currencies, rates, etc., would remain stable. Given the high correlations across risk assets, for most portfolios, shocking individual factors in isolation (i.e., without propagation) will underestimate exposure to loss.

Even with propagation, in practice there is another flaw in how investors have applied this framework. It relates to the well-known issue of unstable correlations and betas that we discussed in Chapter 9. During stress events, such as the crisis of 2020, the beta between equity and rates is likely to become more negative, while almost all other betas are likely to jump higher. Yet most risk models rely on *recent* rather than *stress* betas. (Many investors realized in 2020 that they had more credit risk in their portfolio than they expected, and that this credit risk was essentially indirect equity risk.)

When we shock a risk factor and infer movements in other related risk factors, we should use stress betas. To use a simple example, as of February 28, 2019, based on the last 12 months, the beta between the equity and credit factors was 0.13. Hence, a shock of –10% on the equity factor would translate into a loss of $0.13 \times -10\% = -1.3\%$ for credit factor exposures. However, on December 31, 2008, the trailing 12-month beta was 0.48, which would translate into a propagated shock to credit of –4.8%.[12]

Stacy Cuffe and Lisa Goldberg (2012), in their article "Allocating Assets in Climates of Extreme Risk," explain how the sensitivities (covariances/ betas) that we measure to propagate shocks can be adjusted based on the nature of the stress tests:

> It may be prudent to go back in history to find a consistent covariance matrix forecast. For example, a manager who believes that the U.S. economy is on the brink of a prolonged period of disinflation might wish to impart this view to his or her asset allocation in the context of a stressed covariance matrix taken from a disinflationary historical period. The financial crisis of 2008 spawned a disinflationary regime that led to deflation. To assess how asset class returns may behave during a period of disinflation or deflation, a manager can either construct a covariance matrix from an equally weighted sample of observations from relevant historical periods or take a historical EWMA covariance matrix using an analysis date from the relevant regime.

Despite these complications, the approach is quite useful because it allows investors to specify shocks or a combination of shocks that may not have happened before but that may be possible given current conditions. The propagation framework allows the investor to express views on a limited number of factors.

There is no crystal ball. To the extent an investor lacks insights about possible future shocks, the framework will be of little help. The banker who told me that no one could have predicted the spread moves that occurred during the 2008 crisis wouldn't have gained much insight from the framework unless someone identified the risk of a significant jump in structured credit spreads. The logic is circular. It depends heavily on the investor's views, which are the true value-added. The framework itself is simply there to impose consistency and scale the approach to multiple portfolios and factors.

Offense Versus Defense

So far, we've discussed how to use scenario analysis to play defense, i.e., to better understand fat tails and to calibrate and hedge exposure to loss. In practice, if pressed, most investors will admit that they use scenario analysis after portfolio construction has taken place, as a back-office exercise to appease clients and perhaps reassure themselves that their portfolio isn't exposed to undue risks. But I've rarely seen scenario analysis influence portfolio construction in a meaningful way.

However, investors and analysts who formulate forward-looking macro views can use scenario analysis to play offense as well. In a tactical framework, we can specify various macro scenarios in quadrants across growth and inflation. Then we can map which trades would do well in which state of the world. These trades can be implemented across currencies, countries, rates, spread sectors, etc. They can represent long, short, or long-short positions. Some trades might be designed to generate alpha, while others may mitigate tail risks. Probabilities can be assigned to each scenario.

The important part of such a process, as always, is to understand market expectations and how deviations from market expectations can impact asset returns. Easier said than done, but the idea is that scenario analysis can influence investment decisions more than many investors seem to appreciate. When we discuss single-period portfolio optimization in Chapter 14, we will see how to integrate scenarios directly into asset allocation decisions.

The Most Common Risk Forecasting Error

Fat tails are difficult to predict. Even after the fact (looked at in retrospect), they often lead to the mismeasurement of risk. Regime-based models and scenario analysis can alleviate these forecasting errors.

Before we move to portfolio construction, we must cover one additional source of risk forecasting error. This error is surprisingly common. Even investment experts and risk managers frequently get it wrong. Yet its impact is greater than anything we've discussed so far. Once revealed, it becomes obvious and intuitive.

On December 31, 2017, I met with three old friends in Newport Beach, California, for a champagne brunch. We got into a debate on Bitcoin, which had closed above $14,000 the week before. Two of my friends were bullish on the cryptocurrency. I said it was a bubble, about to burst. (I don't trade Bitcoin.) I converted our fourth compadre to my view. Two against two. To settle the disagreement, we decided to bet on Bitcoin's direction in 2018. We would meet again for brunch in a year. If Bitcoin went below $5,000—a 64% drop—the other bear and I would win.

This bet was ambiguous, because we didn't specify whether we would win if Bitcoin dipped below $5,000 *at any point* in 2018 or whether it had to *end the year* below $5,000. It's a perfect example of the key source of risk forecasting error: accounting for within-horizon risk. There are many scenarios in which Bitcoin could dip during the year but recover before the end of the year. The probability that it would dip below $5,000 at least once during 2018 (the "first-passage probability") was higher than the probability that it would end the year below that threshold. We kept debating whether we should use the first-passage or end-of-horizon outcome over text messages through the year. Bitcoin ended 2018 at $3,600, down 74%.

Mark Kritzman and Don Rich (2002) explain this important distinction between *within-horizon* and *end-of-horizon* risk measurement in "The

Mismeasurement of Risk." They begin with a famous quote from John Maynard Keynes: "In the long run, we are all dead."

Then they add the sentence that followed it in the original text *A Tract on Monetary Reform* (1923): "Economists set themselves too easy, too useless a task, if in tempestuous seasons they can only tell us that when the storm is long past, the ocean will be flat." This quote isn't as well-known, but it speaks to within-horizon exposure to loss.

The authors introduce two new risk measures based on first-passage probabilities. Within-horizon probability of loss, noted above, is the probability that the asset or portfolio dips below a threshold at some time, and continuous value at risk is an improved version of value at risk (minimum loss at a given confidence level) that measures exposure to loss throughout the investment horizon. The authors present several examples of why within-horizon risk matters: an asset manager might get fired if performance dips below a threshold; a hedge fund might face insolvency even if the losses are temporary; a borrower must maintain a given level of reserves per the loan covenants; etc.

Shorter-horizon risk measures don't address these concerns, because while they provide an estimate of exposure to loss—say, one day forward—they don't reflect losses that may accumulate over time. Maximum drawdown, while a useful measure of peak-to-trough exposure, doesn't consider the initial level of wealth. Hence, it doesn't differentiate between a case when the portfolio's value goes up 20% and then down 10% versus a case when the portfolio is flat and then down 10%, which is clearly a worse outcome.

Kritzman and Rich explain the mathematics behind first-passage probabilities in an intuitive and transparent way. They provide examples that show a significant difference in exposure to loss, whether we measure risk within or at the end of the horizon. For some experts, this distinction is obvious. But those who consume risk reports too often don't realize that the numbers are based on end-of-horizon probabilities. Then they get surprised when, along the way, realized risk "feels" much higher than what was forecasted.

In my Bitcoin example, the $5,000 threshold was more likely to be breached at some point within the year than precisely at the end of the year. For a more generic example, suppose you hold a plain-vanilla portfolio invested 60% in US stocks and 40% in US bonds. What is the probability that this portfolio could be down –5% over the next 12 months? If we use monthly data from February 1976 to January 2019 and account for fat tails, the traditional, end-of-horizon estimate is about 6%. However, the probability that the portfolio may be down –5% at any point over the next year is 21%. The difference between within-horizon and end-of-horizon probabilities increases as the time horizon gets longer. With a five-year horizon, the probability that the portfolio will be down –5% five years from now is only 1.4%, compared with the within-horizon probability of 28%.[13] These numbers suggest that from the perspective of first-passage probabilities, time diversification does not work. The idea that over time, risk goes down as good years diversify bad years only holds if we use end-of-horizon estimates. Otherwise, within-horizon exposure to loss *increases* as the time horizon gets longer.

Next time someone shows you a report with risk forecasts, the first question you should ask, even before you ask if fat tails were considered, is whether the numbers are based on end-of-horizon or within-horizon probabilities. Odds are, these are typical end-of-horizon numbers, and therefore they underestimate your exposure to loss along the way.

Rules of Thumb for Risk Forecasting

To summarize our discussion on risk forecasting, here are my top 10 rules of thumb:

1. When in doubt, use short data windows, even for medium-term forecasts.
2. Use higher-frequency data, including for low-frequency volatility forecasts.
3. If available, use information derived from options prices (implied volatility).
4. Account for the fact that volatility is most persistent over shorter horizons.
5. Do not worry too much about the need to use highly sophisticated models.

6. Expect some mean reversion for long-term forecasts (over five or more years).
7. Recognize that fat tails matter and should be included in your risk forecasts.
8. Separate your dataset into regimes, and assign probabilities to each regime.
9. Build historical and forward-looking scenarios to stress-test exposure to loss.
10. Model exposure to loss both at the end of and within the investment horizon.

Notes

1. http://nassimtaleb.org/tag/fat-tails/.
2. https://www.nytimes.com/2007/04/22/books/chapters/0422-1st-tale.html.
3. All numbers in this section are estimated with the Windham Portfolio Advisor. Indexes: MSCI USA for US stocks and Barclays U.S. Aggregate for US bonds. Monthly data from February 1976 to January 2019 were used.
4. Windham Portfolio Advisor. Based on monthly returns for the Merrill Lynch High Yield Index from February 1994 to January 2019.
5. All sector weights are from Bloomberg Finance L.P., compiled at the end of each year mentioned. Recent data are as of March 17, 2019. See SPX Index, MEMB function.
6. Jonathan Wheatley, 2017, "Emerging Market Assets Are Trapped by an Outdated Cliché," *Financial Times*, FT.com, June 26, 2017. Used under license from the Financial Times. All Rights Reserved. https://www.ft.com/content/3f2d69ea-575e-11e7-9fed-c19e2700005f.
7. Sources for this section on the Barclays U.S. Aggregate: Thrivent Asset Management, https://www.thrivent.com/literature/29311.pdf; and Bloomberg Barclays Indices, from the Barclays Data Feed; Bloomberg Finance L.P.
8. As of Q3, 2018. *Source:* Federal Reserve Bank of St. Louis, https://fred.stlouisfed.org/series/GFDEGDQ188S.
9. Factor exposures and factor returns are from MSCI Barra, POINT, and proprietary in-house systems (T. Rowe Price). As of January 31, 2019.
10. Bloomberg Finance L.P. TRA Function; SPX Index; LC09TRUU Index. Numbers reported are for total returns.
11. See Cuffe and Goldberg (2012).

12. Examples are constructed based on monthly data from Bloomberg Finance L.P. The equity factor is approximated with the price return of the S&P 500. The credit spread factor is estimated as $-7 \times$ the change in the OAS of the Barclays Credit Index (LUCROAS).
13. All estimates are from the Windham Portfolio Advisor, using a block bootstrap with 12-month blocks. As of January 31, 2019.

PART THREE

PORTFOLIO CONSTRUCTION

Modern Portfolio Theory is simple, because it is developed based on a finite horizon (one period). In a multi-period context, the risk-free rate and the betas can change.
—JPP

Now that we have covered return forecasting across short and long horizons, through equilibrium, valuation, and momentum lenses, as well as risk forecasting from volatility to higher moments, fat tails, and scenarios, a logical progression is to focus on portfolio construction. How do we put it all together?

First, before they optimize the trade-off between forecasted return and risk, multi-asset investors must choose the building blocks. Should we allocate across asset classes, or should we follow a more recent trend and allocate across risk factors? Then we must determine a target risk level, which we can express broadly via the stock and bond mix. This decision requires us to solve a multiperiod optimization problem. Next we must decide whether (and how) to use single-period portfolio optimization to populate the stock and bond mix with the appropriate underlying building blocks.

On the choice of asset classes or risk factors, there are pros and cons to each approach. My view is that both are useful if used in the right context. Most asset allocators still invest across traditional asset classes. Nonetheless, risk factors can be quite useful in improving return and risk forecasts, and in some limited cases, they can be used as stand-alone investments. A tired analogy is that risk factors are the "nutrients" of asset classes. A few essential factors—such as interest rate, equity, currency, and liquidity—cut across all asset classes, just like all foods can be decomposed into fats, carbs, and proteins.

Unfortunately, there's a lot of hype around risk factors. Major firms (and many startups) have developed commercial applications and products based on factors. Often their goal is to define factors as "asset classes" to raise assets. They do so because the governance process for institutional asset owners is typically quite rigid, such that new types of products face an uphill battle. "Where does it fit within our asset allocation?" is almost always the question. If an investment strategy can have its own "bucket"/asset class, it becomes much easier for its provider to win business. Every time someone presents you with a new asset class, watch your wallet, because that's where that person's hand is going.

However, factor analysis and investing are very broad areas of investment management. Many of their applications are quite useful. The important question here is whether factor analysis can improve the portfolio construction process. Rest assured—I'm not trying to sell a factor-based investment strategy.

12

Asset Classes Versus Risk Factors and Something About Dr. Strange

While volatilities are easy to visualize, covariances are more difficult. Academics have standardized the measure into the concept of beta, which is easier to interpret.
—JPP

BACK IN 2010, A FEW WEEKS AFTER I JOINED PIMCO, MARK Taborsky—who was a multi-asset portfolio manager at the time—suggested that we compare the diversification properties of risk factors with traditional asset classes. We eventually published an editorial in 2011 in the *Journal of Portfolio Management* on the topic. To my surprise, our two-pager received a lot of attention (unlike most of my publications) and was the most downloaded article in the *Journal of Portfolio Management* for over a year. It has been cited by 16 subsequent articles . . . although not all of them are complimentary.

When they think of risk factors, most people think of equity-based, Fama-French factors such as market beta, size, value, momentum, and quality. Some comprehensive models also include sector and country factors.

But fixed income portfolio managers have long decomposed portfolios into risk factors as well, probably even before equity investors did so. Almost all fixed income risk models are factor-based. Duration is a risk factor (or to be more precise, the interest rate is the risk factor, and duration is the exposure to it, or beta). Over time, many fixed income investors have expanded their factor-based approach to multi-asset portfolio management. To do so, they have connected two separate sets of factors (equity and fixed income), typically housed in two separate systems.

This process is not as complicated as it seems. We just need to measure the correlations between fixed income and equity factors. It *can* be made very complicated if we try to remeasure exposures across asset classes. For example, we can try to assign interest rate duration to stocks, equity beta to credit bonds, etc. In my experience, it's better to keep it simple. It's OK to allow for correlated factors. The correlation matrix will add up the risks in a consistent manner.

It's in that multi-asset context that Mark Taborsky and I wanted to help institutional investors with their asset allocation decisions. If asset classes are combinations of risk factors, why not diversify the portfolio directly across these factors? And if we diversify across factors, are the portfolios more resilient to market turbulence than are those allocated across asset classes?

To investigate, first I compiled returns for various factors. I used equity factors such as market beta, size, value, and momentum. For fixed income, I used interest rate duration, two slope factors, and a few flavors of credit spreads. I also added real estate and commodity as alternative factors. There is no industry consensus on how to map asset classes to risk factors. In a monograph I mentioned earlier, "Factor Investing and Asset Allocation: A Business Cycle Perspective" (2016), my coauthors and I provide an overview of methodologies to define factors, which include statistical methods (principal components analysis, regression analysis, etc.), fixed income mathematics, and long-short equity portfolio construction. (Earlier in this book, we also discussed macro factors. While they drive asset returns, these factors are not directly investable. You can't invest in GDP growth.)

For asset classes, I used the traditional building blocks: large and small cap US stocks, international stocks, core bonds, etc. We found that the average correlation across risk factors was much lower than the average correlation across asset classes. Also, during periods of market stress, the average correlation across risk factors did not jump by nearly as much as the correlation across classes.

This result was to be expected, because several of the factors were represented by long-short portfolios, while asset classes were all long-only benchmarks. If we allow for short positions, we can drastically lower correlations and make the portfolio's volatility more stable. When we discussed extreme correlations in Chapter 9, I mentioned that there's nothing magical about risk factors. If we constrain risk factors to be linear combinations of asset classes and allow for short positions in both asset classes and risk factors, we arrive at the same portfolio optimization result. No efficiency gains.

The problem is that we didn't explain this nuance in the editorial. I worry that we contributed to the hype around risk premiums as asset classes, which was not our goal. However, the fact remains that risk factors are often less constrained than asset classes. They are typically defined as long-short portfolios. And they sometimes cover a broader investment universe than asset classes, which also leads to efficiency gains.

Importantly, as we discussed in the context of scenario analysis, asset classes' exposures to risk factors change over time. Examples of such changes abound. For instance, the interest rate duration of the Barclays U.S. Aggregate has increased by more than 40% since the 2008 crisis (from 4.5 to 6 years). Before the global financial crisis, the financials and energy sectors represented 31% of the S&P 500 index. They now represent only 19% of the index. Six years ago, energy and materials represented about 25% of the emerging markets equity index, while technology represented less than 15%. These percentages have now flipped.

No Need to Build a New Optimizer—We Can Use Risk Factors Behind the Scenes

This instability in factor exposures has consequences for portfolio construction. It motivates the use of risk factor models (rather than asset class–based models) in portfolio optimization *even if we continue to invest across asset classes*. A typical multi-asset portfolio optimization process solves for the asset class weights that maximize the portfolio's expected return for a given risk level. But if we can measure each asset class's risk factor exposures, as well as the non-factor-based ("idiosyncratic") risk, there is a simple mathematical transformation that allows us to estimate asset class volatilities, correlations, and tail risks from their current factor exposures. The intuition is that we can multiply current factor exposures with historical factor returns to rebuild an asset class return series. (We can simulate the non-factor-based volatility to scale up the risk accordingly.) Then we can use our traditional *asset class*–based portfolio optimization tools on *asset class* risk estimates *that have been derived from risk factors*. It all adds up beautifully. There's no need to build a new optimizer.

The downside of this hybrid factor-based/asset class–based approach is that sometimes risk factor exposures can change rapidly. In these cases, point-in-time estimates may be misleading. Suppose you allocate to hedge funds. Hedge fund managers may shift their equity market beta up and down tactically as part of their mandate. If the manager has de-risked the portfolio and gone to cash, and you estimate volatility and correlations based on current factor exposures, you will underestimate exposure to loss. The solution is to measure how exposures change over time. If they change rapidly, it may be preferable to use average exposures over a longer period and assign the rest of the volatility to the non-factor-based bucket, which in this case represents market timing skill.

Remember that the goal, as always, is to forecast risk based on what we know about the asset class or strategy. What's the most relevant risk estimate for the future? The answer may differ based on the length of our investment horizon. In the case of dynamic strategies like hedge funds, average exposures are more relevant for relatively long horizons. For an estimate of risk one day, one week, or one month ahead, current exposures often work best.

Smart Betas, Alt Betas, Style Premiums, Risk Premiums, and All the Hype

Beyond the commendable use of risk factor models to forecast risk, our industry has recently embraced direct investment in risk factors (or smart betas, alternative betas, style premiums, etc.). We discussed the theoretical foundations for this trend in Chapter 1. Factors should deliver a positive return if they represent compensation for undiversifiable risk (risk premiums) or a persistent anomaly caused by investor behavior. In that context, not all factors qualify as risk premiums. Most risk factor models include country, currency, yield curve slope, and sector factors. These types of factors help measure risk, but they're not expected to deliver a risk premium.[1]

Over time, equity markets deliver a risk premium (over bonds or cash), as modeled in the capital asset pricing model. Relative to bond investors, stock investors get compensated for their investment in the riskiest part of companies' capital structure. Hence, equity market beta is the most basic risk premium.

Similar risk premium arguments have been made for value (long high book-to-market, short low book-to-market stocks), size (long small capitalization, short large capitalization stocks), momentum (long stocks with high recent returns, short stocks with low recent returns), and a variety of other factors. These factors, in theory, deliver returns that compensate for higher risk.[2]

But for factors such as momentum, we don't know whether excess returns represent compensation for risk or a behavioral anomaly. Some authors have argued that momentum is caused by investors who extrapolate recent performance. These investors like to buy stocks that have gone up in price and sell stocks that have gone down in price.[3] It's easy to see how such behavior can create bubbles. Prices may increase for fundamental reasons, but then continue to increase due to momentum investors, which leads to further price appreciation, which leads to more demand by momentum investors, and so on. A vicious circle, of sorts. The same effect can occur on the downside, when a price decline precipitates sell orders, which leads to further price declines, which leads to . . . You catch my drift.

However, value-oriented investors often take the other side of the trade. They seek to buy low and sell high. They sell inflated assets that have levitated away from fundamentals and buy deflated assets at bargain prices. Momentum investors often buy high and want to sell *higher*. This push and pull between momentum and value investors should lead to some equilibrium. Only if momentum investors are more numerous or aggressive will the momentum risk premium persist. It will likely persist at a relatively short time horizon—typically one month, as I showed in Chapter 5 in the context of return forecasting. At longer horizons, prices tend to revert to fundamentals. This mean reversion rewards value investors. I suspect this difference in time horizon between momentum and value investors also explains why the value and momentum factors are uncorrelated month to month.

Another risk premium that comes with a plausible story is the low-risk anomaly. There are several versions of the strategy, and a variety of smart beta products provide exposure to it (minimum volatility, low beta, etc.). The main idea is that low-risk/low-beta stocks tend to outperform high-beta stocks due to investors' leverage constraints. As Frazzini and Pedersen (2014) explain in "Betting Against Beta":

> Many investors—such as individuals, pension funds, and mutual funds—are constrained in the leverage that they can take, and they therefore overweight risky securities instead of using leverage. . . . This behavior of tilting toward high-beta assets suggests that risky high-beta assets require lower risk-adjusted returns than low-beta assets, which require leverage.

Makes sense. The authors show that a strategy that levers low-risk assets and shorts high-risk assets ("betting against beta") delivers "significant positive risk-adjusted returns" across markets. Even lower-risk Treasury and corporate bonds seem to outperform their higher-beta counterparts. They make a credible case. They control for other factor exposures such as size, value, momentum, and liquidity, and they uncover similar risk premiums across a wide range of assets, including country bond indexes, commodities, and currencies.

Still, to rely on this strategy, we must reject the CAPM's idea that risk is rewarded. In a recent paper with the amusing title "Betting Against Betting

Against Beta," Robert Novy-Marx and Mihail Velikov (2018) disagree with the interpretation that low-beta assets offer a free lunch. But first they acknowledge the success of the paper:

> Frazzini and Pedersen's "Betting Against Beta" (2014) is an unmitigated academic success. It is, at the time of this writing, the fourth most downloaded article from the *Journal of Financial Economics* over the last 90 days, and its field-weighted citation impact suggests it has been cited 26 times more often than the average paper published in similar journals. Its impact on practice has been even greater. It is one of the most influential articles on "defensive equity," a class of strategies that has seen massive capital inflows and is now a major investment category for institutional investors.

Then comes the hammer. Novy-Marx and Velikov describe the concept as a "fairly simple idea" (which may sound like an insult in the academic world, but for experienced practitioners, simple is good), and add that the risk premium's "astonishing performance cannot be achieved in practice." The methodology, partly because of its weighting scheme as well as how it uses leverage, "achieves its large, highly significant alpha, by hugely overweighting micro- and nano-cap stocks. . . . These stocks have limited capacity and are expensive to trade."

Nonetheless, since its discovery several decades ago, the low-risk anomaly has persisted over time.[4] As with most risk premiums, investors just need to temper their expectations. Good results are achievable in practice, but for due diligence purposes, they should require live track records rather than backtests.

Covered call writing, which we discussed in Chapter 7,[5] is a strategy that delivers another risk premium with sound theoretical foundations and persistence over time: the volatility risk premium. There are several options strategies to access this risk premium, and it works across asset classes. The big picture is that investors who sell insurance get compensated over time, in exchange for exposure to tail risk. They can (and should) also hedge directional market risk. With such a "delta hedging" program, they capture the difference between implied and realized volatility. This difference tends to be positive across markets and over time, but it is also sensitive to tail events.

The Diversification Argument, Once Again

Part of the appeal (and the hype) behind risk premiums as building blocks for portfolio construction is their low correlation with each other and with traditional asset classes. The main reason for this low correlation, of course, is that most risk premiums employ short positions. Yet many of them, as we discussed in Chapter 9 in the context of our research on when diversification fails, are "long carry," "long credit," or "short optionality," which means they have implied equity beta, especially when markets sell off.

The study titled "Value and Momentum Everywhere" (2013) by Cliff Asness, Toby Moskowitz, and Lasse Heje Pedersen shows the power of diversification across risk premiums. When the authors combine value and momentum strategies across markets (individual US, UK, European, and Japanese stocks, equity country indexes, currencies, global government bonds, and commodity futures), they obtain a stratospheric, hardly-ever-seen-in-practice Sharpe (return-to-risk) ratio of 1.59.

Of note, value and momentum strategies that invest from the top down, across countries' indexes, government bonds, and currencies, are essentially a form of systematic GTAA (global tactical asset allocation). These strategies are often referred to as "style premiums" because they differ from other risk premiums that are constructed as long-short portfolios of individual stocks. A carry factor—which is another way to measure value—can be added to style premium strategies to capitalize on the predictive power of yields that we discussed in Chapter 2.

Backtest Buyer Beware

Risk premium strategies are too easy to build. It has been estimated that there are at least 300 published factors, with roughly 40 newly discovered factors announced each year.[6] In the real world, it's not that easy to beat markets on a risk-adjusted basis. In the paper "Will Your Factor Deliver?"

(2016), Noah Beck, Jason Hsu, Vitali Kalesnik, and Helge Kostka explain the issue as follows:

> Few serious investors are likely to believe that all the 300-odd factor strategies would actually deliver reliable premiums in the future. Aside from a few egregious cases of research "mistakes" in which a claimed factor premium could not be replicated by other researchers, there are many other reasons to question the validity of the various exotic new sources of excess returns, which some academics mock as a "zoo of factors." Skeptics argue that many of the documented factor premiums are the fruit of massive, intentional data mining.

After they apply several robustness tests, which include a more realistic assessment of transaction costs, they find that size and quality, two of the most prominent risk premiums, show "weak robustness," while momentum, illiquidity, and low beta are more robust. But they add that "liquidity-demanding factors, such as illiquidity and momentum, are associated with significantly higher trading costs than other factors. Investors may be better off accessing these factors through active management rather than indexation."

Even well-intentioned researchers often fall into the trap of data mining/overfitting. And when they don't, they most likely rely on prior studies that were data-mined.[7] Out-of-sample backtests are never truly out-of-sample, because researchers can look at simulated results and tweak their models to improve performance. Even if model inputs rely only on data that would have been available at the time, researchers get several passes at history. Wouldn't it be nice in the real world to be able to say: "Wait, I think I should have bought the top 5 and bottom 5 stocks instead of the top 10 and bottom 10, and I should have weighted them based on volatility rather than use equal weights. Let's ask Doctor Strange[8] to reverse time, so I can get another pass"? In such a world, we'd see as many realized Sharpe ratios of 1.5 as we see in paper backtests.

To be fair, it can be useful to look at backtest data to improve a model, if we have a good reason to believe the improvement is going to work in the future. Data mining is not a black-and-white issue. It's tricky. It helps if we can add truly out-of-sample analysis, with untouched data from another time period or from another market.

But another issue with risk premiums is that they can get crowded. As investors pile on these strategies, performance deteriorates. In the paper "Does Academic Research Destroy Stock Return Predictability," R. David McLean and Jeffrey Pontiff (2016) show that after publication, risk premium performance deteriorates by 58%. They attribute 26% of this deterioration to data mining and the remaining 32% to crowding, or "publication-informed trading." They also raise two other red flags related to risk premium backtests: *postpublication declines are greater for predictors with higher in-sample returns, and returns are higher for portfolios concentrated in stocks with high idiosyncratic risk and low liquidity.*

Risk factors won't replace asset classes for portfolio construction. Investors should use the factor approach in risk models and roll up factor-based risk forecasts to the asset class level. (They can continue to use asset class–based portfolio optimization tools.) They should consider small allocations to risk premiums if they believe they can identify a handful of robust strategies. These risk premiums provide access to long-short portfolios and dynamic, uncorrelated sources of returns. But if someone shows you a backtest, don't buy all the hype. Ask for a live track record and the theoretical foundations behind the risk premiums, as well as an analysis of tail risks and tail correlations—and *be mindful of crowding.*

Notes

1. For example, in "Factor Investing and Asset Allocation: A Business Cycle Perspective" (2016), we show that adding sector, regional, and currency effects improves the CAPM's fit to month-to-month data.
2. See, for example, Fama and French (1992 and 2012) and Asness, Moskowitz, and Pedersen (2013).
3. For a recent review of the literature on momentum, see Dhankar and Maheshwari (2016).
4. A quick overview of the massive literature on the subject is available at https://en.wikipedia.org/wiki/Low-volatility_anomaly.
5. Page 102 provides references.
6. See Beck et al. (2016) and Harvey, Liu, and Zhu (2016).
7. See McQueen and Thorley (1999).
8. My son Charlie is 11, and he's a Marvel fan, so I'm "forced" to sit through comic book movies with him. At least, that's my excuse.

13

Stocks Versus Bonds and Something About Precision Weapons

Utility theory is meant to represent someone's tolerance for risk.

—JPP

WE'VE JUST DISCUSSED WHY WE SHOULD NOT GIVE UP ON asset classes. Though the debate on asset classes versus risk factors is relatively recent, the perennial, most fundamental debate in asset allocation is on stocks versus bonds. How much should an investor allocate to each asset class? This decision, more than any other portfolio construction decision, drives the risk level in investors' portfolios. Ultimately, it drives outcomes with respect to an individual investor's retirement security (or lack thereof) or ability to meet any kind of liability. *It is, without a doubt, the most important portfolio construction decision an investor makes.*

While I worked at a bond powerhouse (PIMCO), I drank the fixed income Kool-Aid. I often ended my presentations with the exclamation: "Bonds are awesome!" To assuage concerns about rising rates, I would emphasize how bonds diversify portfolio risk and hedge liabilities. Bond cash flows are known in advance, so you know how much you'll be able to spend in the future. You can even hedge inflation risk with Treasury Inflation-Protected Securities (TIPS).

Now that I work at a stock-picking powerhouse (T. Rowe Price),[1] I often declare: "Stocks are awesome!" To assuage concerns with high valuations and short-term exposure to loss, I explain how a substantial allocation to stocks is the only way to reach long-term retirement goals when an investor can't contribute enough. Stocks can provide an upside that can't be achieved with bonds. They're the engine of growth in investor portfolios.

Clearly, the question is not as simple as one versus the other. There's a role for both stocks and bonds in balanced portfolios. Investors must calibrate their stock-bond allocation based on their risk tolerance. But how do we determine the appropriate mix, given an investor's risk tolerance? Or an even more difficult question: How do we estimate an investor's risk tolerance? The so-called glide paths used in target-date funds (TDFs) provide a useful guide to adjust the stock-bond mix as a function of when an investor expects to retire.

In a 2016 *InvestmentNews* editorial, I officially turned my coat on my PIMCO days. My colleague Jim Tzitzouris, an industry thought leader on life cycle investing, and I argued that many investors may need a higher allocation to stocks than they think. Jim had convinced me through a series of fun and intense debates over afternoon coffees (Jim drinks "quad" espressos, i.e., four shots). To make our case, we discussed personal finance and the role of human capital.

Some Background on Personal Finance[2]

At a 2006 Boston University conference, Nobel Prize–winning economist Paul A. Samuelson asked the audience whether personal finance was an exact science. Then he answered his own question: "Of course, the answer to that is a flat no. If this disappoints anyone in the audience, now is a good moment to rectify your miscalculation by leaving."[3]

One of Samuelson's many contributions to the field of economics has been to build mathematical models to better understand how to optimize personal finance decisions. How much should individuals save for retirement? How should they allocate their investment portfolio throughout their lifetime?

Samuelson's models have evolved over time. Expanding on them, Bob Merton, Zvi Bodie, and others have argued that human capital—the present value of an individual's future salary income—is an "asset" just like stocks and bonds and should be considered as part of the life cycle asset allocation decision.[4]

Human capital also drives the retirement liability. When they reach retirement, individuals need an income stream to meet their spending goals, usually some portion of their salary just before retirement. With defined benefit (DB) plans, this liability is explicitly defined; accordingly, a majority of DB plans employ liability-driven investment strategies. This approach has also been making its way into portfolio construction models for target-date funds, which are used in defined contribution plans.

Overall, the concept of human capital makes a lot of sense. However, Jim and I argued that the conclusion reached by most industry participants regarding its impact on portfolio construction is wrong.

Because salary payments are relatively steady month to month, conventional wisdom is that human capital is bond-like, and therefore, it should be hedged with bonds. In recent years, Bodie has even gone so far as to suggest that most individuals should invest 100% of their retirement savings in a TIPS portfolio, to safely match their retirement spending goal.

Is that sound advice? Echoing Mr. Samuelson: the answer is a flat no. While bonds will always have their place in balanced portfolios, ultimately Jim and I explained that individuals are more likely to reach their retirement goals with stocks. This conclusion leads to a key tenet of portfolio construction: in addition to risk tolerance, investors' goals should guide their stock-bond mix.

The asset-side case for stocks is unambiguous. A recent study published in 2019 reported that only 10% of Americans are confident that they'll have enough put away for retirement.[5] People are severely underfunded, and the media refers to this situation as a retirement crisis.

With 30-year nominal bonds currently yielding 2.86% (and 30-year TIPS currently yielding 0.96%),[6] bonds will not bridge the underfunding gap for individuals. In such a low-rate environment, the benefits of compounding are too small. Suppose TIPS generate 0% real return (lower than 0.96%, but bear with me for this example), and a couple save 10% of their consumption per year to buy TIPS. In this zero-rate environment, it will take the bond investor roughly *10* years to save enough to replace *1 year of consumption* in retirement, assuming salary remains constant (or 9 years if we replace postsavings consumption). If you're healthy and expect to live 30 years in retirement, you need to save for 270 years before you can retire (9 years of savings for 30 years of consumption postsavings). While this example assumes you earn nothing on bonds after inflation and therefore get zero benefit from compounding, until yields increase, reality is not that far off. With such low rates, investors can't afford a 100% bond allocation. The math doesn't add up.

This example illustrates how ultra-accommodative monetary policy has pushed investors toward risky assets. It explains the thirst for yield that has compressed corporate spreads and led to increased demand for high-dividend stocks. In general, it explains the demand for stocks and the structurally higher valuations of US and global stocks over the last two decades.

In contrast, in countries with higher rates and a lower equity risk premium, portfolio construction focuses on bonds. Recently, on a trip to Brazil, I met with several institutional investors who explained why they hold very little, if any, stocks: in the past, they've been able to meet their return target with short-term government bonds. From 1999 to 2019, the short-term interest rate in Brazil averaged close to 15%.[7] Of course, these high rates have come with periods of hyperinflation, but real rates have been high as well, and ultimately, the major Brazilian investors and wealth managers I met with still hold less than 10% in stocks.

Human Capital: Does It Look Like a Bond or a Stock?

Most people think that bonds hedge human capital better than stocks. Salaries look like bond coupons because the amount and timing of paychecks are known in advance. As we approach retirement, our human capital depletes. If I ever retire, it will probably be 20 or 25 years from now. In theory, I have plenty of human capital left, as long as my health holds out. My total portfolio contains a large allocation to an "asset" that represents the present value of my future paychecks. But one year from retirement, I will have almost no human capital left. If my risk tolerance doesn't change, I should replace my human capital, as it depletes, with similarly behaved bonds. This way, my total portfolio allocation, and ipso facto its risk profile, does not change.

However, this approach is too academic. First, it assumes constant risk aversion. Yet it seems to me that most people become more risk-averse as they approach retirement and as the balance of their savings (their "pot") grows.

Next, Jim and I argued that human capital is more stock-like than bond-like. When stocks do well, salaries tend to increase due to earnings growth (and vice versa when stocks do badly). From that perspective, human capital has a "positive equity beta." In the asset management and banking industries, a significant portion of our income is incentive compensation. And for many in these industries, job security seems linked to the economic cycle. Our "equity beta" is quite high. Employees and entrepreneurs in cyclical industries (housing, materials, transportation, etc.) seem to be in the same boat. At the other end of the spectrum, perhaps tenured professors, medical professionals, and government workers have lower "equity beta."

Although we recognized that exposures should and do vary across industries, Jim and I guessed that aggregate wage data would reveal significant equity exposure. We calculated the correlation between wages and the returns on stocks and bonds. To avoid issues with short-term volatility in financial assets, we focused on rolling three-year return correlations. We found that, net of inflation, the average-wage index was more correlated to stocks (+53%) than to bonds (+30%), based on data from 1952 to 2014. Hence, if we hold risk aversion constant, stocks may be the better replacement for human capital as it depletes.

Of course, stocks have greater exposure to loss than bonds, and their volatility can keep retirees up at night. As individuals approach retirement, they can mitigate this downside risk with bonds. But in the final analysis, which is the best long-term retirement portfolio? Is it bonds or a balanced portfolio with a healthy allocation to stocks? In our *InvestmentNews* article, Jim and I echoed Samuelson. We said, "We believe the answer is a balanced portfolio with a healthy allocation to stocks. And if this conclusion disappoints any of our readers, now is a good time to rectify your miscalculation by moving on to another *InvestmentNews* article."

Target-Date Funds as the Default Allocation

In the United States, as defined contribution plans have grown, we have given individuals responsibility for portfolio construction. Individuals are presented with a menu of investment options, and they must choose how much to allocate to stocks versus bonds. Then, within each asset class, they must choose how much to allocate between different strategies and sub–asset classes. These choices aren't easy to make for those who are not investment professionals.

Recently, I discussed this topic with a financial advisor. He argued that it was unreasonable to ask individuals to solve their life cycle portfolio construction problem on their own. "Most people don't have the expertise required to make these investment choices. Would your surgeon ask you to perform surgery on yourself?" he asked rhetorically. Most individuals simply don't make a choice. Those involved with defined contribution plans in the United States know that inertia seems to be the most powerful force that drives portfolio construction. The do-nothing option is always the most popular.

Inertia has given rise to the importance of default options. Whether individuals elect to contribute a percentage of their salary toward their retirement or, as is often the case, they are automatically enrolled by their employers, they don't construct their portfolios; instead their employers (who are their plans' sponsors) must decide how to allocate the funds.

For many years, the default option was cash. But this default has led to poor returns. If an individual has a long time horizon before retirement, it's hard to argue that cash is a good investment. In fact, it may be the worst choice. It's not even the "risk-free" choice, because cash needs to be reinvested along the way, at uncertain rates. We can't predict the cumulative return for cash over multiyear horizons. In theory, the "safest choice" is a long, inflation-protected bond that delivers cash flows that match what we want to spend in retirement.[8] Such an asset does not exist, but long bonds are typically used as a proxy. However, long bonds, as we have just discussed, are also a suboptimal choice when rates are low, especially when individuals are underfunded (and they can't *afford* risk-free).

Stocks are awesome. But they also expose investors to significant short-term losses. How much should individuals allocate to stocks throughout their life cycle? That is the key portfolio construction question. As mentioned, it affects investment outcomes in a way that no other portfolio construction decision does.

Following the Pension Protection Act of 2006, plan sponsors can automatically enroll employees for monthly contributions to their retirement plan. They can use a multi-asset fund as the default option. These measures make inertia work in favor of employees. They can opt out or change their asset allocation, but if they do nothing (which is often the case), they automatically get exposure to a diversified portfolio with a healthy allocation to stocks. A popular default option is a target-date fund. A TDF starts with a high allocation to stocks when the employees (or "plan participants" in defined contribution jargon) are early in their career, and the allocation gradually shifts from stocks to bonds as they approach retirement (the glide path). Participants are assigned a TDF vintage based on their age.

As a disclaimer, our Global Multi-Asset Division at T. Rowe Price oversees over $250 billion in TDF assets (as of May 2019). We are the largest provider of actively managed TDFs.[9] Here's how research director Jim Tzitzouris introduces our approach to glide path construction, i.e., how we determine how much stock an individual should hold as a function of the person's age:

We believe that investors' utility (satisfaction) is derived from two sources: consumption and wealth. Investors' levels of risk aversion, impatience, and wealth affinity lead to different glide paths. We choose a glide path that maximizes utility for as many plan participants as possible.

Utility is essentially the satisfaction an individual derives from various levels of income and wealth in retirement, given the person's tolerance for risk. It's a measure that relies on probabilities. To measure expected utility at each point during an individual's life cycle, we need to calculate the present value of multiple, probability-weighted future investment outcomes. Each investment outcome is mapped to a utility score. To generate the scenarios, we use Monte Carlo simulations, which embed forward-looking, long-term capital markets assumptions on the equity risk premium, interest rates, inflation, etc. (We will discuss direct utility maximization, also called "full-scale optimization," in Chapter 14.)

This approach sounds technical, and it is, but we can summarize it as follows: *We design the glide path in a way that considers what individuals are trying to achieve and how much risk they're willing to bear in order to get there. It's the good old return versus risk portfolio construction process, but across multiple time periods and with multiple objectives.*

Our "utility lab" has been developed over more than 15 years, and our portfolio construction is difficult to replicate as a simple formula or recipe. Some of the objectives and constraints are "behavioral" in nature in that they don't fit neatly within classical utility functions. Often, they represent plan sponsor needs. Also, our portfolio managers and researchers use judgment and experience in combination with data and models. They adjust portfolio weights on the margin to account for the uncertainty in the models and specific market needs. It's an iterative process.[10]

Separately, we also optimize allocations to sub–asset classes and strategies. This second optimization process is how we "fill the buckets" within stocks and bonds. To do so, we use a variety of portfolio optimization techniques, scenario analyses, and, again, judgment and experience.

We'll discuss portfolio optimization in more detail shortly. But for now, in the absence of any other information (such as taxes, other sources of income, goals, bequest motive, risk tolerance, etc.), what allocation of stocks versus bonds would we deem "best practice" as a default option for individuals? We have two different TDF series, one with higher stocks allocation than the other. Our higher-stocks glide path is by far the most popular. It has a longer track record, and it has delivered higher returns over time, because, well, stocks are awesome. However, there's a role in the marketplace for a lower-stocks glide path, for plan sponsors and participants who are more averse to short-term losses and are better funded. These participants may have higher account balances, as well as higher savings rates, and perhaps access to a defined benefit pension.

Figure 13.1 charts our stocks versus bonds mix for our flagship, higher-stocks glide path, as a function of how many years the individual is from retirement (negative numbers show years *in* retirement). As shown, when an individual is 25 years away from retirement, allocation to stocks is 90%. The time horizon is quite long, so risk tolerance is higher. This allocation then gradually decreases as time passes. The at-retirement allocation to stocks is 55%, which may seem high, but again, most individuals are underfunded and need a nest egg to keep up with inflation and last for 20+ years *in* retirement.

FIGURE 13.1 Retirement glide path

Years from Retirement (and Postretirement in Negative Values)

■ Stocks ▦ Bonds

To summarize, how much to allocate between stocks and bonds is the most important asset allocation decision. And it often requires a multiperiod optimization. We invest for individuals throughout their life cycles, and they spend over multiple periods in retirement. Defined benefit pension plans use an asset liability approach. They define the risk-free asset as the liability-matching portfolio. But if we think about the goal of defined contribution plans in the United States, and retirement-oriented plans throughout the world, the goal is always the same: to meet future income needs in retirement. To me, it's a puzzle that different investors around the world use different approaches to solve the *same problem*. I pontificated about this issue at a pensions and investments conference back in 2016.[11] Endowments and sovereign wealth funds may seem like they have different objectives from each other, but essentially both entities invest to meet future cash disbursements.

The level of funding matters. It's easy to simply recommend, "Match the liability," or a favorite of consultants, "Match the liability with bonds, and then invest the rest in risk assets." However, when expected returns on bonds aren't high enough, you can only match a liability if you're very close to fully funded. As an extreme example (just to make the point), suppose I have $1,400 in savings, and I want to go on a vacation that will cost $2,000, five years from now. And suppose real interest rates are 0.5%. How can I "match the liability" with bonds? Impossible. Five years from now, if I invest in bonds, I'll have $1,435. The only two ways forward are to either contribute more or take some investment risk and hope for higher returns. If I take some investment risk, I need about a 7.4% return annualized to reach my $2,000 target. Underfunded investors *need* high returns. When consultants say, "Match the liability with bonds, and then invest the rest in risk assets," *this advice can only apply to overfunded investors.*

Once we have solved the stocks versus bonds question, we have (roughly) calibrated the asset mix to the investor's risk tolerance. Next, investors must populate the stocks and bonds "buckets" with multiple asset classes and strategies. For these granular portfolio construction choices, I submit that single-period optimizations work best. Single-period optimization models are more flexible and transparent than the multiperiod utility framework, and they are reviewed more often (every one to five years). Think of the multiperiod utility lab as the heavy artillery and the single-period optimizations as lighter, precision weapons. (I'm clearly not a military expert, but you get the idea.) Note that I refer to portfolio optimization*s*, plural. For robustness, it's better to test various methodologies than to rely on a single model. As I've mentioned before, judgment and experience must always play a role in portfolio construction.

In Chapter 17, we will populate the stock-bond glide path with sub–asset classes. We will review in detail the sample asset mixes that are broadly representative portfolios that are used to manage a total of more than $250 billion in retirement assets. Because retirement platforms in the United States are typically focused on US assets and cost minimization (hence, alternatives are rarely included), we will look at a less constrained, more global multi-asset portfolio.

Before we review the end product, let's discuss how we can use single-period optimization tools in the process, as well as cover two key topics in portfolio construction: the role of private assets and the active versus passive debate.

Notes

1. We also have a very strong fixed income franchise, but it is smaller than our equity franchise.
2. This section is from Page and Tzitzouris (2016).
3. See Horan (2009).
4. See, for example, Bodie, Merton, and Samuelson (1992), Merton (2003), and Chen, Ibbotson, Milevsky, and Zhu (2006).
5. https://www.cnbc.com/2019/06/27/how-many-americans-have-nothing -saved-for-retirement.html.
6. As of May 8, 2019. *Sources:* Federal Reserve Bank of St. Louis and cnbc.com.
7. https://tradingeconomics.com/brazil/interest-rate.
8. For an intuitive description of how to think about the risk-free rate as a function of your time horizon, see *An Economist Walks into a Brothel, and Other Unexpected Places to Understand Risk* by Allison Schrager (2019).
9. Morningstar.
10. Jim Tzitzouris recommends the book *Strategic Asset Allocation* by Campbell and Viceira (2002) as a good reference for several of the methodologies that we use.
11. See video.pionline .com/media/Different+approaches%2C+same+problem/ 0_ebr4ogkk.

14

Single-Period Portfolio Optimization and Something About Controlled Substances

Simply, we seek to describe models that improve
the odds of making better decisions.
—JPP

A COUPLE OF YEARS AFTER I JOINED STATE STREET, MARK Kritzman asked me to stop by his office, where he handed me a mysterious piece of paper. It was handwritten, full of incomprehensible equations, and had arrived by fax, which was antiquated even in 2002.

A comment had been written sideways in the document's margin. It read, "And therefore, Mark, both you and Markowitz are wrong."

The author turned out to be economist Paul A. Samuelson, who had been debating portfolio construction with Harry Markowitz for years. This salvo was a response to an article in which Mark described various useful applications of mean-variance portfolio optimization. Using a theoretical example and complicated mathematical derivations, Samuelson argued that higher moments (the deviations from "normality" that we discussed earlier, such as fat tails) matter a great deal, and therefore, mean-variance optimization leads to "gratuitous deadweight loss," i.e., suboptimal portfolios. If we account for higher moments in portfolio construction, we arrive at better solutions, Samuelson said.

This fax kicked off a strand of research for Mark and me on direct utility maximization, which accounts for higher moments in portfolio construction. But first, Mark called Harry Markowitz. When he tells this story, Mark likes to joke that he asked Markowitz: "What did you do wrong?"

Do higher moments matter? It was a remarkable opportunity to get involved in research on a (perhaps *the*) key question in portfolio construction, with one degree of separation from two intellectual giants. And despite the academic nature of the debate, this question matters for all asset allocators. For example, it drives decisions such as how much to allocate to asset classes with relatively fat tails (corporate bonds, hedge funds, smart betas, and so forth).

To frame the problem, let us start with the standard mean-variance optimization approach, as outlined by Markowitz in 1952. A book on asset allocation wouldn't be complete without it. With mean-variance optimization, we solve for the portfolio weights that maximize

Expected return – risk aversion × volatility

where volatility is expressed as the variance of returns (standard deviation squared).

In contrast, with direct utility maximization (also called "full-scale optimization"), we must translate each potential outcome to a level of investor satisfaction (utility). (We mentioned this approach in the context of our discussion on glide path design.) This approach accounts for all features of the return distributions, higher moments included. Although most investors don't define their utility functions, they do so indirectly when they try to express their goals and tolerance for risk. When they solve for the associated trade-offs in portfolio construction, they (again, indirectly) seek to maximize their utility. In the end, portfolio construction *is* utility maximization.

How happy will the investor be if the portfolio returns 11%, compared with 10%? What about 9%? 8%? 7%? How worried is the investor about potential losses? And so on. These preferences must be modeled as functions of the return (or terminal wealth, which is just initial wealth times the return). Each potential outcome corresponds to a quantifiable level of satisfaction.

It's a complex problem. Investors don't express their preferences that way. Never in the history of financial advice has a client walked into an advisor's office and declared, "Hi, my name is John, and I have log-wealth utility preferences." Plus it's nearly impossible for financial advisors to build a utility function from scratch.

Fortunately, utility theory has been a rich field of research in financial economics. Several functions have been suggested to describe investors' attitudes toward risky outcomes. Most of them are some version of "power utility." For example, investor utility can be defined as to the natural log of wealth, or its square root, or any other exponent applied to wealth.[1] Suppose I have a log-wealth utility function. To calculate the utility of a given outcome (return), say +5%, I simply apply the "ln" function, as follows:

Utility = ln (1 + 5%) = 0.049

The number 0.049 doesn't mean much by itself. But if we apply the log function to all possible future returns and then calculate the sum of these numbers, we obtain our total expected utility. *That's the number we want to maximize.* We can try different portfolio weights until we find the allocation that generates the highest total utility.

Utility maximization may seem technical, but it is the essence of portfolio construction. *To understand this concept is to understand all there is to know about portfolio optimization, and generally how we invest in the presence of risk.*

Let's expand this example to build more intuition. We can use a simple case or "toy model," like those Samuelson used in his note to Mark.

Suppose we want to construct a portfolio composed of two asset classes: stocks and bonds. Also, assume that the probability of a recession is 10%, during which stocks will sell off and lose 20%, while bonds will return +9%. Otherwise, there is a 90% probability that we will stay in an expansion, and stocks will return +11%, while bonds will return +7%.

We can easily build a utility maximizer in Excel. In Table 14.1, I show the outputs for all interim steps if the investor has a log-wealth utility function. Any interested reader can replicate this example in about five minutes. Terminal wealth is simply 1 + return; portfolio wealth is the weighted average return based on the stocks and bonds weights; utility is the natural log of (terminal) portfolio wealth, i.e., ln (portfolio wealth); and probability-weighted utility is the probability-weighted sum of the utility numbers (based on the 10%, 90% probabilities).

TABLE 14.1   Simple Example of Utility Maximization

Weights		Constraint
Stocks	70%	100%
Bonds	30%	
	Returns	
	Recession	Expansion
	10%	90%
Stocks	−20%	11%
Bonds	9%	7%
	Terminal Wealth	
	10%	90%
	Recession	Expansion
Stocks	80%	111%
Bonds	109%	107%
	Portfolio Wealth	
	88.70%	109.80%
	Utility	
	−0.120	0.093
	Probability-Weighted Utility	
	0.07215	

The goal is to maximize probability-weighted utility. To do so, we can try different stocks and bonds weights until we find the mix that produces the highest number.

It may be hard to believe, but this small optimizer that we built in five minutes represents the state of the art in portfolio construction technology. We just need to add more scenarios and assets. This framework is much more powerful than mean-variance optimization, because it accounts for all features of the data, such as fat tails, *and* it allows for any type of utility functions.

However, there's a catch. As we add more assets, we can't manually test all possible portfolio weights to find the asset mix that maximizes utility. Call it the "curse of dimensionality." With two assets, if we move weights by increments of 1% (which is not very precise but probably good enough), we need to test 101 portfolios. With 3 assets, we need to test 5,151 portfolios. With 5 assets, the number of portfolios to test grows to 4.5 million, and so on. It's a combinatorial problem. The number grows so fast that at 10 assets, we need to test over 4 *trillion* portfolios. At 20 assets? 5 million trillion (4,910,371,215,000,000,000,000) portfolios, if we round to the nearest trillion.[2] Imagine the scale of the problem if we want to be more precise and vary weights by increments of 0.1% instead of 1%.

In practice, this search-optimization process is computerized, and mathematical shortcuts are taken to converge to a solution faster than if we tried every possible set of weights. Many different tools and software packages are available to approximate a solution. The question is, which tool works best?

To answer this question, shortly after we started our research on full-scale optimization, I set up a "battle of the search algorithms." I wanted to find out which software would perform best. The answer surprised me and everybody else involved.

First, I set up a sample problem in Excel. I used 20 hedge funds, which I selected because they had highly nonnormal historical return distributions. I applied some constraints to avoid concentrated portfolios.

I used a utility function with two inflection points ("kinks"). These inflection points represent a sharp drop in investor satisfaction. Most investors have a significant aversion to loss, beyond what can be modeled with classical, smooth utility functions. Hence, their utility function drops significantly around zero. (For an example, see Kahneman and Tversky's, 1979, famous s-shaped value function, derived from prospect theory.)

Suppose that for a specific reason (such as the risk of bankruptcy), you want to avoid a one-year return below −10%, at all costs. In this case, your utility function should drop significantly at −10% as well. Any asset that may contribute to such a scenario (−10% or worse) is heavily penalized or eliminated from your portfolio. Essentially, this drastic kink in the utility function eliminates any solution that may breach the −10% loss barrier, *no matter how small the probability of breach or how high the expected return that you need to forgo to eliminate the offending asset. (Remember:* There are no free lunches in portfolio construction—only trade-offs.)

I expected this case to be difficult to solve. It involved a relatively large number of assets, with nonnormal return distributions and the added complexity of constraints and kinks in the utility function. I wrote an email to a long list of colleagues to kick off the contest. I included people from our IT department who had access to massive computing power (through a "grid" platform), quant finance whizzes, Harvard PhD economists, etc. My question was simple: "Which set of weights maximizes utility?"

The underlying, more interesting experiment was to find out who would get the highest utility number. All the participants had the same information. They could use any tool they wanted. There would be a clear winner: whoever solved for the highest utility.

My best guess was that a genetic algorithm would win. One colleague had started to work on genetic algorithms. A genetic algorithm uses a wide range of randomly selected starting points, lets them "compete" toward a higher utility number, kills off the least promising areas, and reconcentrates computing power on the most promising searches. (Beyond this simple description, I have no idea how to write a genetic algorithm. But it sounds cool.) Or perhaps someone in IT would win, through the brute force of computing power.

I certainly didn't expect that *I* would win. But I did. I generated the highest utility number with the most mundane of all tools: Microsoft Excel's solver. My takeaway is to never underestimate Microsoft. It turns out that anyone with a basic version of Excel can build a remarkably powerful and flexible full-scale portfolio optimization tool.

While I thought my contest was clever, a few colleagues commented that it wasn't fair. A fair comparison should cover multiple optimization cases, with different assets, utility functions, and constraints. It should include portfolios with hundreds of individual stocks and bonds. My contest was anecdotal at best. Nonetheless, applied to a utility maximization framework like the one we built in five minutes, the Excel solver works very well. (Of course, multiperiod optimizers, as mentioned earlier in the context of target-date funds glide path design, are much harder to build and represent a whole separate set of challenges.)

Though they impose rigor on the process, utility models don't always represent investor preferences very well. As we have discussed in the sections on return and risk forecasting, it's extremely difficult to model risky outcomes. We have two interconnected problems: we apply models that poorly represent investor preferences to estimates that poorly represent investment returns and risks. Yet, to echo the story from my introduction to this book, if we don't think we can do a *reasonable* job at both, perhaps we shouldn't be in the investment business.

A Middle Ground Between Simplicity and Complexity

To approximate utility functions and asset return distributions, it helps to simplify the portfolio construction problem. As Harry Markowitz found, mean-variance optimization achieves this goal remarkably well. Higher moments don't matter, as Markowitz showed in his debate with Samuelson on the subject. In our research on full-scale optimization, initially we found similar results.

Problems with mean variance start to occur when the utility function includes a sharp drop, a kink that represents significant aversion to loss beyond a threshold. As mentioned, such situations are quite common— most investors define their tolerance to risk as "I can't lose more than x% in one year." In these cases, mean-variance optimization allocates too much to assets with low volatility but large exposure to loss (negatively skewed assets that sell volatility). Jan-Hein Cremers, Mark, and I (2005) published these findings in a paper titled "Optimal Hedge Fund Allocations: Do Higher Moments Matter?," and Tim Adler and Mark (2007) published a more general paper with similar conclusions: "Mean-Variance Versus Full-Scale Optimisation: In and Out of Sample."

Mean-variance and full-scale portfolio optimization models are bookends on a spectrum from simplest (mean variance) to most complex (full scale). Between these bookends, there are several modified versions of mean-variance optimization that account for fat tails but don't require us to define a utility function in detail.

For example, in Chapter 11 we discussed risk regimes and how we can model a fat-tailed distribution as a mixture of two probability distributions, each of which may be normal. In a paper that contains the best footnote in the history of the *Financial Analysts Journal* (more on that shortly), "Optimal Portfolios in Good Times and Bad," George Chow, Eric Jacquier, Mark Kritzman, and Kenneth Lowry (1999) suggest a blended regime approach. They modify mean-variance optimization to make it more sensitive to exposure to loss. To do so, they use two separate sets of volatilities and correlations ("covariance matrices"): one for the normal regime and one for the turbulent regime. The goal is to find the portfolio weights that maximize

Expected return – [risk aversion 1 × volatility (quiet) +
risk aversion 2 × volatility (turbulent)]

where risk aversion 1 represents aversion to volatility in quiet markets and risk aversion 2 represents aversion to risk in times of market stress. As in the original version of mean-variance optimization, volatility is measured as the squared standard deviations of returns.

The authors also multiply the risk aversion terms by the relative probabilities of the quiet and turbulent regimes. Turbulent regimes typically have low probability but significant exposure to loss. Ultimately, regimes can be defined in different ways. In this paper, Chow et al. propose a powerful method that accounts for correlation effects.

They define the regimes based on a measure of multivariate distance, also called the Mahalanobis distance. The Mahalanobis distance is a measure of the distance between a point and the center of a distribution, a multidimensional generalization of the idea of measuring how many standard deviations away the point is from the mean of the distribution. It has a long history of applications in scientific research, and several useful animated tutorials on how to calculate it are available online. It was first used in 1927 to measure similarities in skulls. In 2010, Mark Kritzman and Yuanzhen Li published a paper titled "Skulls, Financial Turbulence, and Risk Management" in the *Financial Analysts Journal.*

In addition to how far it is from the average, an observation—usually a month in a data sample—is more likely to be a multivariate outlier if it represents an unusual *interaction* between assets. What does this have to do with skulls? Kritzman and Li explain:

Mahalanobis (1927) used 7–15 characteristics of the human skull to analyze distances and resemblances between various castes and tribes in India. The skull characteristics used by Mahalanobis included head length, head breadth, nasal length, nasal breadth, cephalic index, nasal index, and stature. The characteristics differed by scale and variability. That is, Mahalanobis might have considered a half-inch difference in nasal length between two groups of skulls a significant difference whereas he considered the same difference in head length to be insignificant. . . . He later proposed a more generalized statistical measure of distance, the Mahalanobis distance, which takes into account not only the standard deviations *of individual dimensions but also the correlations between dimensions.* [Italics added]

It turns out that the approach is useful in an investment context to estimate financial turbulence and define risk regimes. Chow et al. provide an easy visualization of the methodology for two assets. In our State Street PowerPoint presentations, we used a 3D rotating ellipsoid, which helped us explain the concept as applied to three assets (and show off what at the time were impressive animated GIF capabilities). But when we try to visualize an outlier in more than three dimensions, i.e., for four assets or more, it gets much harder. This leads me to a fun footnote. I don't know how Chow et al. managed to get it passed the referees, but here it is:

> If we were to consider three return series, the outlier boundary would be an ellipsoid, a form that looks something like a football. We are unable to visualize an outlier boundary for samples that include more than three return series—at least not without the assistance of a controlled substance.

There are several other modified versions of mean-variance optimization that account for nonnormal (non-Gaussian) higher moments, in particular fat tails.[3] For example, we can replace volatility with a measure of tail risk. In Chapter 10 we discussed conditional value at risk (CVaR), a measure of expected loss during market sell-offs. If we use CVaR as our measure of tail risk, we can modify mean variance to solve for the weights that maximize[4]

– risk aversion × CVaR

CVaR can be replaced with any tail-risk measure of choice, such as probability of a loss greater than –10%, value at risk (VaR), etc.

We can also use tail-risk constraints. For example, suppose we don't want CVaR to go below –10%. We can define the optimization problem as

Expected return – risk aversion × volatility
subject to CVaR <–10%

In this framework, any constraint should work. For example, we can solve for the mean-variance optimal portfolio, subject to a constraint that the portfolio not lose more than 15% under a 2008 historical scenario. This constrained framework also allows for multiple scenario constraints—for example, we can combine 2000 and 2008 scenarios. We can also use forward-looking scenarios.

We can combine volatility and tail risk directly into one objective function. To do so, we can use the same approach as we did for the risk regimes above, but replace the regime-specific aversion parameters with aversions to volatility and tail risk:

Expected return – [risk aversion 1 × volatility (quiet) + risk aversion 2 × tail risk]

Again, tail risk can be measured as CVaR, VaR, probability of loss, 2008 scenario, etc. It can be probability-weighted within the objective function. Essentially, every tail-risk measure we discussed in the risk forecasting section can be used, and beyond. With this approach, we optimize the portfolio in three dimensions: return, volatility, and tail risk. For the same return and volatility, we want the solution with the lowest possible tail risk. Hence, again we penalize assets with low volatility but high tail risk (those pesky "short-volatility" assets, such as hedge funds, credit, and the like).

In Chapter 8 we discussed higher moments. Another methodology is to add these higher moments directly into the objective function, as follows:[5]

Expected return – risk aversion × volatility + skewness aversion × skewness – kurtosis aversion × kurtosis

Note the positive sign for skewness, as positive skewness is preferable to negative skewness for loss-averse investors. The effect of this modification to mean-variance optimization is generally the same as for the other modified approaches: assets with undesirable downside risk are penalized beyond what would be captured by volatility.

How Should We Address Issues with Concentrated and Unstable Solutions?

Anyone who has used optimizers for portfolio construction knows that they often yield concentrated portfolios. Also, these concentrated solutions can be sensitive to small changes in inputs, which compounds the problem. Counterintuitively, it could be argued that these issues are moot. Before I explain why most people worry too much about them, let me review how they have been addressed in the financial literature.

First, we can apply constraints to the weights. For example, we can limit the hedge fund allocation to 10% of the portfolio. Such constraints can be applied to any of the methodologies described above, from full-scale optimization to all flavors of tail-risk-sensitive mean-variance optimizations.

We can define "group" constraints. Suppose that in addition to stocks and bonds, we allocate to hedge funds, liquid alternatives, and real estate—all asset classes that are part of the "alternatives" category. In this case, we could set up a constraint such that no more than 20% of the portfolio should be allocated to alternatives. (I didn't pick this example randomly. Alternative assets often have artificially low volatilities and unreasonably high expected returns, which leads to "corner" solutions in which the optimizer allocates the entire portfolio to alternatives. *A classic example:* If you add private real estate to a stocks and bonds portfolio, and you don't carefully calibrate your inputs, the optimizer will want to allocate 100% to private real estate.)

There are many other ways to deal with these issues beyond simple weights constraints. Indeed, the literature on how to overcome problems with concentrated portfolios and unstable solutions in portfolio optimization is extensive. A popular approach, pioneered by Richard Michaud, has been to use resampling.[6] The idea is to repetitively reoptimize the portfolio on subsamples of our dataset. This process reveals that small changes in data samples can lead to very different solutions. But if we calculate the average of the solutions, we stabilize the outcome.

When short positions are not allowed, this process yields portfolios that are less concentrated. When it resamples, every time the optimizer finds a solution that shorts an asset class, it substitutes the negative weight for a zero allocation. Therefore, the average optimal weight for a given asset is more likely to be positive than if we ran a mean-variance optimization on the full sample. (At least that's how I understand the process. I believe Michaud employs a few "secret sauce" ingredients as well.)

Though it doesn't improve our risk and return forecasts per se, this approach can help determine confidence intervals for the optimal weights. We can use it to estimate an optimal "zone" rather than a point estimate. This zone reflects the uncertainty in our estimates.

Another way to impose stability in optimal weights and avoid concentrated portfolios is to use "Bayesian shrinkage" methodologies. Jorion (1986, 1991) proposes an approach that compresses return estimates toward a reference point, such as the average return of the minimum-risk portfolio. This shrinkage process takes into account relative volatilities and correlations across assets to impose consistency in return estimates.

The popular Black-Litterman model uses related concepts, as explained in their 1992 paper, "Global Portfolio Optimization." The model blends discretionary (what some quants would call "made-up") views with equilibrium returns (from the CAPM, which we discussed in Chapter 1). This blending process takes into account our level of confidence in our views, as well as volatilities and correlations.

Like the Jorion approach, the Black-Litterman model imposes consistency. If we don't use views, or if we have very little confidence in them, the solution converges to market capitalization weights. Views that run counter to equilibrium or that would lead to concentrated portfolios are adjusted, or "tamed." For example, if we expect negatively correlated assets to both experience high positive returns are the same time (which is unlikely since the assets are negatively correlated), the model will likely "shrink" the offending estimate(s) closer to a value consistent with the CAPM.

These shrinkage models are relatively technical, but for quants (or quant-lites like me), the best way to familiarize yourself with them is to recode the example in Black and Litterman's paper. The authors use a simple three-asset example and provide a step-by-step guide to the process.

These models aren't *that* useful for nonquants. They require too many assumptions, and they blur the line between the process to estimate inputs and portfolio construction. If you're an expert in these models, you can trace back what drives your final estimates: the reference point that you shrink the estimates toward, volatility effects, correlation effects, risk aversion parameters, or other aspects of the models. For everyone else, it is better to cleanly separate return forecasting, risk forecasting, and portfolio construction (incidentally, this is how I've organized this book). This separation provides transparency and makes it easier to apply judgment to our estimates.

Another way to avoid concentrated portfolios, with a clearer separation between inputs and portfolio construction than resampling and shrinkage methods, is to add a peer group risk (tracking error) constraint to mean-variance optimization. Even better, as Chow (1995) suggests, we can add tracking error directly to the objective function; i.e., we can maximize

Expected return – risk aversion × volatility – tracking error aversion × tracking error

The tracking error term is like an elastic that pulls portfolio weights toward a benchmark (typically market capitalization weights or the average allocation of a peer group). Tracking error aversion determines the strength of that elastic. In the same way as for the other expanded objective functions we have just reviewed, the aversion parameters enable us to specify the importance of one goal relative to the other. In this case, we can specify whether we care more about absolute risk (volatility) or relative risk (tracking error). Chow shows how this approach yields an efficient *surface*, as opposed to a traditional efficient *frontier*. A frontier maps return to risk for optimal portfolios across risk aversion levels. A surface maps return, risk, and tracking error in three dimensions. Chow provides an intuitive visualization:

- For the same return and volatility, the optimization finds the portfolio with the lowest tracking error.
- For the same volatility and tracking error, it finds the portfolio with the highest return.
- For the same return and tracking error, it finds the portfolio with the lowest volatility.

To move across the surface, we vary the strengths of the risk aversion and tracking error aversion "elastics." This idea that the solution set represents an optimal surface, as opposed to a frontier, applies to all optimizations with two risk terms in the objective function, such as the mean-variance–CVaR optimization we discussed above.

Are Optimizers Worthless?

Given the issues with unstable and concentrated portfolios, some academics and practitioners have suggested that optimizers are useless. *I disagree. Optimizers are helpful tools if used correctly.* If used incorrectly, they can lead to dangerously misallocated portfolios (recall the GIGO critique from the Introduction in this book). In a widely cited paper, DeMiguel, Garlappi, and Uppal (2007) show that equally weighted portfolios outperform mean-variance optimal portfolios across a wide range of assets. *I disagree with this conclusion as well.*

In "In Defense of Optimization," Mark Kritzman, Dave Turkington, and I (2010) counter that DeMiguel, Garlappi, and Uppal unfairly penalize mean-variance optimization. These authors feed the mean-variance optimizer the wrong inputs. They use rolling 60-month realized returns as expected returns. But no one would use these assumptions in practice, as they include pathological cases with negative expected equity risk premiums, and broadly speaking, they ignore everything we have discussed in the first section of this book on return forecasting.

In our study, we show that when we use basic expected returns instead of rolling short-term realized returns, mean variance outperforms equally weighted portfolios. We don't assume any forecasting skill. We model expected returns with long-run averages (estimated out-of-sample) and constant risk premiums. We also use equal returns across assets, which yield the minimum-risk portfolio.

In Chapter 2, I mentioned that risk minimization, without forecasting skill, outperformed the market capitalization–weighted benchmark. In "In Defense of Optimization," we find similar results across a much broader range of backtests. Again, the takeaway is that without *any* return forecasts (which is better than with poor return forecasts), optimization performs remarkably well. This result is due to the persistence in volatility and correlations that we discussed in the context of risk forecasting, and perhaps the low-beta effect that we discussed in Chapter 12. Our paper won a 2011 Graham and Dodd Scroll Award for excellence in research.

In the follow-up paper "In Defense of Portfolio Optimization: What If We Can Forecast?," Allen, Lizieri, and Satchell (2019) expand this research to cases that assume various levels of forecasting skills. Their results reinforce our conclusions. In their words:

> We challenge academic consensus that estimation error makes mean-variance portfolio strategies inferior to passive equal-weighted approaches. We demonstrate analytically, via simulation, and empirically that investors endowed with modest forecasting ability benefit substantially from a mean-variance approach. . . . We frame our study realistically using budget constraints, transaction costs and out-of-sample testing for a wide range of investments.

Besides, the concerns with unstable solutions and concentrated portfolio may be overblown. In a paper titled "Are Optimizers Error Maximizers?,"[7] Mark Kritzman (2006) demonstrates that the issue with sensitivity to small changes in inputs *only occurs when assets are highly correlated*, and therefore they can be substituted for each other without a large impact on the portfolio's return and risk characteristics. Thus, large shifts in weights barely change the risk and return of the optimal solution. And when assets aren't highly correlated, optimal solutions are more stable.

What About Risk Parity?

With risk parity, we can greatly simplify portfolio construction. I agree that we should put risk at the center of the asset allocation decision and that we should strive for robustness (i.e., find solutions that may be suboptimal under a precise set of return and risk forecasts, but that work reasonably well under a wide range of possibilities). However, asset allocators should not rely naïvely on the approach.

The idea is to equalize asset classes' contribution to portfolio risk. Think of risk parity portfolios as equal risk portfolios, instead of equal weights. To increase risk contributions from lower-volatility assets, such as bonds, we must lever them. Typically, we assume that all asset classes have the same expected return-to-risk ratio.

Simplifying assumptions are often made for correlations as well. These assumptions are thought to make the process more "robust" because they are somewhat "agnostic" and reduce forecast errors. This idea of robustness has become quite popular with investors, especially after several strategies outperformed the traditional 60% stocks, 40% bonds portfolio during the sell-off of 2008.[8] Risk parity products offered by quantitative asset managers have grown to as much as USD 500 billion in AUM, as of 2018.[9]

In 2016, I reviewed Edward Qian's book *Risk Parity Fundamentals*, for the *Quantitative Finance Journal*.[10] Over the last few years, the asset management industry has been divided on the topic of risk parity. Some prominent asset managers seem to religiously believe that it offers better risk-adjusted performance compared with traditional asset allocation approaches, irrespective of where and how it is implemented. Others believe that risk parity is a fad fueled by misleading interpretations of finance theory and dubious backtests.

The debate reached a critical point a few years ago with the publication of an article by Robert Anderson, Stephen Bianchi, and Lisa Goldberg (2012) in the *Financial Analysts Journal*, titled "Will My Risk Parity Strategy Outperform?" The authors showed that over an 80-year backtest, risk parity *underperforms* the 60% equities/40% bonds portfolio, after accounting for the historical cost of leverage and turnover.

The response by proponents of risk parity was thoughtful and quite clear. Anderson, Bianchi, and Goldberg's backtest of risk parity was misleading because it misrepresented how the approach is implemented in practice. Ultimately, our industry seems to have reached the "Let's agree to disagree" stage of the debate.

Qian's book is certainly one-sided in favor of risk parity. In almost every chapter, he repeats the mantra that risk parity provides better diversification, and ipso facto better risk-adjusted performance, than traditional balanced portfolios. Toward the end of the book, I started to wonder whether Qian would claim that risk parity can cure cancer. He certainly makes a strong case that to improve portfolio returns, investors should use high return-to-risk ratio, low-beta assets (usually bonds). Such results are consistent with the theory of leverage aversion, which we discussed earlier in the context of the low-beta risk premium.

Most chapters read like a rebuttal to risk parity skeptics. Here are some liberal paraphrases of his questions and answers:

Q: Aren't bond yields too low?
A: The slope of the curve and what's priced in matter more than the level of rates.

Q: Does risk parity rely on an unsafe amount of leverage?
A: No. In fact, if we account for the implicit leverage in stocks, risk parity leverage is similar to balanced portfolios.

Q: What if both stocks and bonds become positively correlated, for example, during unexpected rate increases?
A: Historical evidence shows that risk parity portfolios recover well from such episodes. Moreover, commodities provide an additional layer of diversification beyond stocks and bonds. (The events of 2020 may put into question this answer. As liquidity completely dried up, for a while investors sold Treasuries *at the same time that equity and commodity markets sold off.* These events were a perfect storm for risk parity investors.)

Q: Does risk parity ignore liabilities?
A: The approach can be easily adjusted to account for liabilities and funded ratios.

Unfortunately, across all his backtests and examples, Qian does not address one of the most important issues: the critique by Anderson, Bianchi, and Goldberg regarding the cost of leverage and transaction costs. In the current low-rate environment, the cost of borrowing is extremely low. But for backtests that go back 40+ years, he should adjust for historical LIBOR rates that were as high as 9+%. Qian does not provide his assumptions on this question, and the reader is left wondering whether the consistent drumbeat of "Risk parity beats balanced portfolios" would become muted after leverage and turnover costs adjustments.

Overall, it's not clear whether risk parity is inherently superior to traditional portfolio construction approaches. Skeptics may take issue with the overemphasis on risk concentration, as opposed to exposure to loss. (A 60% equities/40% bonds portfolio may have 95% exposure to the equity risk factor, but it still has a lower exposure to loss than a 95% equities/5% bonds portfolio.) Though most quantitative investors understand and manage tail risks, it's not always obvious how risk parity portfolios, most of which are constructed based on volatility, account for nonnormal distributions. Risk parity can be implemented in many ways, which can lead to a wide range of outcomes. Technical details on how covariance matrices are calculated, how and when portfolios are rebalanced, and whether a specific risk is targeted over time matter a great deal.

Nonetheless, for investors who have access to cheap leverage, it's hard to refute the arguments that we should put risk at the heart of the portfolio construction process and that we should increase exposures to uncorrelated, high return-to-risk ratio assets. Valuation-focused investors who don't believe that return-to-risk ratios are always equal across all asset classes (or don't believe that correlations are all the same across asset classes) may arrive at a different portfolio than "risk parity," but they will still benefit from these insights.

Notes

1. See, for example, Levy and Markowitz (1979), Adler and Kritzman (2007), and Cremers, Kritzman, and Page (2005).
2. See Cremers, Kritzman, and Page (2005).
3. For reviews of some of the literature on this topic, see Harvey, Liechty, Liechty, and Müller (2010), Beardsley, Field, and Xiao (2012), and Rachev, Menn, and Fabozzi (2005). Note that the literature on this topic is extensive (see Greiner's 2012 comment to the *FAJ*, for example)—apologies in advance for any reference I may have missed. Here I discuss applications that I and many others have used in practice.
4. See Xiong and Idzorek (2011) as an example.
5. See, for example, Beardsley, Field, and Xiao (2012).
6. Visit https://www.newfrontieradvisors.com/research/articles/optimization -and-portfolio-construction/ for a list of references.
7. This paper also won an award—the 2006 Bernstein-Fabozzi/Jacobs Levy Outstanding Article Award. Perhaps a good topic for those who hope to

win an award from a financial practitioner journal is to find a way to defend portfolio optimization.

8. See Mercer (2013).
9. Bridgewater, AQR, Panagora, and many others offer such strategies. See www.forbes.com/sites/simonconstable/2018/02/13/how-trillions-in-risk -parityvolatility-trades-could-sink-the-market/#3e6a7a362e2f.
10. Parts of this section are from this book review, with permission. http:// www.tandfonline.com.

15

Private Assets and Something About Ostriches

Any investment decision, and any decision made within an enterprise, must account for risk. Discounted cash flow valuations are completely invalid, have no significance whatsoever, and are useless for decision-making if they don't properly account for risk. Market values derive from an estimation of risk.

—JPP

NO MATTER WHICH OPTIMIZATION METHODOLOGY WE use—multiperiod, full scale, mean variance, tail-risk-aware versions of mean variance, risk parity, and/or judgment and experience—a perennial challenge in portfolio construction has been to determine the optimal allocation to alternative asset classes. Institutional investors such as public pensions and endowments have grappled with this question for years. Recently, alternative asset classes have grown in popularity with individual investors as well.

The comparison between public and private equities is particularly important given the size and growing popularity of private equity as an asset class. Also, this comparison can be generalized to different alternative asset classes, because it relates to the broader question of how to allocate between liquid and illiquid markets.

What's the role of private equity in investors' portfolios? What's the optimal mix between private and public equities? As I mentioned in Chapter 9, a naïve answer—often reinforced by consultants armed with mean-variance optimization results—is that private equity is *awesome*. It's essentially a free lunch. If the investor's time horizon is long enough, perhaps the entire portfolio should be invested in private markets because they seem to deliver high returns, low volatility, and low correlation to the business cycle. *Based on my extensive review of the literature, and my own research, I would argue that private equity is not a free lunch. It has a role to play in some investors' portfolios, but it's a smaller role than suggested by a naïve interpretation of the data.*

A study by Hamilton Lane, an asset management company in private markets, claims that as of September 30, 2018, the 20-year return-to-risk (Sharpe) ratio of private equity was *270%* higher than that for public markets (as proxied by the MSCI World Index). Moreover, from 2000 to 2018, the same study claims that the lowest five-year annualized return for developed markets buyouts (a large sub–asset class within private equity focused on leveraged buyouts) was +2.4%, compared with –5.7% for the MSCI World Index. Essentially, from this five-year lens, *cash* has more downside than buyouts, as global cash rates have dipped to zero and below.[1]

Similarly, in an article by Austin, Thurston, and Prout (2019) that encourages wealthy individual investors to invest in private equity, the consulting firm Cambridge Associates finds that the more an institution invests in private equity, the higher the returns. The article implies that a 40% allocation to private equity might be optimal:

[Our analysis] highlights the meaningful returns that institutions with higher allocations to private investments have achieved over the last 20 years. The median annualized return for a greater than 15% average allocation was 8.1%, 160 basis points higher than the group with a less than 5% allocation. [It] also shows that the higher the allocation the better and . . . top decile performers have steadily increased their allocations over the years to a mean of 40%.

The message seems to be that private investors should emulate sophisticated endowments. The authors add that "illiquidity does not translate into greater risk, unless liquidity needs have been miscalculated. In fact . . . institutions with higher allocations to private investments fared better in most major market downturns."

Public pensions apparently also benefit from private equity's advantage over public markets. The American Investment Council, in its 2018 Public Pension Study, claims that across 163 US public pension funds, on a 10-year annualized basis, private equity returns were 8.6%, compared with 6.1% for public equities.

Despite higher valuations and the usual disclaimer that past returns aren't indicative of future returns, private equity investors remain optimistic. In its *2018 Global Private Markets Review*, McKinsey reports that 90% of limited partners (the asset owners that provide capital to private equity managers) expect private equity to continue to outperform public markets. "And so, capital keeps flowing in," the McKinsey folks observe. The Hamilton Lane study shows that more than $6 trillion has flowed into private market investments over the last 10 years.[2] This flood of money should only intensify over the next decade. Hamilton Lane projects that between $11 trillion and $15 trillion will be raised over the next 10 years.

Footnotes and Fine-Print Disclaimers Matter

From the perspective of finance theory, and common sense, it's hard to justify why private companies should consistently outperform public companies. Imagine two companies that provide the same products and services. Suppose they have the same expected cash flows, have no debt, and are managed by twin sisters with the same business acumen and experience. The only difference is that one is a private company, while the other is publicly traded.

To value companies, investors discount their expected cash flows. These two hypothetical companies have the same expected cash flows. The discount rate for both should vary as a function of the risk-free rate and a premium for risk. Over time, why would a stake in the private company appreciate much faster than a stake in its public twin if they are both valued based on discounted cash flows? And why would the private company's business risk be lower than the public company's?

Perhaps there's a premium for illiquidity. Shareholders in the private company may require a higher rate of return in exchange for the inability to buy or sell shares easily on the open market. The puzzle remains, however, whether this premium justifies a 270% increase in the Sharpe ratio, as reported in the Hamilton Lane study.

Answers may lie in the footnotes and fine print of the studies reported above, which contain statements such as "Performance results do not reflect the deduction of any applicable advisory or management fees" and "based on internal rates of returns." These studies and projections are from firms that have skin in the private equity game: Hamilton Lane is a private equity manager; Cambridge Associates and McKinsey count many private equity investors as clients; and the American Investment Council is an industry advocacy group that represents private equity firms.

Academics, on the other hand, are incentivized to let their data speak and to provide as much transparency as possible with regard to their assumptions. Perhaps they provide more of a truth-seeking assessment of private equity's performance compared with that of public markets.

Remarkably, the academic consensus appears to be that private equity does *not* outperform public markets over time. For most of my career, I've tried to provide a bridge between academic research and practice. This conclusion may represent one of the biggest chasms between academic research and conventional wisdom that we have ever faced as an industry.

A wide range of biases in marketing presentations may explain the chasm. The three key issues are that private equity returns are *levered*, *locked up*, and *self-reported*. These biases interreact and compound each other. First, leverage amplifies returns, and when those returns are smoothed, risk-

adjusted returns are automatically overstated. Second, private equity managers ask investors to precommit capital that they can deploy and return
as they see fit, typically over long lockup periods. Portfolio managers in
public markets, in contrast, have no control over capital inflows and outflows. Third, private equity firms are granted substantial flexibility in how
they report the value of their investments, as these investments don't trade
frequently, if at all.

In "Private Equity Performance: Returns, Persistence, and Capital Flows,"
Steven N. Kaplan and Antoinette Schoar (2005) conclude that "average
[private equity] fund returns approximately equal the S&P 500." Their sample covers a 21-year period, from 1980 to 2001. They do not control for
leverage. Hence, they assume that private equity investments have a market
beta (sensitivity to the S&P 500) of 1.0. They do not control for the possibility that private equity funds may be more exposed to systematic risks than
public equities.

The only adjustment they make is to account for the "locked-up" component, i.e., the timing of cash flows. Internal rates of returns (IRRs) for
private equity funds are value-weighted, while public market benchmarks
are time-weighted (all years get the same weight in the calculation). Because
private equity managers benefit from significant flexibility on the timing of
cash flows, this comparison may favor private markets.

To adjust for this bias, Kaplan and Schoar calculate a public market equivalent (PME) benchmark. PMEs provide a value-weighted version of the
S&P 500's returns that assumes the same cash inflows and outflows as for the
private equity fund. Hence, they neutralize the timing advantage for private
equity.[3] PMEs are typically reported as a ratio between public and private
market returns. A ratio above 1.0 means that private equity outperforms the
public market, and vice versa for a ratio below 1.0.

To illustrate, suppose the S&P 500 returns +5% one year and +20%
the following year, for a compound (time-weighted) annual rate of return of
+12.2%. Let us assume that over the same period, a private equity fund's
investments delivered the exact same returns as the S&P 500. However, the
private equity manager deployed $10 million in capital at the beginning of

the first year and added $100 million before the second year. In this case, the private equity manager had more dollars exposed to the very good year ($110 million invested at +20%) than the "just OK" year ($10 million invested at +5%)—good timing.

The private equity manager would have been able to return $132.6 million to the investor at the end of two years, for a value-weighted IRR of +18.6%. If we compare the IRR of +18.6% with the S&P's return of +12.2%, should we conclude that private equity outperformed public markets by more than +6%? Is this outperformance true "alpha"? In this case, PME is obviously 1.0, as the underlying returns were the same each year. *All we did was adjust for the timing of cash flows, and alpha went from +6% to zero.*

Kaplan and Schoar found that the average PME for 746 private equity funds was 0.96 if calculated on an equally weighted basis and 1.05 if calculated on a size-weighted basis (large funds tend to perform better). These results were not statistically different from 1.0. Recent studies have confirmed these PME-based results for a wide range of datasets and time periods.[4]

These studies mainly adjusted for the timing of cash flows. Others have highlighted additional biases in published private equity returns. In the first few sentences of their 2009 article "The Performance of Private Equity Funds," Ludovic Phalippou and Oliver Gottschlag get straight to the point:

> The performance of private equity funds as reported by industry associations and previous research is overstated. A large part of performance is driven by inflated accounting valuation of ongoing investments and we find a bias toward better performing funds in the data. We find an average net-of-fees performance of 3% per year below the S&P 500. Adjusting for risk brings the underperformance to 6% per year.

These numbers are remarkably far from those reported by Hamilton Lane, Cambridge Associates, the American Investment Council, and others. They tell a completely different story about private equity as an asset class. Let's investigate how Phalippou and Gottschlag assert that private equity underperforms public equities by –6%. Their study provides a good example of meticulous, truth-seeking academic research.

First, as in other studies, they use PMEs (which they call profitability indexes). Their PME methodology also adjusts for biases in how fund returns are aggregated. Traditional methodologies use total capital committed at inception to determine the weights used to calculate averages. However, these weights don't reflect the present value of money invested. It's a technical adjustment, but the authors find that "standard aggregation choices bias performance estimates upward."

Next, they control for the "self-reported" bias. Net asset values (NAVs), which are part of private equity return calculations, tend to be smoothed and inflated. To correct for this bias, Phalippou and Gottschlag only select funds that have been terminated. Curiously, many terminated funds report a residual NAV in private equity databases, even though cash inflows and outflows have stopped and the funds have been closed. The authors write off those "living deads," residual NAVs, because they don't represent actual cash returned to the investor. In a sense, living deads may represent the aggregate effect of the overvaluation of NAVs over the life of the investment. In the words of the authors, "Funds that have reached their normal liquidation stage still report large accounting valuations for ongoing investments, which biases performance estimates upward."

To adjust for the sample bias—the fact that only funds with good returns report to the main databases—they add funds that aren't available in commercial databases. These funds underperform the broader universe.

Then they adjust for "levered" bias. They account for systematic risks, which include leverage in leveraged buyouts and small/growth factors in venture capital. Other studies have shown that these types of systematic risk adjustments *alone* can equalize the returns of private and public equity.[5] One study (Phalippou, 2014) has shown that leveraged buyout funds underperform a levered-up benchmark composed of small and value public market indexes by –3.1% per year. Moreover, even without leverage, some studies (Stafford, 2017; Ilmanen, Chandra, and McQuinn, 2019) have shown that private equity underperforms small value stocks quite significantly after private equity fees are considered. Other studies (Kinlaw, Kritzman, and Mao, 2015) have shown that sector effects matter.

Last, Phalippou and Gottschlag estimate that fees represent more than 25% of the value invested in private equity (–6% per year, which matches their reported level of underperformance for private versus public equities). To the extent that marketing presentations for private equity use gross-of-fee returns, this bias may be the most worrisome. The first question any investor should ask is whether returns are gross or net of fees.

Some Practitioners Don't Buy the Private Equity Hype

Many sophisticated investors are also skeptical of private equity's supposed superiority as an asset class. In the 2006 article "You Can't Eat IRR," Howard Marks, cofounder of Oaktree Capital, first explains that the IRR methodology has some advantages. With conventional time-weighted returns, large percentage gains on a small amount of capital ("big percentage gains on small dollars") inflate returns. In contrast, IRRs adjust returns for the amount of capital deployed.

However, Marks also points out a major issue with IRRs: they adjust for when the capital was *called*, not *actually deployed*, by the private equity manager. He concludes that "a high internal rate of return does not in and of itself put money in one's pocket." To illustrate, he uses a real-life example. An investor received a report that showed his private equity manager had delivered an IRR of +27.1%. But the investor only grew his $750,000 investment into $1,023,000 in 4.5 years, for an annualized rate of return of +7.3%—a staggering difference.

Cliff Asness of AQR recently introduced a satirical private equity fund called S.M.O.O.T.H.[6] The fund will be invested in liquid assets, but it will deliver remarkably low volatility and great diversification. The small print reveals that the fund will be afforded extra leverage, lockups, and flexible NAV valuations and reporting. Asness jokes that "due to our new proprietary S.M.O.O.T.H. process, even if we fail to deliver this lack of correlation, the S.M.O.O.T.H. Fund will still report returns mostly unrelated to normal markets." He goes on to say:

This proprietary process involves implementing our normal hedged liquid alternative process, but only marking to market occasionally, and then reporting some combination of the weighted average of the prior few years' prices, with a healthy weight also given to our own unaudited estimates of what the Fund is likely worth (based on how we think it should've performed).

Satire aside, a 2019 article by my former colleagues Megan Czasonis, Mark Kritzman, and David Turkington shows significant biases in how private equity managers report performance. Private equity valuations are reported after the fact, over the course of the following two or three months. Returns for 2018 are calculated in Q1 2019, for example. This differs from mutual funds, which publish returns daily. This study reveals an asymmetry in how public market returns affect private equity valuations: private equity managers tend to mark *up* their investments when public market returns are positive, while they don't mark them *down* as much when public market returns are negative.

During bear markets, or more generally, when investors rush for the door, the fact that private assets' reported valuations can levitate above their true market value becomes painfully obvious. Illiquid assets embed a short option position. When liquidity abounds, the "liquidity option" pays a premium, but when liquidity disappears, the investor must pay up. In 2009, Harvard faced a liquidity crisis and received bids at *60 cents on the dollar* on its private investments. A *Forbes* article (2009), "How Harvard's Investing Superstars Crashed," on the topic quotes the investment bank involved in the transactions: "The big discounts are due to 'unrealistic pricing levels at which funds continued to hold their investments' and 'fantasy valuations.'"

In 2019, in the United Kingdom, investors in the Woodford Equity Income Fund were denied redemptions. The fund froze more than GBP 3.7 billion in investors' money. This fund was marketed to be as liquid as a US mutual fund. The issue, according to the *Financial Times*, was excessive investments in unlisted and generally illiquid assets.[7]

In a 2016 article published on Alpha Architect, David Foulke sums up why many practitioners have started to take the side of academics on the private versus public equity debate:

> Indeed, how meaningful is it to claim some performance advantage over public markets when you use leverage to buy small, cheap private companies, and exercise substantial discretion in measuring NAV? And then to say this "advantage" justifies an all-in ~7% fee?

Can Public Equity Fund Managers Deliver Private Equity–Like Returns?

Unlike private equity fund managers, public equity managers must provide daily liquidity. They must always be invested (plus or minus a small cash buffer). They must buy securities as investors give them cash to invest, even though markets may be overvalued, and sell securities as their clients redeem cash, even though it may be the worst time to sell. In other words, several of their buy-and-sell decisions are nondiscretionary. Unlike private equity managers, they can't wait for the best opportunities to deploy or return capital.

In a 2019 study that raises questions about the supposed superiority of index strategies over active management, titled "Do Mutual Funds Trade on Earnings News? The Information Content of Large Active Trades," Linda Chen, Wei Huang, and George Jiang analyze a large sample of nearly 2,000 US public equity mutual fund managers' trades from January 1998 to March 2015. They show that discretionary trades (large active trades) by skilled mutual fund managers add significant value over passive benchmarks.

In contrast, "forced" trades—those generated by fund flows (subscriptions and redemptions)—detract from returns. The authors explain that public equity managers offer two benefits to investors: professional portfolio management and investment liquidity. The latter comes at a cost, because fund flows are typically "uninformative."[8] If it weren't for fund flows, the study shows, skilled public equity managers would outperform the bottom quintile of managers by +1.27% per year, after adjustments for market beta, size, style (value versus growth), and momentum factors.

In the 1999 article "Investor Flows and the Assessed Performance of Open-End Mutual Funds," Roger M. Edelen explains this effect from a theoretical perspective:

> The conventional analysis [which shows that mutual fund managers underperform passive benchmarks on average and have no market timing skill] gives no consideration to the fact that fund managers provide a great deal of liquidity to investors and thus engage in a material volume of uninformed, liquidity-motivated trading. . . . In an asymmetrically informed market with costly information production, equilibrium is attained only when liquidity-motivated traders sustain losses to informed traders. . . . Thus, any trader forced to engage in a material volume of liquidity-motivated trading in a financial market that is in informational equilibrium will be unable to avoid below-average performance, ceteris paribus.

Academic theories that rely on assumptions of "an asymmetrically informed market with costly information production" and "informational equilibrium" may seem opaque to investors, but the idea is simple: if we believe in a zero-sum game, stock pickers who trade just to provide liquidity to their investors are at a disadvantage to those who trade based on information. Edelen provides an intuitive example:

> Consider the performance of an open-end fund manager who occasionally has private information that leads to positive risk-adjusted returns, but who also satisfies investors' liquidity demands. A well-functioning performance measure should identify this manager as being informed. Yet fund flows force the manager to engage in liquidity-motivated trading. Depending on the timing and relative magnitude of information arrival and investor flows, the fund's average risk-adjusted return could very well be negative even though the manager is informed. Thus, the very act of providing a liquid equity position to investors at low cost, arguably the primary service of an open-end mutual fund, can cause an informed fund manager to have negative abnormal returns.

Basing his findings on a time period that varies across funds (with a mean start date of May 1985 and mean end date of July 1989), Edelen calculates that for every unit of flows-based trading, defined as 100% of the fund's assets in a year, performance deteriorates by −1.5 to −2%. Based on his analysis of a sample of 166 mutual funds, he concludes that "controlling for this indirect cost of liquidity changes the average fund's abnormal return (net of expenses) from a statistically significant −1.6% per year to a statistically insignificant −0.2%."

This result raises an important question: *What if we allowed lockups in public market portfolios?* Edelen estimates that for the median fund, about *half of all trading volume is due to liquidity provision*, as opposed to informed trading.

What if we went one step further and completely leveled the playing field? What if we allowed public market fund managers the same flexibility across the board (use of leverage; when to call, deploy, and return capital; etc.) as private market fund managers? If we set aside return-smoothing shenanigans, there is no reason why we must limit private equity–like structures to private markets.

For an ongoing research project, my colleagues Rob Sharps, Rob Panariello, Camila Arbelaez, and I have surmised that many long-term investors in public markets would be prepared to accept similar terms as those afforded private equity managers in exchange for enhanced performance. Unlike with private market investments, the investors would benefit from the added confidence of transparent and unbiased valuations, as well as the confidence that in a crisis, the underlying investments would remain liquid.

Many institutional investors may want to go one step further and encourage public market fund managers to use appraisal accounting on such a product. These investors might think that appraisal-based returns help them manage their career risk. Appraisals often cushion losses, at least in the short run. Smoothed returns look great in asset liability studies. (One manager selection professional once told me that if we could deliver a smoothed version of the S&P 500 index, many asset owners would be prepared to pay very high fees for it, even though the underlying return stream can be obtained for about 5 bps in an index fund.) But to use self-reported appraisals when marked-to-market data are available would be bad practice from a risk management perspective, akin to how ostriches put their head in the sand.

In our research, we will estimate the benefit of leverage and lockups as applied to actively managed public market funds. Simple lockups don't necessarily provide an advantage, especially if they lead to other agency and tax issues. For example, there's a lack of evidence that closed-end funds (which eliminate liquidity provision) outperform open-end funds after leverage adjustments.[9] These funds don't have full discretion on when to return capital. In fact, most of them are focused on the provision of a high and predictable yield. However, private equity terms, which include the ability to call, deploy, and return capital at will, can magnify an investor's ability to generate alpha. When combined with leverage, we surmise that such terms would let active public market fund managers go toe-to-toe with private markets fund managers. They would no longer be required to bring the proverbial knife to a gunfight.

Of course, if there is a liquidity risk premium, private assets may still outperform public markets. But with the amount of money deployed in private markets, which seems to have reached bubble-like levels, one could question whether these markets will deliver a liquidity risk premium going forward.

In prior studies focused on PMEs, authors have assumed that private equity fund flows would have been deployed into an index (usually the S&P 500). In our study, we will substitute index exposures for actively managed funds. We will also adjust for the liquidity provision component in public funds. Essentially, we will calculate PMEs on reverse-engineered, "locked-up" versions of a large sample of public fund managers' track records. Depending on the outcome, we may also consider a product development effort to create private equity–like, actively managed public equity vehicles.

The bottom line is that private equity is not necessarily a free lunch. Still, private equity and other alternative asset classes can have their place in investors' portfolios, if the asset allocator can identify good managers and model risk thoughtfully.

Portfolio Construction with Alternative Assets

In Chapter 17, we will review portfolios that broadly incorporate the body of research and best practices we have discussed throughout this book on return forecasting, risk forecasting, and portfolio construction. Many of these portfolios won't include alternatives because most tax-deferred US retirement plan sponsors seek to minimize fees and maximize liquidity. Other model portfolios will include about 10%. *For qualified investors who can forgo some liquidity in their portfolios, all things considered, a 10% allocation to alternatives seems reasonable.* This weight is close to the market portfolio's allocation (Doeswijk, Lam, and Swinkels, 2014); and as we have discussed in Chapter 1, when in doubt, the market portfolio provides an anchor to portfolio construction. Other investors, such as endowments and wealthy individuals with a long time horizon, may want to allocate more to alternatives. But they should remain mindful that alternatives are not a free lunch, and that the "alternatives" category remains ill-defined and includes a wide range of investments (hedge funds, private real estate, private equity, infrastructure, agriculture, etc.).

Notes

1. Hamilton Lane, Investor Conference, April 2, 2019, http://www.hamilton lane.com.
2. Broadly defined, including private equity, venture capital, private credit, private real estate, and infrastructure.
3. To be fair, it could be argued that private equity fund managers have better market timing skill than public equity managers, but this "skill" would be hard to measure because public equity managers don't have the same flexibility on how they deploy cash.
4. Harris, Jenkinson, and Kaplan (2016) found that private equity provided zero alpha versus public markets from 2005 to 2014. L'Her, Stoyanova, Shaw, Scott, and Lai (2016) adjusted for other factors and improved on the PME methodology and found zero alpha. Brown, Harris, Jenkinson, Kaplan, and Robinson (2015) compared four private equity datasets and found that leveraged buyouts (the main style of private equity investing) did not outperform public markets from 2006 to 2014.
5. See Franzoni, Nowak, and Phallipou (2012) and Gupta and Van Nieuwerburgh (2019) as examples.
6. See Asness (2019).
7. https://www.ft.com/content/82bab25c-972c-11e9-9573-ee5cbb98ed36.
8. See Edelen (1999).
9. See, for example, the article by Elton, Gruber, Blake, and Shacar (2013), which is quoted in an exhaustive review of the literature on closed-end funds by Cherkes (2012).

16

Active Versus Passive and Something About the "Pharma Bro"

We can't measure directly if the market is efficient
from a capital allocation perspective. But indirectly,
we can study whether abnormal profits are possible.
—JPP

NOW THAT WE HAVE DISCUSSED RISK FACTORS AND THE role of alternative assets, we must discuss one more important question on portfolio construction: Should we allocate to active or passive building blocks?

In recent years, index strategies have gained market share over active managers. The common narrative is that on average, active managers don't outperform index-tracking strategies. In my view, this narrative is flawed. Not every active manager is "average." Skilled active managers—with a repeatable and disciplined process, significant resources, the right culture, reasonable fees, and a long time horizon—have delivered excess returns to investors over decades and, ultimately, have contributed to better retirement outcomes. There are many examples of skilled active managers, so let's use a hypothetical example (which will please my legal department because it simplifies the compliance requirements for this book), albeit one that's not divorced from reality.

Suppose that through active security selection (via fundamental research), tactical asset allocation (as described earlier in this book), and structural portfolio design advantages (also based on many of the concepts we reviewed in this book), an actively managed target-date fund has outperformed a target-date fund that allocates to index-based strategies by 82 bps per year since inception, after fees. Is that a meaningful difference?

Let us assume that twin sisters Mary and Lucy have the exact same savings patterns but at two different employers. Mary's employer uses the active target-date fund as the default investment option, while Lucy's employer uses the index-based option. Suppose the sisters each contribute $12,000 per year toward their retirement. Let's assume that the index-based strategy returns 6% per year (after fees), compared with 6.82% (after fees) for the actively managed strategy, for a difference of 82 bps.

There are many ways to run this simulation. For example, we can include stochastic asset returns, salary growth, employer match, inflation, etc. But for illustration purposes, we can get a reasonable estimate with the "FV" function in Excel. This function calculates the future value of a stream of payment for a given rate of return and time horizon. We find that over her entire career (40 years, from age 25 to age 65) Mary accumulates a retirement balance of $2,287,248 with the active strategy (isn't compounding great?), compared with $1,857,243 for Lucy's index-based target-date fund.

In this example, the total active management advantage is $430,104. If both employers have 5,000 employees, or "plan participants," the decision of the plan sponsor at Mary's company to rely on a skilled active manager has created, over time, a staggering total of over $2.15 billion (5,000 × $430,104) in extra retirement security for the employees at Mary's company compared with the choice of a passive strategy. That's meaningful.

Though inspired by actual results, this example is "cherry-picked," as participants would be invested in different vintages and experience different entry and exit dates. Also, most individuals contribute less than $12,000 per year. Selecting an active manager involves the risk of underperformance. For every buyer of a security, there's a seller. For every seller, there's a buyer. In that context, it's hard to imagine how *average* active performance could be much higher than . . . average. But again, not every active manager is average. Like almost everything in investment management, the active versus passive decision boils down to a risk versus return decision. Investors who want to take active risk can be rewarded for it.

In the end, though, financial markets have room for both active and passive investment management. Investors who prefer to minimize fees, even at the cost of possibly higher after-fee returns, should choose passive strategies.

The Revenge of the Stock Pickers

A recent trend popular with asset owners globally has been to invest in blend strategies, which optimize the asset mix between passive and active building blocks. Blend portfolios give investors exposure to active management within a specified fee budget. With massive, bubble-like inflows into index strategies in recent years, there's an argument to be made that even fee-sensitive investors can benefit from *some* exposure to active management. In the 2018 article "The Revenge of the Stock Pickers," my colleagues Hailey Lynch, Rob Panariello, Jim Tzitzouris, David Giroux, and I provide empirical evidence that the more assets flow into index strategies, the easier it gets for active stock pickers to outperform the index.

In that context, before we review our portfolios, let us take a short detour into the world of stock picking. This detour will help us better understand the active versus passive decision. My coauthors and I show that index investors distort security-level pricing, which creates opportunities for active managers, especially stock pickers. We focus on the stock-picking opportunities created by the popularity of exchange-traded funds (ETFs).

ETFs now account for 30% of all trading volume on US exchanges, up from less than 2% in 2000.[1] This trend may have created opportunities for stock pickers. When an ETF trades heavily around a theme, correlations among its constituents increase significantly. Even some securities that have little or negative exposure to the theme itself begin to trade in lockstep with other ETF constituents. In other words, because ETF investors are blind to security-level information, they often "throw the baby out with the bathwater."

The events of 2020 have provided additional evidence of this effect. As the prices of individual stocks get dragged up or down with ETFs, mispricings can become significant, and the profits realized by taking advantage of them may represent one of the hidden costs of ETF investing. In a 2017 editorial, *Financial Analysts Journal* coeditor Daniel Giamouridis calls for more research on this topic. He refers to "higher trade commonality in ETF constituent stocks (in down markets), increased commonality in their liquidity/ market impact, and less idiosyncratic risk compared with nonconstituent stocks." He emphasizes that future research should clarify how volatility and correlations change as well as the likelihood of price deviations from fundamentals (and reversions).

To answer this call for research and, importantly, to estimate the size of this opportunity for stock pickers, we have designed a simple, contrarian trading strategy that buys oversold constituents when an ETF sells off in a high-volume panic. We focus on the downside because, as we discussed in Chapter 9, investors are less rational when faced with losses than when faced with gains; i.e., diversification fails much more often on the downside than on the upside. Hence, extreme downside correlations are almost always higher than upside correlations. As Rob Panariello and I (2018) argued, in financial markets, fear is more contagious than optimism.

We identify oversold constituents by their beta to their ETF. We use nine sector ETFs because they are more susceptible to speculative, retail-oriented trading than broad index ETFs. We also use an S&P 500 ETF and a small cap ETF.

Giamouridis specifically calls for research to cover "not only stocks in broad market indexes that are ETF constituents but also specific segments of the equity market," such as sectors.

We don't suggest that anyone implement this strategy without fundamental oversight, but our results are striking: when high-volume sell-offs occur, ETF investors may be leaving as much as 200–300 bps of alpha on the table for stock pickers to capture over the following 40 days. Across ETFs, such events occur an average of 30 times per year, for a total of 240 events throughout our study period (January 4, 2010 to December 29, 2017).

This strategy doesn't require any stock-picking skills other than the ability to measure a stock's beta to its ETF. We suspect stock pickers can capture even more alpha from ETF investors. They can carefully analyze why the ETF is selling off and whether certain constituents are simply being dragged down with it for no good fundamental reason. Our goal is merely to estimate the size of the opportunity, because it's impossible to backtest a discretionary, fundamental approach.

Cahan, Bai, and Yang (2018) suggest that most ETF investors ignore the fundamentals of the underlying constituents.[2] The authors refer to the "arbitrage opportunity" that arises when "the short-term trading activity in an ETF is inconsistent with the real-world fundamentals of the underlying stocks." They use the term "arbitrage" in an informal way, not in the academic sense of riskless profit. But they show that investors can generate alpha if they select ETFs based on constituent fundamentals.

They find that sector ETFs are the most disconnected from fundamentals, but the effect is also present for broad market and smart beta ETFs.

Although we reach similar conclusions, our approach is different in that we pick stocks (i.e., we look for mispricings within ETF constituents), whereas Cahan et al. pick ETFs (they look for mispricing across ETFs, based on stock-level analysis).

Similarly, others have documented evidence of the effects of indexing on security-level comovements. When a stock is added to an index, its correlation with its peer index constituents immediately increases.[3]

As a corollary, Xiong and Sullivan (2012) argue that in general, index investing contributes to systematic equity market risk. Regarding ETFs specifically, Da and Shive (2017) show that the higher the turnover on an ETF, the higher the correlation between its constituents. They conclude that these comovements are excessive—that is, not driven entirely by fundamentals.

Note, however, that such research does not mean indexing is bad for markets per se. Wurgler (2010), for example, says that "for the sake of balance, it is important to start by acknowledging the many considerable benefits that indexes and index-linked investment products provide." Similarly, Hill

(2016) explains that the natural tension between macro investors, who trade ETFs and other index products in response to dynamic market conditions, and fundamental investors, who take the long-term view, is healthy for financial markets: "Each type of investor depends on the presence of the other to provide liquidity and to drive prices to appropriate levels."

Brown, Davies, and Ringgenberg (2018) approach the issue from a different angle. Unlike Cahan et al.'s loose definition of "arbitrage," they study the true arbitrage between an ETF's price and its net asset value. [To take advantage of the discount or premium, arbitrageurs simultaneously sell (buy) the ETF and buy (sell) the underlying securities.] Their dataset provides a unique and transparent view of arbitrage activities. They show that an increase in ETF arbitrage activity signals nonfundamental demand shocks (perhaps because of sentiment, or "thematic," trading). In turn, these shocks appear to predict subsequent return reversals at the one-month horizon for both ETFs and their constituents.

This wide body of research all points to the same conclusion: index/passive investing may cause mispricings and abnormal correlations (or "correlation bubbles").[4] Surprisingly, Madhavan and Morillo (2018) arrive at the opposite conclusion. They use a factor model to analyze what drives correlations over time and find that macro factors are more important than the increase in ETF assets in driving cross-stock correlations higher. One of their key arguments is that "although cross-stock correlations rose in the period when ETF assets increased, they are not at unprecedented levels relative to the past, well before the rise of passive indexing." But as our research shows, averages can be misleading. If we isolate days with high ETF volume, the picture is quite different and supports the mainstream conclusion that indexing causes correlation abnormalities.

Also in the skeptical camp is an earlier study that supports Madhavan and Morillo's (2018) critique. Glosten, Nallareddy, and Zou (2016) suggest that jumps in cross-constituent correlations could be explained by macro shocks or, more generally, systematic fundamental information. In this case, some illiquid ETF constituents may even benefit from ETF trading volume because they become more efficiently priced (i.e., they react more promptly to macro fundamental news). But the authors reach mixed conclusions. They find that systematic price discovery only partially explains ETF activity.[5]

If ETF volumes improve the pricing of systematic shocks but don't distort the pricing of nonsystematic information, we shouldn't observe predictable reversals, such as those reported by Brown et al. (2018). Moreover, Ben-David, Franzoni, and Moussawi (2018) observe that ETFs attract "high-frequency demand" and, based on observed reversals, confirm that "demand shocks in the ETF market translate into non-fundamental price changes for the underlying securities."

To build on this body of research, we posit that the main reason for the distortions and reversals is that some ETF constituents aren't exposed to macro shocks in the same way—or to the same extent—as their peers. We call these constituents "outsiders." We recognize that the list of outsiders can change as a function of the nature of the macro shock. Ultimately, the more different constituents are from one another, the more opportunities there are for distortions.

We show that these abnormalities present an alpha opportunity for stock pickers who can distinguish between systematic shocks and ETF-driven price distortions. We suggest a practical shortcut: focus on the behavior of outsider constituents around significant jumps in ETF volumes. This approach is different from everything else we have found in the literature. For example, Brown et al. (2018) sort stocks based on ETF-driven volume, without considering whether a given stock is an outsider or not.

Ultimately, while we recognize the role of index products in financial markets, we conclude that stock pickers may be able to "pick off" the rising number of ETF investors if they can answer two simple questions: Why is the ETF selling off, and should this constituent be selling off with it? *The implication for asset allocators is that they should allocate at least part of their portfolios to skilled active managers if they want to hedge against bubble-like situations in index-based products. This research supports the idea of active-passive diversification. It also provides a warning sign to avoid a recent trend (a fad?) toward niche ETFs.*

A Case Study: Pharmaceuticals, Hillary's Tweet, and the Valeant Subpoena

As an illustration, consider the behavior of US healthcare and pharmaceutical stocks in September 2015. Between September 18 and 28, the Health Care Select Sector SPDR ETF (XLV) plummeted by −10.7%, compared with −5.4% for the S&P 500. Volume on the ETF over these seven trading days jumped to its 99th percentile, whereas volume on the S&P 500 remained in its 33rd percentile.[6]

Two important events appear to have driven most of the sell-off in healthcare stocks. First, on September 21, Hillary Clinton tweeted that she would unveil a plan to curtail "price gouging" by pharmaceutical companies.[7] (The day before, the *New York Times* had published an article on how Turing Pharmaceuticals had just increased the price of a lifesaving drug from $13.50 to $750.00.[8] The media nicknamed Martin Shkreli, Turing's young and brash CEO, the "pharma bro.") Second, on September 28, Democrats in the US House of Representatives asked to subpoena Valeant Pharmaceuticals for documents on drug price increases.[9] XLV volume on that day reached an all-time high.

Both events threatened to put pressure on pharmaceuticals-sector revenues, but not necessarily those of other healthcare stocks. Although some companies were directly in the line of fire, it's hard to imagine how regulation aimed at human drug pricing would affect companies that make animal medicines and vaccines, such as Zoetis, or medical equipment, such as Baxter International.[10] Yet all XLV constituents—without exception—sold off over these seven trading days.

Pharmaceuticals contribute a significant percentage to XLV's total volatility. Such high-beta stocks tend to be at the center of most high-volume thematic sell-offs in this ETF. In contrast, stocks with a low beta to XLV are often unaffected by the theme behind the sell-off, at least from a fundamental perspective. Nevertheless, they get dragged along, like the baby thrown out with the bathwater. Hence, an easy way to identify outsiders within a list of ETF constituents is to look for stocks that have a low beta to their ETF.

We would have identified five "outsiders" stocks on September 28, 2015, if we had ranked XLV's constituents by their ETF beta and selected the bottom 10%. These stocks should not have been affected by the drug pricing controversy. These companies sell such products and services as dental equipment, pet supplies, and lab tests. Yet they sold off on the political posturing around drug pricing. Because of an increase in constituent correlations—which is common when ETF volumes spike—they sold off more than expected based on their ETF betas. An equally weighted portfolio of these five stocks returned –8.3% during the seven-day sell-off compared with an ETF beta-implied return of –6.1%.

This overreaction created an opportunity for stock pickers. Suppose an investor had bought the five outsider stocks (equal weights) at the end of the sell-off and levered the portfolio to an ETF beta of 1.0 (we levered the portfolio to calculate alpha versus the ETF). Over the next 40 days, the investor would have outperformed XLV by +4.2% after transaction and borrowing costs.[11]

Another Case Study: Financials, the Impact of Interest Rates, and REITs

On February 11, 2016, then US Federal Reserve Chair Janet Yellen concluded her semiannual testimony to Congress with an indication that the Fed was not in a rush to raise rates. "Financial conditions in the United States have recently become less supportive of growth,"[12] she said, adding that negative rates were "not off the table."[13] These comments hurt the Financial Select Sector SPDR ETF (XLF) because financials tend to benefit from rising rates. For example, when rates rise, banks can lend at a rate that is higher than their overnight borrowing costs and thereby increase net interest revenues.

From February 4 to 11, 2016, XLF returned –6.6%. Although higher trading volumes on this ETF had been recorded around the financial crisis, its volume for those six trading days in February 2016 was in the 91st percentile for all six-day periods over the previous five years. Volume on the S&P 500 was also elevated relative to the previous five years. It was in the 94th percentile, which reflected the systemic importance of monetary policy and, presumably, Yellen's comments on weaker economic growth.

However, marketwide selling was not as intense as in financials: the S&P 500 returned –4.4%. What happened to the outsiders within XLF? Among the eight stocks with the lowest beta to XLF (the bottom 10%), seven were REITs and the eighth was American Express. Unlike banks, REITs tend to trade as positive duration assets. Real estate assets are almost always valued based on discounted cash flow models. Cash flows (i.e., rents) are fairly predictable. When rates go down, the value of real estate assets goes up; when rates go up, their value goes down (i.e., these assets behave like bonds).

As for American Express, the company's 2015 annual report explains that its revenues have positive duration: "Amex is negatively exposed to interest rates."[14] According to the American Express Company (2015), "The detrimental effect on our annual net interest income of a hypothetical, immediate 100 basis point increase in interest rates would be approximately $216 million."

Therefore, as the market suddenly had to digest the possibility of lower rates, REITs and American Express should have performed better than other financials. In fact, because the growth shock was downplayed (Yellen said that despite weaker expectations, it would not "be fair to jump to any conclusion about the state of the economy"),[15] perhaps they should have rallied. Treasuries were up, for example.

But an equally weighted portfolio of the eight outsiders returned −8.5% during the six days leading up to and including the end of Yellen's testimony on February 11. We surmised that REITs and American Express were oversold because of the spike in ETF trading volume, which led to indiscriminate selling across financials. As in our first case study on healthcare stocks, if a stock picker had bought the outsiders (equally weighted portfolio) after the sell-off, levered them to an ETF beta of 1.0, and held the portfolio for 40 days, she would have outperformed the ETF significantly—in this case, by +20.0% after transaction and borrowing costs. It is worth noting that later that year, REITs were spun off from financials and reclassified as a separate sector.

Such ETF-driven stock-picking opportunities appear to be pervasive. Beyond our two case studies, there are correlation bubbles everywhere. For example, suppose a company's earnings disappoint. Investors may use an ETF to sell exposure to the entire sector, even though from a fundamental perspective, several competitors should not be affected (and perhaps some should benefit from a gain in market share). Macro factors also seem to matter. For example, a drop in oil prices may lead to a sell-off in an energy-sector

ETF, dragging down companies that may have little or negative exposure to oil. Emerging markets ETFs may also sell off with oil prices, even though some markets and companies within the emerging markets index are net importers. And so on.

The challenge for stock pickers is twofold. First, they must look for situations when an ETF sells off with very high volume, based on a specific theme. Second, they must identify the outsiders—the oversold companies that should not be affected by the theme from a fundamental perspective. The good news is that simple filters may work quite well: we found that most spikes in ETF trading volume lead to abnormal correlations, and low ETF betas appear to be a good way to identify outsiders.

These correlation abnormalities can create a plethora of buying opportunities at the security level. To illustrate, we backtest a simple systematic strategy. For each volume spike accompanied by a negative return, we systematically buy the outsiders and hold them for 40 days. We do so across all 11 ETFs in our sample and across time. We identify outsiders the same way we did in our pharmaceutical and financials case studies: we rank constituents by ETF beta and build an equally weighted portfolio of the bottom 10%. Then, to calculate alpha versus the ETF, we lever the portfolio to an ETF beta of 1.0. Essentially, we replicate our case studies but on a much bigger scale, across a total of 240 volume spikes. All our data are out-of-sample, based on what would have been available at the time.

We calculate the average cumulative alpha (the return for the levered outsider portfolio minus the ETF) across all events, from 1 to 40 days after the volume spike and before and after trading costs.[16] Average alpha on the first post-spike day is slightly negative, which indicates that even if we lagged the implementation time by one day, the strategy would still work. Then, as the time window expands, average alpha cumulates positively and consistently—all the way to 40 days.

The strategy does not work perfectly for all ETFs or at all time horizons, but on average, it generates significant after-cost alpha.[17] Because we force the outsider portfolios' ETF betas to 1.0, the strategy is not expected to take on any systemic factor exposure—such as market beta, value, or momentum exposures—relative to the ETF. Because we measure performance relative to the ETF, we expect these alphas to be "idiosyncratic" (i.e., stock-picking alphas).[18]

Notably, the strategy does not work well for the Materials Select Sector SPDR ETF (XLB), and although it works in the short term, it ends in negative territory for the Technology Select Sector SPDR ETF (XLK). These outcomes highlight the risk of systematic, simple trading rules. In these cases, the trading rules lead to large positions in low-ETF-beta stocks that underperformed their ETFs after the high-volume sell-offs.

Perhaps fundamental analysis would have helped. A stock picker would have analyzed the theme behind each sell-off. She would have taken into consideration whether the low-ETF-beta outsiders were truly outsiders to the theme and, if so, whether these companies presented a risk of short-term underperformance for other reasons. Then she would have scaled the positions relative to the theme according to a risk-return analysis. Once the long positions were established, she would have applied discipline to determine when to sell them, considering market developments and the health of the sector and the companies involved.

Last, although the strategy identifies ETF volume spikes and conditions them on down days, it does not condition on the size or duration of the sell-off. Focusing on the largest sell-offs, with a flexible time horizon, might have enhanced performance. Volumes across ETFs and index funds also need to be monitored, of course, because several index products may trade in the same sector. Ultimately, a lot more can be done when the strategy incorporates fundamental analysis. Hence, our goal is to indicate the potential size of the opportunity, not to design a purely systematic approach.

Takeaways

Are ETF investors increasingly at risk of getting "picked off"? Because of the growing popularity—as well as the liquidity and tax benefits—of passive investing, the percentage of trading volume on US exchanges from ETFs has increased significantly. Some ETF investors focus on top-down market views or themes, whereas others believe that markets are efficient and simply want broad index exposures. In all cases, when they trade, most ETF investors—and index investors in general—ignore security-level fundamentals. They simply buy or sell all securities in the index in proportions determined by the index provider (typically, market capitalization weights).

As a result, we find that when ETF volumes spike, correlations among constituents increase to levels that are not justified by company-level fundamentals. Our study of 240 events between 2010 and 2017, compiled across 11 ETFs, suggested that these correlation bubbles may create opportunities for stock pickers. Investors who buy oversold constituents after high-ETF-volume days and hold them as they mean-revert over the next 5 to 40 days may generate alpha at the expense of index investors. Are we witnessing the revenge of the stock pickers?

My view is that there's a place for both passive and active management in financial markets. Passive investors and stock pickers can happily coexist. We report gains for stock pickers that are of practical significance, but these results don't mean ETFs are "bad." They simply mean that different investors can make markets more liquid and efficient together. Market efficiency remains a paradox: profit opportunities, such as the one we have identified (and which indicates inefficiencies), are necessary to make markets more efficient. Such are the ebbs and flows of financial market equilibrium.

Rules of Thumb for Portfolio Construction

We have covered a lot of ground in this section on portfolio construction. We discussed the choice of building blocks and whether risk factors can replace asset classes—not really; but risk factor analysis is useful in portfolio construction. Then we pondered the stocks versus bonds question in the context of life cycle investing. We reviewed a wide range of approaches to portfolio optimization, from single-period to multi-period optimization and from mean-variance to various tail-risk-aware approaches. Last, we took a slight detour into the world of stock pickers, to frame the active versus passive debate and illustrate the role of skilled active management in markets and in investors' portfolios.

To summarize, following are my top seven rules of thumb for portfolio construction. These recommendations assume that the hard work on return and risk forecasting has been done, as discussed in Parts One and Two of this book:

1. Don't use factors as substitutes for asset classes—no need to overhaul portfolio construction.
2. Use risk factor models to assess portfolio diversification, forecast risk, and enhance scenarios.
3. Consider risk premiums as possible small stand-alone investments, but beware of backtest results.
4. Solve this question first: What stock-bond mix matches the investor's goals and risk tolerance?
5. Use portfolio optimization models, judgment, and experience to populate the stock-bond mix.
6. Consider alternatives as diversifiers, but beware of inflated returns and underreported risks.
7. Allocate between active and passive strategies as a function of active risk tolerance and fees.

Notes

1. Robin Wigglesworth, "ETFs Are Eating the U.S. Stock Market," *Financial Times* (January 24, 2017). Volume data are from Credit Suisse, as of 2016. In 2016, seven of the ten most traded securities were ETFs, not stocks. The *Wall Street Journal* reports that the ETF industry has grown to $3.5 trillion in size: Asjylyn Loder, "Investors Win from ETF Price War," *Wall Street Journal* (July 12, 2018), www.wsj.com/articles/etf-fees-tumble-as-price-war-heats-up-among-big-fund-firms-1531396800.
2. In a related article, Chao, Shah, Finelli, et al. (2018) showed that a contrarian strategy that buys stocks with high ETF outflows and sells stocks with high ETF inflows generates substantial profits.
3. See Wurgler (2010), Barberis, Shleifer, and Wurgler (2005), and Greenwood and Sosner (2007).
4. For an extreme example, the case of the VanEck Vectors Junior Gold Miners ETF is interesting. See Asjylyn Loder and Chris Dieterich, "How a $1.4 Billion ETF Gold Rush Rattled Mining Stocks Around the World," *Wall Street Journal,* April 23, 2017. The authors say that "money rushing into

exchange-traded funds investing in gold mining stocks sparked wild trading in the stocks while the price of gold was largely flat."

5. The authors didn't find this same increase in informational efficiency "for big firms, stocks with high analyst following, and for stocks with perfectly competitive equity markets." With the exception of IJR (the small cap ETF), all 10 of our other ETFs were made up of firms in the S&P 500, which are generally big firms with high analyst following.

6. Percentiles calculated for all seven-day periods from December 22, 1998 to September 28, 2015.

7. https://twitter.com/hillaryclinton/status/645974772275408896?lang=en.

8. Andrew Pollack, "Drug Goes from $13.50 a Tablet to $750, Overnight," *New York Times,* September 20, 2015, http://www.nytimes.com/2015/09/21/business/a-huge-overnightincrease-in-a-drugs-price-raises-protests.html.

9. Valeant actually began trading under the name Bausch Health Companies Inc. on Monday, July 16, 2018.

10. It could be argued that drug-pricing pressures could ultimately affect the entire medical system and thereby impact medical equipment providers. However, these stocks' reaction still seems exaggerated.

11. Throughout this research project, including in the 2010–2017 backtest, transaction costs were estimated at 10 bps, or 17 bps considering leverage (on average). Borrowing costs were based on LIBOR + 50 bps and depend on how long the position was held. They cumulate to about 10 bps on average after 40 days. Hence, a rough estimate of total costs (transaction and borrowing) for 40 days would be 27 bps.

12. Zacks Equity Research, "Stock Market News for February 11, 2016," NASDAQ, http://www.nasdaq.com/article/stock-market-news-for-february-11-2016-cm578585.

13. Larry Elliott and Jill Treanor, "Stock Markets Hit by Global Rout Raising Fears for Financial Sector," *Guardian,* February 11, 2016, http://www.theguardian.com/business/2016/feb/11/stock-markets-hit-by-global-rout-raising-fears-for-financial-sector.

14. Ben Levisohn, "American Express: No, Higher Interest Rates Won't Help," *Barron's*, December 22, 2016, http://www.barrons.com/articles/american-express-no-higher-interest-rates-wont-help-1482422718.

15. Zacks Equity Research, "Stock Market News for February 11, 2016."

16. Our choice of the 1- to 40-day windows was motivated by prior studies, as well as the need to avoid too many overlapping events. Ben-David et al. (2018) found that "most of the contemporaneous stock-price effect of ETF flows reverts over the next 40 days, in line with the view that the demand shocks in the ETF market translate into nonfundamental price changes for the underlying securities." Brown et al. (2018) used a one-month horizon. Though extending the window beyond 40 days was possible (and we found that alpha continues to accumulate after 40 days), it creates too many overlapping events and makes it more difficult to attribute alpha. The median number of days between ETF spike dates in our sample was 38.

17. See the online supplemental material, available at http://www.tandfonline
    .com/doi/suppl/10.1080/0015198X.2019.1572358, for details of the statis-
    tical test.
18. Brown et al.'s (2018) analysis shows that ETF-driven reversals generate signif-
    icant alphas after controlling for the Fama-French three factors plus momen-
    tum. Using betas calculated over the 252 pre-event days, the expected beta
    to the S&P 500 was slightly higher for the levered outsider portfolio than it
    was for the ETF. Consequently, after adjusting for the exposure to the market
    in the 40 post-event days, we could see a reduction in the alpha generated by
    our strategy of about 20 bps—a fraction of our 300 bps of precost alpha. We
    left it to the reader to interpret whether this slight excess beta constitutes a
    systematic bias, but if so, the impact remains small relative to the magnitude
    of the net alphas. Regarding liquidity, our outsiders have a similar liquidity
    profile, on average, to that of their peer constituents. The distribution is sym-
    metrical: roughly half the low-ETF-beta stocks have above-average liquidity,
    and half have below-average liquidity.

17

Sample Portfolios and Something About Gunslingers

*Asset allocation is simply about seeking
the highest possible return given our risk tolerance.*
—JPP

FOLLOWING ARE STRATEGIC ASSET ALLOCATIONS FOR portfolios that broadly incorporate the principles we've discussed throughout this book. Tactical asset allocation should also be applied around these strategic weights, to take advantage of relative valuation opportunities based on the approach we discussed in Part One of this book.

My goal is to finish this book with practical recommendations. There's a wide range of high-quality multi-asset portfolios offered to investors. In my view, these are the portfolios that best illustrate a thoughtful approach to asset allocation. They have delivered strong risk-adjusted returns and have done well in markets when diversification has failed. I rely on broad market indexes to represent asset classes, again, for illustrative purposes.

In the Global Multi-Asset Division at T. Rowe Price, we manage more than 200 different portfolios/products. These "samples" don't constitute advice. Every investor's situation is different, and an assessment of risk tolerance remains paramount (the hope is not via blood tests, per our earlier discussion in Chapter 11). But these portfolios can serve as good anchor points, or "templates" for portfolio construction.

Target-Date Portfolios

Target-date portfolios, as discussed in Chapter 13, automatically adjust the stock-bond mix over time to account for the investor's time horizon. Investors simply buy a fund that matches their expected retirement date, contribute to it along the way, and "forget it." Meanwhile the fund manager reduces the allocation to stocks and adjusts the components as time passes. This process eliminates the need for the investors to regularly reoptimize their portfolio.

Basically, these funds provide an autopilot solution. They are available in many tax-deferred 401(k) accounts as well as through advisors and as direct investments. In Table 17.1 (in the following section), I show the strategic allocations for a sample of target-date portfolios. As mentioned, these weights don't include tactical deviations, which change over time. For simplicity I show seven key portfolios along the glide path, although a typical target-date series would shift from the asset mix based on the investor's age in smaller increments.

Most portfolio managers of active target-date funds rely on well-staffed, dedicated research teams for strategic and tactical asset allocation. I have used index exposures for illustrative purposes in the table, but each component can be actively managed by portfolio managers who focus on security selection and rely on an army of analysts. Essentially, active target-date funds combine the entirety of an investment firm's capabilities.

Is the Home Bias Really a Bias?

Notice in the table a moderate strategic home bias toward US assets. When we build portfolios outside the United States, we typically allow some degree of home bias as well (we "localize" them). For example, our target-date portfolios in Korea include an allocation to Korean equities and bonds that's larger than their market capitalization weights in the world portfolio. The home bias accounts for liabilities, i.e., the fact that retirees spend their savings in their home country. If the local economy does well or if local prices inflate, retirees will want/need to spend more.[1] In this scenario, the growth of their local assets will hedge the increase in spending needs (all else equal), and vice versa when the economy does poorly. (In this case, the need to spend decreases in a way that offsets portfolio losses.)

The same liability argument applies to bonds. If rates go up, retirees can buy a given income stream with less money, so they'll tolerate losses on their local bond portfolio. If rates go down, retirees will pay more for an income stream, but they'll be able to finance the income stream with appreciated local bond values. This concept is well known in the world of defined benefit plans.

Because defined contribution plans essentially solve for the same problem (accumulate assets to replace one's salary in retirement), the concept applies here as well. The bottom line is that though global diversification remains important for growth and risk management, local assets hedge local spending, and so a home "bias" isn't always a bias per se. Nonetheless, some investors want broad global market exposures, which we provide in various non-home-biased portfolios as well.

Here are other notable features of these sample portfolios:

- They include strategic alpha positions in high-return diversifiers such as high-yield and emerging markets bonds. These asset classes may offer both high-risk-adjusted-beta (index) returns over time and rich alpha opportunities.
- For similar reasons, they tend to allocate slightly more to small and mid cap stocks than their market cap weights would indicate. These market capitalization weights have drifted down over time.

- The real assets class is composed of global stocks that should perform well during inflationary environments (metals and mining, precious metals, real estate investment trusts, and energy companies). It includes US and non-US companies.
- In several of our models, as in the target-date portfolios, we also include allocations to Treasury Inflation-Protected Securities. Often, we debate the strategic role of inflation protection, because inflation has been so low for so long. Though we often underweight inflation-linked assets tactically, we believe inflation remains a "tail risk," so a strategic allocation to inflation protection is warranted in most portfolios.
- In our flagship Target Date Fund series at T. Rowe Price, almost all components are actively managed, although here I use index exposures for illustrative purposes. We also offer active-passive blends, which have recently become popular with 401(k) plan sponsors.
- Stocks are the main engine of growth in investors' portfolios. Despite increased volatility along the way, over the long run, it can pay to allocate to stocks. In our portfolios we tend to allocate slightly more to stocks than our peers do. We manage this strategic equity risk through tail-risk-aware diversification and tactical asset allocation.

In Table 17.1, I also show historical annualized returns over various time periods. "CMA returns" refer to capital markets assumptions—expected returns for the next five years—which reflect our view of the current state of the world. These numbers are lower than historical returns because interest rates are close to an all-time low, as we discussed in Chapter 1, and alphas from active management (security selection and tactical asset allocation) are not included.[2]

TABLE 17.1   Asset Allocations Throughout the Life Cycle*

US Stocks	Index	Years Before and After Retirement (Allocations in %)						
		−20	−15	−5	0	+5	+15	+20
Large Cap Core	S&P 500	9	11	16	19	18	13	12
Large Cap Growth	Russell 1000 Growth	17	15	8	5	3	2	2
Large Cap Value	Russell 1000 Value	17	15	8	5	3	2	2
Mid Cap Growth	Russell Mid-Cap Growth	3	3	3	2	2	1	1
Mid Cap Value	Russell Mid-Cap Value	3	3	3	2	2	1	1
Small Cap	Russell 2000	2	2	2	1	1	1	1
Small Cap Growth	Russell 2000 Growth	2	2	2	1	1	1	1
Small Cap Value	Russell 2000 Value	2	2	2	1	1	1	1
Total US Stocks		*57*	*53*	*43*	*37*	*31*	*23*	*21*
Non-US Stocks								
Int'l Developed Core	MSCI EAFE	7	6	5	4	4	3	3
Int'l Developed Growth	MSCI EAFE Growth	7	6	5	4	4	3	3
Int'l Developed Value	MSCI EAFE Value	7	6	5	4	4	3	3
Emerging Markets	MSCI Emerging Markets	4	3	3	2	2	2	1
Total Non-US Stocks		*24*	*23*	*18*	*16*	*13*	*10*	*9*
Real Assets	Weighted Benchmark	4	4	3	3	2	2	2
Total Stocks		**85**	**80**	**64**	**55**	**46**	**35**	**31**
Core Bonds								
US Core	Bloomberg Barclays U.S. Agg	7	9	14	16	18	20	22
Dymamic Global	3M USD Libor (Cash)	2	3	5	5	6	7	7
Int'l Bond Hedged	Bloomberg Barclays Global Agg Hedged	2	2	3	4	4	5	5
Total Core Bonds		*10*	*14*	*21*	*25*	*27*	*32*	*34*

(continued on next page)

TABLE 17.1   Asset Allocations Throughout the Life Cycle* (continued)

Diversifying Bonds	Index	Years Before and After Retirement (Allocations in %)						
		−20	−15	−5	0	+5	+15	+20
US Treasury Long	Bloomberg Barclays Treasury Long	3	3	3	4	4	4	4
High Yield	JP Morgan Global High Yield	1	1	2	3	3	4	4
Floating Rate	S&P Performing Loan Index	0.2	0.3	1	1	1	1	1
EM Bond	JP Morgan EM Bond Index	1	2	3	4	4	5	6
Total Diversifying Bonds		*5*	*6*	*9*	*11*	*12*	*14*	*15*
Inflation Focused	Bloomberg Barclays TIPS	0	1	6	10	15	20	20
Total Bonds		**15**	**20**	**36**	**45**	**54**	**65**	**69**
Annualized USD Returns as of November 30, 2019 (%)								
	3 Years	14.0	13.9	13.1	12.5	11.8	11.1	10.9
	5 Years	11.3	10.9	9.6	8.8	8.0	7.0	6.6
	10 Years	7.8	7.6	6.8	6.3	5.7	5.1	4.9
	CMA Returns (5 Years)	6.0	5.8	5.4	5.2	4.9	4.7	4.6
Risk (%)								
	Volatility	10.7	10.1	8.1	7.0	5.9	4.7	4.2
Probability of -10% Loss (1 Year, End, in %)		7.2	7.2	6.6	6.0	5.4	4.8	4.2
Probability of -10% Loss (1 Year, Within, in %)		17.5	15.1	10.2	9.0	7.2	7.2	7.2
1-Month Tail Risk (CVAR)		−8.7	−8.2	−6.7	−5.9	−5.1	−4.2	−3.9
Scenario: Global Stocks down −10%		−8.7	−8.1	−6.5	−5.6	−4.7	−3.6	−3.2

Data sources for return statistics: See index providers listed in the table; analysis by T. Rowe Price. *Notes on risk analysis:* All risk analyses are based on MSCI BarraOne Platform (factor-based models). Portfolio volatility as of September 30, 2019. 3M USD LIBOR is proxied by ICE BofAML US 3-Month Treasury Bill Index for target-date index-based strategies. BXM was mapped to the iPath CBOE S&P 500 Buywrite ETN (BWVTF US Equity) for target allocation index-based strategies. Portfolio total risk (volatility) and scenario analysis (−10% shock to MSCI ACWI Index) are calculated based on MSCI Barra MIM with the GEM long-term model. For the scenario analysis, a −10% shock to the World Equity Index (proxied by MSCI ACWI) is applied, as well as correlated (propagated) shocks across asset classes using the covariance matrix from Barra's Global Multi-Asset risk model BIM303L with GEM3L factors. Historical expected shortfall (CVaR) simulation relies on the MSCI BIM303L model, and the holding period is 22 days (confidence level 95%). Probabilities of −10% loss (at the end of and within a one-year horizon) are estimated from the Barra MIM volatilities and CMA returns, based on Kritzman and Rich (2002). The historical-period start date is January 1, 2003, and the end date is September 30, 2019.

Target Allocation Portfolios

Conservative Income

This sample conservative income asset allocation (Table 17.2) provides a high level of current income, with moderate to low volatility, for US-focused investors. (In general, like other retirement-focused portfolios such as target-date funds, income portfolios tend to be "localized," with a focus on the investor's home country.)

It does, however, include a "kicker" of 12.5% in income-oriented stocks to boost returns over time and provide a long-term inflation hedge. Along with other portfolio features, such as diversified credit exposures and security selection alpha (if implemented via actively managed strategies), this equity allocation may help investors accumulate more capital than a pure bond portfolio.

In contrast, many conservative income portfolios invest entirely in fixed income assets. In doing so, they tend to strive for yield and to load up on *indirect* equity risk through high-yield bonds and other lower-rated sectors. These funds miss an opportunity to directly calibrate and benefit from stock-bond diversification. Though it varies greatly over time, this is one of the most robust forms of diversification, as we discussed in Chapter 9.

The fixed income portion of the portfolio is one of the most diversified across all the samples I show in this chapter, which is consistent with the portfolio's large allocation to fixed income in general (87.5%). The dedicated US Treasury Long position helps diversify equity risk. We use this asset class both strategically and tactically in most of our portfolios. From a strategic perspective, it provides significant diversification to equity risk per dollar invested, due to its high-interest-rate sensitivity/long duration—a "risk parity" concept, if you will. For the same reason, from a tactical perspective, US Treasury Long is an efficient and highly liquid building block when we want to manage our total portfolio risk up and down based on our risk-on versus risk-off view of the markets.

The usual high-yielding sectors are present (high yield, floating rate, and emerging markets) to deliver income, and the core bonds components are customized for the conservative income objective. Through security selection, skilled portfolio managers in these asset classes seek to avoid systematic biases that often build up in index exposures, such as large oil risk factor exposures.

Dynamic global bonds, which are also in the Target Date Fund samples, are employed as a type of conservative strategy that is designed to do well when diversification fails elsewhere in the portfolio. The strategy focuses on a cash benchmark, includes direct equity/credit risk hedging positions, and capitalizes on relative value opportunities primarily in rates and currencies. In our portfolios, we classify dynamic global bonds as core bonds, given their conservative nature and volatility closer to core than diversifying sectors, or we categorize them under alternatives, given their focus on absolute return. In all cases, it's the same strategy, but we find it useful to put it in different categories to reflect the role the bonds play in a given portfolio versus other components.

TABLE 17.2 Income Portfolio—Conservative, US Focused*

US Stocks	Index	Weights (%)
Equity Income	Russell 1000 Value	12.5
Total US Stocks		*12.5*
Total Stocks		**12.5**
Core Bonds		
US Core	Bloomberg Barclays U.S. Agg	18
Short Term Bond	Bloomberg Barclays 1-3 Gov/Credit	5.5
GNMA	Bloomberg Barclays GNMA	9.5
Corporate Income	Bloomberg Barclays U.S. Corp IG	5
Dynamic Global Bond	3M USD LIBOR (cash)	4
Int'l Bond Hedged	Bloomberg Barclays Global Agg Hedged	8
Int'l Bond Unhedged	Bloomberg Barclays Global Agg	3
Total Core Bonds		*53*
Diversifying Bonds		
US Treasury Long	Bloomberg Barclays Treasury Long	4
High Yield	JP Morgan Global High Yield	14.5
Floating Rate	S&P Performing Loan Index	4

Diversifying Bonds	Index	Weights (%)
EM Bond	JP Morgan EM Bond Index	8
EM Local Bond	JP Morgan GBI–EM Global Diversified	2
Total Diversifying Bonds		*32.5*
Inflation Focused		
Short Term TIPS	Bloomberg Barclays TIPS	2
Total Inflation Focused		2
Total Bonds		*87.5*
Annualized USD Returns as of November 30, 2019 (%)		
3 years		10.4
5 years		5.4
10 years		4.2
CMA returns (5 years)		3.9
Risk (%)		
Volatility		2.9
Probability of –10% loss (1 year, end, in %)		1.8
Probability of –10% loss (1 year, within, in %)		6.6
1-month tail risk (CVaR)		–3.6
Scenario: Global stocks down –10%		–1.6

*See the footnote to Table 17.1 for disclosures on data sources, methodologies, and "as of" dates.

Diversified Income—Moderate Risk

Here (Table 17.3) we allocate 40% to stocks, compared with 12.5% for the conservative income portfolio. This sample portfolio seeks the highest total return over time consistent with a primary emphasis on income and a secondary emphasis on capital growth. Given the portfolio's dual objectives, a 7% cash allocation provides an important diversifier to equity risk, adds liquidity, and helps anchor the portfolio's risk closer to its benchmark. It also provides a tactical lever to calibrate risk exposure over time.

TABLE 17.3   Income Portfolio—Moderate, Diversified*

US Stocks	Index	Weights (%)
Large Cap Growth	Russell 1000 Growth	10
Large Cap Value	Russell 1000 Value	10
Volatility Premium	BXM Index	3
Small Cap	Russell 2000	3
Total US Stocks		*27*
Non-US Stocks		
Int'l Developed Core	MSCI EAFE	10
Emerging Markets	MSCI Emerging Markets	2
Total Non-US Stocks		*11*
Real Assets	Weighted benchmark	2.0
Total Stocks		**40**
Core Bonds		
US Core	Bloomberg Barclays U.S. Agg	22
Int'l Bond Hedged	Bloomberg Barclays Global Agg Hedged	6
Total Core Bonds		*28*
Diversifying Bonds		
US Treasury Long	Bloomberg Barclays Treasury Long	2
High Yield	JP Morgan Global High Yield	4
Floating Rate	S&P Performing Loan Index	1
EM Bond	JP Morgan EM Bond Index	5
Total Diversifying Bonds		*12*
Total Bonds		**40**
Cash + Alts		
Money Market	3M USD LIBOR (cash)	7
Alternatives	HFRI Fund of Funds Conservative	13
Total Cash + Alternatives		*20*
Total Cash + Alts		**20**
Annualized USD Returns as of November 30, 2019 (%)		
	3 years	10.9
	5 years	7.3
	10 years	5.3
	CMA returns (5 years)	4.7

	Risk (%)
Volatility	5.1
Probability of –10% loss (1 year, end, in %)	6.0
Probability of –10% loss (1 year, within, in %)	7.8
1-month tail risk (CVaR)	–5.1
Scenario: Global stocks down –10%	–4.0

*See the footnote to Table 17.1 for disclosures on data sources, methodologies, and "as of" dates.

In this asset allocation, alternatives play an important role. We classify the volatility premium within US stocks, although it could also be classified as an alternative. We reviewed this strategy in Chapter 7 when we discussed my presentation at the CFA Institute in Montreal and looked at the correlation between covered call writing—the actively managed strategy we use to access the volatility premium—and a managed volatility strategy. Also, we revisited the topic when we discussed risk factors in Chapter 12. As mentioned, the volatility risk premium may be one of the few "factors" that appear to deliver robust performance over time. This strategy typically focuses on equity index options and comes with a targeted equity exposure ("delta hedging").

Diversified Global Portfolio

This sample asset allocation (Table 17.4) is meant to represent a flagship fund of funds that can be offered to investors globally. Its opportunity set includes developed markets and emerging markets equities, a wide range of global developed markets and emerging markets bond strategies, and various diversifying strategies designed to improve risk-adjusted returns. It's the quintessential one-stop-shop solution. The strategic asset allocation is 60% stocks (without home bias), 28% global fixed income, including exposure to below-investment-grade securities, and 12% alternative investments. Alternative investments may include hedge funds and a dynamic global bond strategy (here classified as an alternative). The government credit allocation is structured with a longer-duration profile as a diversifier, or "hedge," to equity volatility/potential fat-tail exposure in alternatives, with the long end focused on higher-quality bonds and Treasuries.

This type of asset mix is slowly rebuilding an investor base outside the United States, in Europe in particular. Over the last few years, European investors have poured billions into highly dynamic, absolute-return-oriented multi-asset products. The most popular strategies did well during the 2008–2009 sell-off and caught the subsequent upswing in asset prices. But I believe that a significant shift in preferences may have begun, as many of these "gunslinger" strategies have underperformed good old balanced strategies over the last several years. In Chapter 1, I made a snide comment on promises of "stock-like returns for bond-like volatility," supposedly delivered through a handful of big macro bets made by very smart investors. European investors have grown more skeptical of this approach. It's hard to deliver durable performance without breadth and diversification in active management activities, from strategic, to valuation-based tactical, to security selection. Without breadth and without the long-term tailwind of long positions in stocks, credit, and duration premiums, many macro gunslingers have struggled over the last few years.

TABLE 17.4   Balanced Portfolio—Global, Diversified*

US Stocks	Index	Weights (%)
Large Cap Growth	Russell 1000 Growth	11
Large Cap Value	Russell 1000 Value	11
Volatility Premium	BXM Index	5
Small Cap	Russell 2000	5
Total US Stocks		*32*
Non-US Stocks		
Int'l Developed Core	MSCI EAFE	6
Int'l Developed Growth	MSCI EAFE Growth	3
Int'l Developed Value	MSCI EAFE Value	3
Europe	MSCI Europe	4
Japan	MSCI Japan	2
Int'l Small Cap	S&P Global ex-US Small Cap	4
Emerging Markets	MSCI Emerging Markets	4

Non-US Stocks	Index	Weights (%)
Total Non-US Stocks		*25*
Real Assets	Weighted benchmark	3
Total Stocks		**60**
Core Bonds		
Gov Credit	Bloomberg Barclays U.S. Gov/Credit	12
Int'l Bond Hedged	Bloomberg Barclays Global Agg Hedged	1
Int'l Bond Unhedged	Bloomberg Barclays Global Agg	3
Total Core Bonds		*16*
Diversifying Bonds		
High Yield	JP Morgan Global High Yield	2
Floating Rate	S&P Performing Loan Index	1
EM Bond	JP Morgan EM Bond Index	4
Em Local Bond	JP Morgan GBI–EM Global Diversified	2
Total Diversifying Bonds		*9*
Inflation Focused		
Short Term TIPS	Bloomberg Barclays TIPS 1-5	1
Broad TIPS	Bloomberg Barclays TIPS	2
Total Inflation Focused		*3*
Total Bonds		**28**
Alternatives	HFRI Fund of Funds Conservative	12
Annualized USD Returns as of November 30, 2019 (%)		
	3 years	11.2
	5 years	8.4
	10 years	5.7
	CMA returns (5 years)	5.5
Risk (%)		
	Volatility	7.5
	Probability of –10% loss (1 year, end, in %)	6.6
	Probability of –10% loss (1 year, within, in %)	11.5
	1-month tail risk (CVaR)	–7.2
	Scenario: Global stocks down –10%	–6.0

*See the footnote to Table 17.1 for disclosures on data sources, methodologies, and "as of" dates.

Growth Portfolio

This high-octane asset allocation (Table 17.5) seeks the highest total return over time consistent with a primary emphasis on capital growth and a secondary emphasis on income. It invests in a diversified portfolio of about 80% stocks; 16% bonds, money market securities, and cash reserves; and 4% alternative investments. It provides a simple yet diversified set of building blocks, which corresponds to the preferences of US-domiciled investors.

TABLE 17.5   Growth Portfolio—US Focused*

US Stocks	Index	Weights (%)
Large Cap Growth	Russell 1000 Growth	20
Large Cap Value	Russell 1000 Value	20
Volatility Premium	BXM Index	6
Small Cap	Russell 2000	6
Total US Stocks		*53*
Non-US Stocks		
Int'l Developed Core	MSCI EAFE	19
Emerging Markets	MSCI Emerging Markets	3
Total Non-US Stocks		*23*
Real Assets	Weighted benchmark	4
Total Stocks		*80*
Core Bonds		
US Core	Bloomberg Barclays U.S. Agg	9
Int'l Bond Hedged	Bloomberg Barclays Global Agg Hedged	2
Total Core Bonds		*11*
Diversifying Bonds		
US Treasury Long	Bloomberg Barclays Treasury Long	2
High Yield	JP Morgan Global High Yield	1
Floating Rate	S&P Performing Loan Index	0.2
EM Bond	JP Morgan EM Bond Index	1
Total Diversifying Bonds		*5*
Total Bonds		**16**
Alternatives	HFRI Fund of Funds Conservative	4

Index	Weights (%)
Annualized USD Returns as of November 30, 2019 (%)	
3 years	13.1
5 years	10.5
10 years	7.4
CMA returns (5 years)	5.8
Risk (%)	
Volatility	9.8
Probability of –10% loss (1 year, end, in %)	7.2
Probability of –10% loss (1 year, within, in %)	14.5
1-month tail risk (CVaR)	–8.4
Scenario: Global stocks down –10%	–7.9

*See the footnote to Table 17.1 for disclosures on data sources, methodologies, and "as of" dates.

Specialized Portfolios and Thoughts on Change in Our Investment Division

Target Volatility—"Defensive Equity"

This sample portfolio (Table 17.6) directly targets volatility, based on the managed volatility strategy we discussed in Chapter 7. It can be used as a defensive US equity exposure as part of an investor's asset allocation. Half the portfolio is allocated to US stocks, while the other half is allocated to a dynamic sleeve composed of three ETFs: US stocks, US bonds, and "cash"/ short-term bonds. Allocations within this sleeve change based on the volatility environment. When volatility increases, the strategy decreases the allocation to the stocks ETF, and vice versa when volatility decreases. As we have discussed earlier, this process helps manage the failure of diversification in times of market stress.

TABLE 17.6   Target Volatility—Defensive Equity*

US Stocks	Index	Weights (%)
Large Cap Core	S&P 500	50
Total US Stocks		*50*
Volatility Management Sleeve		
S&P 500 Index ETF		**Dynamic Weights**
US Agg Index ETF		
Short Term Bond Index ETF		
Total Volatility Management		*50*
Target Volatility		14%
Range		13–16%
Equity Exposure Range		50–100%
Cash Allocation Range		0–50%

*See the footnote to Table 17.1 for disclosures on data sources, methodologies, and "as of" dates.

These portfolios represent only a few examples of a much broader set of asset mixes that can be appropriate for various investors. Recently, in our Global Multi-Asset Division, we have made a substantial investment in our solutions capabilities. We have launched several localized multi-asset portfolios for non-US investors, based on a range of goals: income, absolute return, liability-driven, retirement, etc. The key to a successful solutions business is to start with client needs.

Also, we have built customized asset allocation models for intermediaries. These models are quite popular with advisors and their clients. Increasingly, advisors spend more time on financial planning and tax management questions, while they rely on third-party models to guide their clients to the appropriate asset mix. These models can be built as variations, or "tweaks," on the sample portfolios I have presented in this chapter. They can be "proprietary," i.e., allocated to building blocks managed by one single investment firm, or "open architecture," i.e., allocated to multiple managers.

In the alternatives space, we have built an absolute return-oriented, multisleeve strategy that leverages our entire investment platform and includes allocations to long-short equity portfolios. One of our most interesting liquid alternative strategies is best described as an unconstrained, long-short multi-asset strategy that harvests a highly focused set of our platform's best ideas (across macro, individual stocks, commodities, credit, special situations, etc.). The bottom line is that asset allocation and multi-asset investment management continue to evolve at a rapid pace.

The evolution of these capabilities illustrates how our Global Multi-Asset Division has gone through a period of accelerated change and modernization over the last four years. We have faced unprecedented competition. To continue to deliver value to our clients, we have developed and improved our capabilities at a breathless pace.

But unlike many competitors, we didn't start with a blank canvas. We've built from a position of strength, with a large asset base and a strong, multidecade history of success in multi-asset investment management. We've had the usual ups and downs that come with an aggressive change agenda. We've had to work hard to maintain our core principles (our strong culture, our focus on existing clients and investment performance, etc.) and embrace new ideas and accelerated innovation.

About three years ago, when I met with our board of directors, I quoted one of the best race car drivers of all time, Mario Andretti: "If everything seems under control, you're not going fast enough." I suspect some of our directors felt uneasy with this quote. But I think others, especially those from the private sector, got the idea: no matter how successful a business, standing still is rarely a good option.

Notes

1. At least in nominal dollars.
2. T. Rowe Price Capital Markets Assumptions, 2019, https://www.troweprice
   .com/content/dam/ide/articles/pdfs/2019/q2/capital-market-assumptions
   .pdf.

Conclusion

Finance evolves constantly. It provides endless intellectual satisfaction to those who study it and move it forward.
—JPP

THE PROFESSOR LOOKED AT HIS STUDENTS WITH AN intense gaze. Silence. He knew how to use pauses to captivate his audience.

"Let me ask again," he said. "What does this mean?"

Another pause. He pointed at the blackboard behind him, which was full of quasi-indecipherable equations and numbers. "Think!" he said. "You're here to learn to use your *judgment*, not just memorize things!"

Another pause. He pointed to his right temple and repeated this mantra about judgment in almost every class, but the bottom line is that most students were a little scared of his reactions when they gave the wrong answer. That day, no one in the class seemed to want to risk an answer.

In most of my other finance classes, I sat in the first few rows. I often volunteered answers. But not in this class. As usual, that day I sat in the last row and kept my head down. And as usual, this professor asked a tricky question. A puzzle that forced everyone to think beyond the numbers. It was a corporate finance question. It had something to do with how to link the financing and investing decisions, and the Modigliani-Miller theorem, which shows that the value of a firm should *not* depend on how it finances its operations. The professor had just walked the class through a hypothetical example, which highlighted the perverse effects of conventional cost-of-capital analysis to evaluate projects.

He added, "Maybe I should invest the firm's capital in T-bills? Put everything in T-bills?"

A lightbulb went off in most students' heads. To invest the firm's capital in cash instruments should not maximize shareholder value. Yet based on the model, the net present value of a cash investment would be positive. Clearly, the assumptions on the firm's cost of capital were wrong.

At the time of this discussion, the professor was about to retire, after a remarkable 40-year career. He had built the university's masters in finance program and published the main textbooks used throughout the undergraduate and graduate programs. Several other universities had adopted his textbooks as well.

Without a doubt, he's the best professor I ever had.

But I might be biased, because he's my father, Jean-Paul Page ("JPP"). That's why I sat in the back of the class and kept my head down. The "JPP" quotes I used in this book are from his massive, 1,000+ page textbook, published in French, titled *Gestion financière et création de valeur* (*Financial Management and Value Creation*).[1]

My father is now retired. He has happily reorganized his life around fishing, hunting, snowmobiling, skiing, traveling, and chopping wood. He has gone cold turkey on his academic activities but continues to write short viewpoints to friends and family, for fun. He writes about political and economic issues, always with a right-leaning, pro-capitalism point of view.

Throughout our journey into return forecasting, risk forecasting, and portfolio construction, I have attempted to take the baton from my father. He always insisted that practitioners should seek to improve the quality of the decision-making process, rather than focus on theoretical considerations. He told his students that quantitative analysis was quite useful, but not a substitute for judgment. He firmly believed that a deep understanding of shareholders' expectations (i.e., what's priced in by the markets) was key to financial decision-making.

On return forecasting for relatively long horizons, we discussed how the strong theoretical foundations of modern finance—the capital asset pricing model in particular—help us assess the impact of low rates on expected returns. The same framework also suggests that risk-proportional returns and market capitalization weights can provide useful reference points around which to debate future returns. Mark Kritzman, the mentor I mentioned several times throughout this book, once told me after I had complained to him about my slow career growth, "Sébastien, the secret to happiness in life is to lower your expectations." Given current conditions, with extraordinary low rates, investors may need to lower their expectations.

Valuation-based expected return models also point to lower returns over the next 5 to 10 years, across a wide range of equity and fixed income asset classes. Although if we express expected returns for equity asset classes as dividend yield, plus long-term growth and valuation change, the numbers are somewhat more optimistic. In that context, it may be prudent to use a few different models and incorporate a good dose of judgment. The good news is that valuation-based models for fixed income asset classes, even those that simply rely on yield to maturity, tend to be remarkably predictive.

As for shorter-term return forecasts, we have seen that valuation ratios and momentum can be useful, but they offer relatively limited predictability (again, except for relative yields across fixed income asset classes, which work well). In a tactical asset allocation context, we have discussed how valuation, fundamental, and macro factors can be combined through a discretionary framework, in which experienced investors play a key role. For such a process, dashboards provide rigor and help filter and organize data in a way that generates trade ideas.

On risk forecasting, the good news is that volatility seems fairly predictable (at least more than returns). Short data windows with higher-frequency sampling (for example, daily or weekly rather than monthly) appear to work best. Investors can take advantage of this predictability through *risk-based investing* strategies, such as managed volatility strategies and covered call writing.

However, under the surface of predictable volatility lies a plethora of risk monsters: diversification almost always fails when we need it the most; so-called tail risks are much harder to model and predict than volatility itself; risk regimes can shift portfolio risk exposures drastically over time; and so on. Thankfully, our industry has advanced beyond models that rely on the normal probability distribution. Investors are now equipped with various methodologies to deal with—though not eliminate—these issues.

On portfolio construction, we have reviewed the debate on asset classes versus risk factors. Risk factor analysis can be quite useful to forecast risk and generate scenarios, but there's a fair amount of hype around factor premium products. It helps to clarify what we mean by "risk factors." Investors do not necessarily need to substitute asset classes for risk factors as the key building blocks for asset allocation. Rather, they can combine these approaches.

Perhaps the key portfolio construction question investors face is how much risk they are prepared to assume to reach their goals. The calibration of the stock-bond mix usually comes next. To answer these types of *life cycle investing* questions, target-date funds can provide a useful reference. With these types of funds, the stock-bond mix changes over time and is determined by the investor's retirement date/age. This "glide path" is typically constructed with the help of multiperiod optimization models. These *utility-based* models seek to integrate capital markets projections with investor preferences, as well as behavioral and demographic considerations.

On single-period portfolio optimization, we have seen that no single approach works perfectly. Each model has strengths and weaknesses. Tail-risk-aware optimization models can be quite useful, but investors must use them carefully to avoid issues with small data samples. Once again, it helps to combine different methodologies.

In doing so, investors must use a healthy dose of judgment. Over my career, I have found that many investors take a dogmatic view on portfolio optimization. The topic is surprisingly polarizing, especially among quants. Some believe that portfolio optimization should not be used at all. Others believe firmly in a specific model. My view is that investors should use various models and assumptions to better understand the trade-offs between asset classes in their portfolio. As JPP said, the key question is not whether a model is flawless or more theoretically elegant than an alternative model. The question is whether the model helps investors arrive at better decisions.

Last, we have addressed two specific challenges in portfolio construction: the role of alternative assets and the role of index-based (passive) building blocks. Alternative assets must be handled with care. Return and risk estimates must be adjusted to reflect the somewhat hidden reality that alternative assets are not a free lunch. To be clear, we didn't rule out the role of alternative assets, but we discussed the need to look beyond published internal rates of return and volatilities.

As for the active versus passive debate, we have discussed a case study that illustrates how both can coexist. The rise in index-based products provides opportunities for active managers. In this case study, we saw that heavy ETF trading volumes lead to abnormally high correlations, providing opportunities for stock pickers. Once again, there's no need to take a dogmatic view. Both passive and active strategies can be useful, depending on investor preferences. But active investment management is not about to disappear. It remains at the heart of our economic system. Not every manager is average, and *skilled* active management, with a repeatable process, can deliver better outcomes than index exposures over time.

Ultimately, how should investors allocate their assets in a way that integrates the key principles discussed in this book? How should they diversify their portfolio when we know that diversification often fails? The model portfolios I have presented in the last section of this book provide some examples. Meanwhile, tactical relative valuation opportunities continue to evolve in real time, and asset allocators continue to improve strategic portfolio construction. I expect the practice and science of asset allocation to continue to merge in a never-ending quest to deliver better outcomes to investors. As my father said, this quest will provide endless intellectual satisfaction to those who move it forward. What a fascinating field indeed!

Note

1. For those interested in corporate governance, the only book he ever published in English is titled *Corporate Governance and Value Creation*, available at https://www.amazon.com/Corporate-Governance-Value-Creation-Jean-Paul/dp/0943205719.

Afterword

Theoretical Foundations of the Asset Allocation Decision

WHEN I RETIRED AFTER 40 YEARS OF TEACHING FINANCE, I left the field entirely. A clean break. I hopped on the snowmobile and started focusing on the next stage in my life. I suppose only Sébastien could convince me to reminisce. I'm glad I did.

Finance is a fascinating field. Its primary goal is to address decisions that lead to better resource allocation, and ultimately, to society's well-being. Every decision that we make in life, including financial decisions, has an impact on our future. But no one can pretend to know the future. Therefore, finance is not about describing the past and publishing what has already happened. Rather, it's about how we handle choices for which we do not yet know the outcome.

Finance is a science, just like physics or chemistry: it relies on solid theoretical foundations, involves rigorous empirical analysis, and leads to important practical applications.

Asset allocation, as presented in this book, provides a credible example of the science and practice of finance as applied to capital markets decisions. The goal is to allow all types of investors, from institutions to individuals, to obtain the highest possible return given the risk they are willing to bear. The steps involved are return forecasting, risk forecasting, and portfolio construction.

Return forecasting is the most popular topic in the literature. To forecast return for a financial asset means to forecast its price—those are two sides of the same coin. If we know the return, we know the price, and vice versa, after we include the income component. The price is not what we hope or imagine an asset is worth. It's what others are willing to pay for it. Therefore, it depends on rational and behavioral factors. The problem is that when we invest, we can't control the future price of an asset. The adage "You make money when you buy" makes a lot of sense: a bad investment decision, in the sense of a bad purchase price, can't be reversed.

In this book, Sébastien explained that some of the theoretical foundations for return forecasting assume efficient markets. From a capital allocation perspective, efficient markets are an important condition for economic development. The best estimate of the price of an asset should be its intrinsic value, and no one should be able to consistently take advantage of the difference between the price and the intrinsic value.

Markets are efficient if all available information is incorporated in the price. Hence, fundamental analysts should get paid as a function of their contribution to making markets more efficient.

Risk forecasting dovetails with return forecasting. Theoretical foundations for risk forecasting include portfolio theory and diversification. Unlike returns, risks aren't additive. Diversification enables investors to increase expected returns without commensurate increases in risk. When we build a portfolio, part of the risk disappears. The risk of an individual asset and its contribution to a portfolio's risk aren't the same. Of course, as Sébastien explained, diversification does not always work as intended.

It's easier to represent the risk of an asset than its contribution to a portfolio's risk. Academics have developed the concept of the "beta," which represents how risky an asset is relative to another asset or relative to the market.

Even if we agree on a risk measure, there are more challenges to address in risk forecasting. Again, we're not trying to explain the past. We must look forward. We must predict the range of possible outcomes around our expected return. Open questions include: Is risk stable through time? Can we use past data to model risk in the future? If so, which time period and data frequency should we use? If risk is not stable, which adjustments should we make?

Portfolio construction is the last step in the asset allocation process. Theoretical foundations for portfolio construction start at the intersection of the capital asset pricing model (CAPM) and utility theory. According to the CAPM, the optimal portfolio is a combination of the market portfolio (which should contain all risky assets) and the risk-free rate. In a portfolio that contains all risky assets, all diversifiable risks have been eliminated. Such a portfolio is said to be "perfectly diversified," and the more we allocate to it, the higher our expected return.

As explained in this book, when in doubt, market capitalization weights provide an anchor to portfolio construction. The weight allocated to the market portfolio depends on the utility function, which represents the investor's risk tolerance.

Never has a theory had so many practical implications in the field of finance. An example of its impact on portfolio management, in particular on asset allocation, has been the popularity of passive, index-based investing. But like all good theories, the CAPM has its flaws. It's a single-period model, and it assumes perfectly efficient markets, to name two. The limitations of the model are therefore important, and its usefulness depends on analysts' and portfolio managers' ability to do their job skillfully. No theory, or model, or "recipe," can replace good judgment.

In the end, better return and risk forecasts and a thoughtful portfolio construction process will allow these theories to perform better in practice. Quantitative methods, as well as the availability and analysis of data and information, have produced sophisticated models that have improved market efficiency. Proponents of the efficient market hypothesis must explain them in simple words, and they must interpret results in the context of their theoretical foundations. Sébastien did a great job on this book. But I'm a tough grader. I give him a solid "A–."

Jean-Paul Page
Retired Professor of Finance
Université de Sherbrooke, Québec, Canada

Acknowledgments

I DECIDED TO WRITE THIS BOOK WHILE OUT ON A LONG trail run. A lightbulb moment, of sorts. My thought was that I could write about complex investment topics in an accessible way, with a "Malcolm Gladwell" lens. After years of writing articles for investment journals, I thought it would be fun to remove the constraints imposed by academic referees. I wanted to focus on the interesting, and sometimes fascinating, conclusions from a wide range of research and from my experience. This book conveys insights from more than 200 academic articles with the goal of helping savvy investors become better asset allocators. Clearly, if you've made it this far, you know that I'm no Malcolm Gladwell. Some chapters remained technical, and I didn't manage to completely eliminate jargon. One book agent told me that this book would "never, ever, be a mass-market book," unless I rewrote it from scratch. I did not. McGraw Hill was happy to work with me to target a more sophisticated audience. I hope that you learned something new. My first thank you must go to Stephen Isaacs and McGraw Hill for believing in this project from day one, and for agreeing not to dilute the content. Also, thank you to Ingrid Case for her excellent edits.

Recently I was interviewed by a reporter at Kiplinger. She asked how people with a full-time job find time to write a book. The short answer is: with a lot of help from my friends.

Parts of this book are heavily inspired by articles I coauthored with T. Rowe Price colleagues Rob Panariello, Jim Tzitzouris, Bob Harlow, Stefan Hubrich, Anna Dreyer, Hailey Lynch, Sean McWilliams, David Giroux, Chris Faulkner-

MacDonagh, David Clewell, and Charles Shriver. It has been, and continues to be, an absolute pleasure to work with every single one of you. I owe a special debt of gratitude to Rob Panariello for help with empirical questions throughout this book; Stefan Hubrich for his thought leadership on managed volatility and several other quantitative topics; Jim Tzitzouris for everything he's taught me about life cycle investing; Jerome Clark and Wyatt Lee for building and leading our Target Date Funds franchise; and David Giroux for showing me how great investors think and for his thought leadership on the macroeconomic dashboards and other relative value analytics for tactical asset allocation. Also, David Clewell has provided continued support of all our "special topics" discussed in our Asset Allocation Committee, and he did yeoman's work on the macroeconomic dashboards. Similarly, Hailey Lynch's empirical analysis for the "Revenge of the Stock Pickers" was outstanding.

I must also thank Charles Shriver, Rob Sharps, and all the members of our Asset Allocation Committee—I'm lucky and humbled to sit at the table with such a distinguished group of investors. Every time we meet, I learn. Working with you makes me less of a dilequant, and more of an investor (you'll have to go back to Chapter 8 if you're not sure or forgot what I mean by "dilequant").

Several colleagues gave feedback on an early draft of the manuscript and helped with a few rounds of edits. Many thanks to Gavin Daly, Peter Austin, Swabi Uus, Shannon Lucas, Stephanie Yankaskas, and Dan Middelton for your thoughtful suggestions. And a special thank you to Swabi Uus and John Zevitas for help with legal and compliance requirements, and to David Oestreicher and Terri Doud for mobilizing the legal resources to get this book reviewed internally. Also, thank you to Sylvia Toense, Head of Global Brand Marketing at T. Rowe Price, for her support of this project.

The more nuanced answers on how one gets to write a book on the side of a full-time job, in addition to help from friends and colleagues, involves synergies, mentorship, time management, and support from family. By synergies, I mean that the content of this book *is* my job. This book shows how we, as an organization, invest money for our clients. Due to our collaborative culture at T. Rowe Price, working there provides an incredible opportunity to learn from others and continue to push the boundaries of best practices for professional asset allocation. We have an outstanding culture, and I'm lucky to be part of this organization.

About mentorship, I often say that everything I've learned about asset allocation, I've learned from Mark Kritzman. Mark mentored me for more than a decade. It was the most rewarding professional collaboration of my entire career. We have remained friends, and I continue to learn from Mark. My career, let alone this book, would never have come to this point without Mark's support throughout the years. As I mentioned earlier in this book, I even steal most of his conference presentation jokes.

At T. Rowe Price, now I benefit from similarly strong mentorship, guidance, and support from Rob Sharps and Bill Stromberg. I can't imagine stronger role models for integrity, humility, investment savvy, and leadership. Our industry suffers from a dearth of skilled investors who can lead people. Rob and Bill are the real deal along both dimensions.

On time management, this book took me more than two years to write, little by little, with moments of self-doubt. I started writing after I read Cal Newport's book *Deep Work*—one of the most impactful books I've ever read. It helped me organize my time. I've never met Cal, but I feel I need to thank him for changing how I think about time management. Mary Rolfe and Dan Middelton deserve a lot of credit as well for their help managing my schedule.

Last, about support from family, in addition to a passion for finance, I learned the importance of a strong work ethic from my father, Jean-Paul Page. He's also taught me how to look at the world with healthy skepticism and to always use judgment in decision-making. I hope you enjoyed reading quotes from him throughout this book. Also, I want to thank my mother, Louisette Hamon. She is a force of nature and has supported me throughout my life.

I wrote parts of this book during nights, weekends, and vacation days. My wife, Anne Ferguson, has been incredibly supportive, and I'm forever grateful to her. She's the love of my life. And to our wonderful kids, Charlie and Olivia, thank you so much for your support. I don't think either of you will have an interest in this book. Robotics, video games, and social media are much more fun than finance, but my hope is that you'll enjoy the fact that I've kept the last few words for you: you're awesome, and I love you!

References and Bibliography

Adler, Timothy, and Mark Kritzman. 2007. "Mean-Variance Versus Full-Scale Optimisation: In and out of Sample," *Journal of Asset Management*, vol. 7, no. 5, pp. 302–311.

Agarwal, Vikas, and Narayan Y. Naik. 2004. "Risks and Portfolio Decisions Involving Hedge Funds," *Review of Financial Studies*, vol. 17, no. 1, pp. 63–98.

Allen, David, Colin Lizieri, and Stephen Satchell. 2019. "In Defense of Portfolio Optimization: What If We Can Forecast?," *Financial Analysts Journal*, vol. 75, no. 3, pp. 1–19.

American Investment Council. May 2018. "Private Equity Delivers Highest Returns for Public Pension Funds," *Annual Public Pension Study*. Retrieved from http://www.investmentcouncil.org/2018-aic-public-pension-study -private-equity-delivers-highest-returns-for-public-pension-funds/.

Andersen, Torben G., Tim Bollerslev, Peter F. Christoffersen, and Francis X. Diebold. 2013. "Financial Risk Measurement for Financial Risk Management," in G. Constantinides, M. Harris, and R. Stulz (Eds.), *Handbook of the Economics of Finance*, Elsevier, pp. 1127–1120.

Anderson, Robert M., Stephen W. Bianchi, and Lisa R. Goldberg. 2012. "Will My Risk Parity Strategy Outperform?," *Financial Analysts Journal*, vol. 68, no. 6, pp. 75–93.

Anderson, Robert M., Stephen W. Bianchi, and Lisa R. Goldberg. 2013. "'Will My Risk Parity Strategy Outperform?' Author Response," *Financial Analysts Journal*, vol. 69, no. 2, pp. 15–16.

Andersson, Magnus, Elizaveta Krylova, and Sami Vähämaa. 2008. "Why Does the Correlation Between Stock and Bond Returns Vary over Time?," *Applied Financial Economics*, vol. 18, no. 2, pp. 139–151.

Ang, Andrew, and Geert Bekaert. 2002. "International Asset Allocation with Regime Shifts," *Review of Financial Studies*, vol. 15, no. 4, pp. 1137–1187.

Ang, Andrew, and Joseph Chen. 2002. "Asymmetric Correlations of Equity Portfolios," *Journal of Financial Economics*, vol. 63, no. 3, pp. 443–494.

Ang, Andrew, Joseph Chen, and Yuhang Xing. 2002. "Downside Correlation and Expected Stock Returns," EFA 2002 Berlin Meetings Presented Paper, USC Finance and Business Economics Working Paper no. 01-25.

Arnott, Rob, Vitali Kalesnik, and Jim Masturzo. 2018. "CAPE Fear: Why CAPE Naysayers Are Wrong," Research Affiliates. Retrieved from http://www.researchaffiliates.com/en_us/publications/articles/645-cape-fear-why-cape-naysayers-are-wrong.html.

Arnott, Robert D., and William J. Bernstein. 2018. "The Long-Run Drivers of Stock Returns: Total Payouts and the Real Economy: A Comment," *Financial Analysts Journal*, vol. 74, no. 1.

Arnott, Robert D., Denis B. Chaves, and Tzee-man Chow. 2017. "King of the Mountain: The Shiller P/E and Macroeconomic Conditions," *Journal of Portfolio Management*, vol. 44, no. 1, pp. 55–68.

Asness, Cliff. 2012. "An Old Friend: The Stock Market's Shiller P/E," AQR. Retrieved from http://www.aqr.com/Insights/Research/White-Papers/ An-Old-Friend-The-Stock-Markets-Shiller-PE.

Asness, Cliff. February 2019. "Introducing the New AQR S.M.O.O.T.H. Fund," AQR Alternative Investing. Retrieved from http://www.aqr.com/ Insights/Perspectives/Introducing-the-New-AQR-SMOOTH-Fund.

Asness, Clifford, Andrea Franzzini, and Lasse H. Pedersen. 2013. "'Will My Risk Parity Strategy Outperform?' A Comment," *Financial Analysts Journal*, vol. 69, no. 2, pp. 12–15.

Asness, Clifford S., Tobias J. Moskowitz, and Lasse Heje Pedersen. 2013. "Value and Momentum Everywhere," *Journal of Finance*, vol. 68, no. 3, pp. 929–985.

Austin, Maureen, David Thurston, and William Prout. February 2019. "Private Investing for Private Investors: Life Can Be Better After 40(%)," Cambridge Associates Research Publications. Retrieved from https:// www.cambridgeassociates.com/research/private-investing-for-private -investors-life-can-be-better-after-40/.

Baele, Lieven, Geert Bekaert, and Koen Inghelbrecht. 2010. "The Determinants of Stock and Bond Return Comovements," *Review of Financial Studies*, vol. 23, no. 6, pp. 2374–2428.

Barberis, Nicholas, Andrei Shleifer, and Jeffrey Wurgler. February 2005. "Comovement," *Journal of Financial Economics*, vol. 75, no. 2, pp. 283–317.

Baumeister, Roy F., Ellen Bratslavsky, Catrin Finkenauer, and Kathleen D. Vohs. 2001. "Bad Is Stronger Than Good," *Review of General Psychology*, vol. 5, no. 4, pp. 323–370.

Beardsley, Xiaoxin W., Brian Field, and Mingqing Xiao. 2012. "Mean-Variance-Skewness-Kurtosis Portfolio Optimization with Return and Liquidity," *Communications in Mathematical Finance*, vol. 1, no. 1, pp. 13–49.

Beck, Noah, Jason Hsu, Vitali Kalesnik, and Helge Kostka. 2016. "Will Your Factor Deliver? An Examination of Factor Robustness and

Implementation Costs," *Financial Analysts Journal*, vol. 72, no. 5, pp. 58–82.

Ben-David, Itzhak, Francesco Franzoni, and Rabih Moussawi. September 2018. "Do ETFs Increase Volatility?," *Journal of Finance*, vol. 73, no. 6, pp. 2471–2535. Retrieved from https://ssrn.com/abstract=1967599.

Bender, Jennifer, Remy Briand, Frank Nielsen, and Dan Stefek. 2010. "Portfolio of Risk Premia: A New Approach to Diversification," *Journal of Portfolio Management*, vol. 36, no. 2, pp. 17–25.

Bernanke, Ben. February 2016. "The Relationship Between Stocks and Oil Prices," *Ben Bernanke's Blog*, Brookings. Retrieved from https://www.brookings.edu/blog/ben-bernanke/2016/02/19/the-relationship-between-stocks-and-oil-prices/.

Bernstein, Peter L. 1991. *Capital Ideas: The Improbable Origins of Modern Wall Street*. Hoboken, NJ: John Wiley & Sons.

Bernstein, Peter L. 1996. *Against the Gods: The Remarkable Story of Risk*. New York: John Wiley & Sons.

Bernstein, Peter L. 2007. *Capital Ideas Evolving*. Hoboken, NJ: John Wiley & Sons.

Bernstein, William J., and Robert D. Arnott. 2003. "Earnings Growth: The Two Percent Dilution," *Financial Analysts Journal*, vol. 59, no. 5, pp. 47–55.

Bhansali, Vineer. 2010. *Bond Portfolio Investing and Risk Management*. New York: McGraw-Hill.

Billio, Monica, Mila Getmansky, and Loriana Pelizzon. 2012. "Crises and Hedge Fund Risk," Yale ICF Working Paper, vol. 7, no. 14. Retrieved from ssrn.com/abstract=1130742.

Black, Fischer, and Robert Litterman. 1992. "Global Portfolio Optimization," *Financial Analysts Journal*, vol. 48, no. 5, pp. 28–43.

Blitz, David C., and Pim Van Vliet. 2008. "Global Tactical Cross-Asset Allocation: Applying Value and Momentum Across Asset Classes," *Journal of Portfolio Management*, vol. 35, no. 1, pp. 23–38.

Bodie, Zvi, Robert C. Merton, and William F. Samuelson. 1992. "Labor Supply Flexibility and Portfolio Choice in a Life Cycle Model," *Journal of Economic Dynamics and Control*, vol. 16, no. 3–4, pp. 427–449.

Bollerslev, Tim. 1990. "Modeling the Coherence in Short-Run Nominal Exchange Rates: A Multivariate Generalized ARCH Model," *Review of Economics and Statistics*, vol. 72, no. 3, pp. 498–505. DOI: 10.2307/2109358.

Bollerslev, Tim, Andrew J. Patton, and Roger Quaedvlieg. 2016. "Exploiting the Errors: A Simple Approach for Improved Volatility Forecasting," *Journal of Econometrics*, vol. 192, no. 1, pp. 1–18.

Booth, James R., and Lena Chua Booth. 1997. "Economic Factors, Monetary Policy, and Expected Returns on Stocks and Bonds," *Economic Review (Federal Reserve Bank of San Francisco)*, vol. 2, p. 32.

Boudoukh, Jacob, Ronen Israel, and Matthew Richardson. 2019. "Long-Horizon Predictability: A Cautionary Tale," *Financial Analysts Journal*, vol. 75, no. 1, pp. 17–30.

Boyd, Johnrac H., Jian Hu, and Ravi Jagannathan. 2005. "The Stock Market's Reaction to Unemployment News: Why Bad News Is Usually Good for Stocks," *Journal of Finance*, vol. 60, no. 2, pp. 649–672.

Brandt, Michael W., and Christopher S. Jones. 2006. "Volatility Forecasting with Range-Based EGARCH Models," *Journal of Business & Economic Statistics*, vol. 24, no. 4, pp. 470–486.

Brightman, Chris, Vitali Kalesnik, and Mark Clements. 2015. "Are Buybacks an Oasis or a Mirage?," Research Affiliates. Retrieved from http://www.researchaffiliates.com/en_us/publications/articles/385_are _buybacks_an_oasis_or_a_mirage.html.

Brown, David C., Shaun Davies, and Matthew C. Ringgenberg. 2018. "ETF Flows, Non-Fundamental Demand, and Return Predictability." Retrieved from https://ssrn.com/abstract=2872414.

Brown, Gregory W., Robert S. Harris, Tim Jenkinson, Steven N. Kaplan, and David T. Robinson. 2015. "What Do Different Commercial Data Sets

Tell Us About Private Equity Performance?," Working Paper. Retrieved from http://ssrn.com/abstract=2701317.

Brown, Stephen J., and Barbara S. Petitt. 2017. "Author Guidelines," *Financial Analysts Journal*. Retrieved from http://www.cfapubs.org/pb -assets/PDFs/FAJ_AuthorGuidelines.pdf.

Brownlees, Christian, Robert Engle, and Bryan Kelly. 2012. "A Practical Guide to Volatility Forecasting Through Calm and Storm," *Journal of Risk*, vol. 14, no. 2, pp. 3–22.

Cahan, Rochester, Yu Bai, and Sungsoo Yang. February 2018. "The ETF Selection Model—Don't Pick the ETF, Pick the Stocks in the ETF," Empirical Research Partners.

Campbell, John Y., and Robert J. Shiller. Winter 1998. "Valuation Ratios and the Long-Run Stock Market Outlook," *Journal of Portfolio Management*, vol. 24, no. 2, pp. 11–26.

Campbell, John Y., and Luis M. Viceira. 2002. *Strategic Asset Allocation: Portfolio Choice for Long-Term Investors*. New York: Oxford University Press.

Campbell, Rachel, Kees Koedijk, and Paul Kofman. 2002. "Increased Correlation in Bear Markets," *Financial Analysts Journal*, vol. 58, no. 1, pp. 87–94.

Cappiello, Lorenzo, Robert F. Engle, and Kevin Sheppard. 2006. "Asymmetric Dynamics in the Correlations of Global Equity and Bond Returns," *Journal of Financial Econometrics*, vol. 4, no. 4, pp. 537–572.

Chao, Alex, Ronnie Shah, Pam Finelli, Hallie Martin, Chin Okoro, Srineel Jalagani, George Zhao, and David Elledge. July 2018. "What Happens When the World Goes Passive? Active ETF Flow Strategies," Deutsche Bank Research, Quantitative Strategy.

Chen, Linda H., Wei Huang, and George J. Jiang. 2019. "Do Mutual Funds Trade on Earnings News? The Information Content of Large Active Trades," Working Paper. Retrieved from http://ssrn.com/abstract=3337928.

Chen, Nai-Fu, Richard Roll, and Stephen A. Ross. 1986. "Economic Forces and the Stock Market," *Journal of Business*, vol. 59, no. 3, pp. 383–403.

Chen, Peng, Roger G. Ibbotson, Moshe A. Milevsky, and Kevin X. Zhu. 2006. "Human Capital, Asset Allocation, and Life Insurance," *Financial Analysts Journal*, vol. 62, no. 1, pp. 97–109. DOI: 10.2469/faj.v62.n1.4061.

Cherkes, Martin. 2012. "Closed-End Funds: A Survey," *Annual Review of Financial Economics*, vol. 4, pp. 431–445. Retrieved from https://doi.org/10.1146/annurev-financial-110311-101714.

Chow, George. 1995. "Portfolio Selection Based on Return, Risk, and Relative Performance," *Financial Analysts Journal*, vol. 51, no. 2, pp. 54–60.

Chow, George, Eric Jacquier, Mark Kritzman, and Kenneth Lowry. 1999. "Optimal Portfolios in Good Times and Bad," *Financial Analysts Journal*, vol. 55, no. 3, pp. 65–73.

Chua, David B., Mark Kritzman, and Sébastien Page. 2009. "The Myth of Diversification," *Journal of Portfolio Management*, vol. 36, no. 1, pp. 26–35.

Clark, Peter K. 1973. "A Subordinated Stochastic Process Model with Finite Variance for Speculative Prices," *Econometrica: Journal of the Econometric Society*, vol. 41, no. 1, pp. 135–155.

Clewell, David, Chris Faulkner-MacDonagh, David Giroux, Sébastien Page, and Charles Shriver. 2017. "Macroeconomic Dashboards for Tactical Asset Allocation," *Journal of Portfolio Management*, vol. 44, no. 2, pp. 50–61.

Cocoma, Paula, Megan Czasonis, Mark Kritzman, and David Turkington. 2017. "Facts About Factors," *Journal of Portfolio Management*, vol. 43, no. 5, pp. 55–65.

Collin, Martin. 2017. "The Hidden Risks of Bond Benchmarks," Schwab Bond Insights. Retrieved from http://www.schwab.com/resource-center/insights/content/hidden-risks-bond-benchmarks.

Corsi, Fulvio. 2009. "A Simple Approximate Long-Memory Model of Realized Volatility," *Journal of Financial Econometrics*, vol. 7, no. 2, pp. 174–196.

Cremers, Jan Hein, Mark P. Kritzman, and Sébastien Page. Spring 2005. "Optimal Hedge Fund Allocations: Do Higher Moments Matter?," *Journal of Portfolio Management*, vol. 31, no. 3, pp. 70–81.

Cuffe, Stacy L., and Lisa R. Goldberg. 2012. "Allocating Assets in Climates of Extreme Risk: A New Paradigm for Stress Testing Portfolios," *Financial Analysts Journal*, vol. 68, no. 2, pp. 85–107.

Czasonis, Megan, Mark P. Kritzman, and David Turkington. 2019. "Private Equity Valuations and Public Equity Performance," *Journal of Alternative Investments*, vol. 22, no. 1, pp. 8–19.

Da, Zhi, and Sophie Shive. 2017. "Exchange Traded Funds and Asset Return Correlations," *European Financial Management*. Retrieved from wileyonlinelibrary.com/journal/eufm.

Dahlquist, Magnus, and Campbell R. Harvey. Spring 2001. "Global Tactical Asset Allocation," *Journal of Global Capital Markets*.

Dalio, Ray. 2017. *Principles: Life and Work*. New York: Simon & Schuster.

De Bondt, Werner F. M., and Richard Thaler. 1985. "Does the Stock Market Overreact?," *Journal of Finance*, vol. 40, no. 3, pp. 793–805. Retrieved from JSTOR, http://www.jstor.org/stable/2327804.

DeMiguel, Victor, Lorenzo Garlappi, and Raman Uppal. 2007. "Optimal Versus Naive Diversification: How Inefficient Is the 1/N Portfolio Strategy?," *Review of Financial Studies*, vol. 22, no. 5, pp. 1915–1953.

Dhankar, Raj, and Supriya Maheshwari. May 2016. "Behavioural Finance: A New Paradigm to Explain Momentum Effect." Retrieved from https://ssrn.com/abstract=2785520.

Doeswijk, Ronald, Trevin Lam, and Laurens Swinkels. 2014. "The Global Multi-Asset Market Portfolio, 1959–2012," *Financial Analysts Journal*, vol. 70, no. 2, pp. 26–41.

Dopfel, Frederick E., and Sunder R. Ramkumar. Fall 2013. "Managed Volatility Strategies: Applications to Investment Policy," *Journal of Portfolio Management*, vol. 40, no. 1, pp. 27–39.

Dowd, Kevin, John Cotter, Chris Humphrey, and Margaret Woods. 2008. "How Unlucky Is 25-Sigma?," *Journal of Portfolio Management*, vol. 34, no. 4, pp. 76–80.

Dreyer, Anna, Robert L. Harlow, Stefan Hubrich, and Sébastien Page. Third Quarter 2016. "Return of the Quants: Risk-Based Investing," *CFA Institute Conference Proceedings*.

Dreyer, Anna, and Stefan Hubrich. 2019. "Tail-Risk Mitigation with Managed Volatility," *Journal of Investment Strategies*, vol. 8, no. 1, pp. 29–56.

Edelen, Roger M. 1999. "Investor Flows and the Assessed Performance of Open-End Mutual Funds," *Journal of Financial Economics*, vol. 53, no. 3, pp. 439–466.

Elton, Edwin J., and Martin J. Gruber. 1995. *Modern Portfolio Theory and Investment Analysis* (5th ed.). Hoboken, NJ: John Wiley & Sons.

Elton, Edwin J., Martin J. Gruber, Christopher R. Blake, and Or Shachar. 2013. "Why Do Closed-End Bond Funds Exist? An Additional Explanation for the Growth in Domestic Closed-End Bond Funds," *Journal of Financial and Quantitative Analysis*, vol. 48, no. 2, pp. 405–425.

Engle, Robert. July 2002. "Dynamic Conditional Correlations: A Simple Class of Multivariate Generalized Autoregressive Conditional Heteroscedasticity Models," *Journal of Business and Economic Statistics*, vol. 20, no. 3, pp. 339–350.

Erb, Claude B., Campbell R. Harvey, and Tadas E. Viskanta. November/December 1994. "Forecasting International Equity Correlations," *Financial Analysts Journal*, vol. 50, no. 6, pp. 32–45. DOI: 10.2469/faj.v50.n6.32.

Fallon, William, James Park, and Danny Yu. 2015. "Asset Allocation Implications of the Global Volatility Premium," *Financial Analysts Journal*, vol. 71, no. 5, pp. 38–56.

Fama, Eugene F., and Kenneth R. French. 1989. "Business Conditions and Expected Returns on Stocks and Bonds," *Journal of Financial Economics*, vol. 25, no. 1, pp. 23–49.

Fama, Eugene F., and Kenneth R. French. 1992. "The Cross-Section of Expected Stock Returns," *Journal of Finance*, vol. 47, no. 2, pp. 427–465.

Fama, Eugene F., and Kenneth R. French. 1993. "Common Risk Factors in the Returns on Stocks and Bonds," *Journal of Financial Economics*, vol. 33, no. 1, pp. 3–56.

Fama, Eugene F., and Kenneth R. French. 2004. "The Capital Asset Pricing Model: Theory and Evidence," *Journal of Economic Perspectives*, vol. 18, no. 3, pp. 25–46.

Fama, Eugene F., and Kenneth R. French. 2012. "Size, Value, and Momentum in International Stock Returns," *Journal of Financial Economics*, vol. 105, no. 3, pp. 457–472.

Feldman, Barry E., and Dhruv Roy. Fall 2005. "Passive Options-Based Investment Strategies: The Case of the CBOE S&P 500 Buy Write Index," *Journal of Investing*, vol. 14, no. 1, pp. 72–89.

Ferreira, Miguel A., and Paulo M. Gama. 2010. "Correlation Dynamics of Global Industry Portfolios," *Journal of Multinational Financial Management*, vol. 20, no. 1, pp. 35–47.

Figelman, Ilya. Summer 2008. "Expected Return and Risk of Covered Call Strategies," *Journal of Portfolio Management*, vol. 34, no. 4, pp. 81–97.

Fleming, Jeff, Chris Kirby, and Barbara Ostdiek. February 2001. "The Economic Value of Volatility Timing," *Journal of Finance*, vol. 56, no. 1, pp. 329–352.

Fleming, Jeff, Chris Kirby, and Barbara Ostdiek. March 2003. "The Economic Value of Volatility Timing Using 'Realized' Volatility," *Journal of Financial Economics*, vol. 67, no. 3, pp. 473–509.

Forbes, Steve. 2014. "Efficient Market? Baloney, Says Famed Value and Momentum Strategist Cliff Asness." Retrieved from http://www.forbes.com/sites/steveforbes/2014/04/22/efficient-market-baloney-says-famed-value-and-momentum-strategist-cliff-asness/#ea770775c6f7.

Fortin, Alain-Philippe, Jean-Guy Simonato, and Georges Dionne. 2018. "Forecasting Expected Shortfall: Should We Use a Multivariate Model for Stock Market Factors?," Working Papers 18-4, HEC Montreal, Canada Research Chair in Risk Management.

Foulke, David. March 2016. "Replicating Private Equity: The Impact of Return Smoothing," Alpha Architect. Retrieved from alphaarchitect.com/2016/03/07/replicating-private-equity-the-impact-of-return-smoothing/.

Franz, Richard. December 2013. "Macro-Based Parametric Asset Allocation." Retrieved from https://ssrn.com/abstract=2260179.

Franzoni, Francesco, Eric Nowak, and Ludovic Phalippou. 2012. "Private Equity Performance and Liquidity Risk," *Journal of Finance*, vol. 67, no. 6, pp. 2341–2373.

Frazzini, Andrea, Ronen Israel, and Tobias J. Moskowitz. April 2018. "Trading Costs," Working Paper. Retrieved from ssrn.com/abstract= 3229719.

Frazzini, Andrea, and Lasse Heje Pedersen. 2014. "Betting Against Beta," *Journal of Financial Economics*, vol. 111, no. 1, pp. 1–25.

Froot, Kenneth A., Paul G. J. O'Connell, and Mark S. Seasholes. February 2001. "The Portfolio Flows of International Investors," *Journal of Financial Economics*, vol. 59, no. 2, pp. 151–193.

Garcia-Feijoo, Luis, Gerald R. Jensen, and Robert R. Johnson. 2012. "The Effectiveness of Asset Classes in Hedging Risk," *Journal of Portfolio Management*, vol. 38, no. 3, pp. 40–55.

Geczy, Christopher C., and Mikhail Samonov. 2015. "215 Years of Global Multi-Asset Momentum: 1800–2014," Working Paper. Retrieved from http://www.investmentpod.com/assets/uploads/whitepapers/ SSRN-id2607730.pdf.

Giamouridis, Daniel. 2017. "Systematic Investment Strategies," *Financial Analysts Journal*, vol. 74, no. 4.

Glosten, Lawrence R., Ravi Jagannathan, and David E. Runkle. 1993. "On the Relation Between the Expected Value and the Volatility of the Nominal Excess Return on Stocks," *Journal of Finance*, vol. 48, no. 5, pp. 1779–1801.

Glosten, Lawrence R., Suresh Nallareddy, and Yuan Zou. December 2016. "ETF Activity and Informational Efficiency of Underlying Securities," Columbia Business School Research Paper no. 16–71. Retrieved from https://ssrn.com/abstract=2846157.

Goodwin, Thomas H. 1993. "Business-Cycle Analysis with a Markov-Switching Model," *Journal of Business & Economic Statistics*, vol. 11, no. 3, pp. 331–339.

Greenwood, Robert M., and Nathan Sosner. September/October 2007. "Trading Patterns and Excess Comovement of Stock Returns," *Financial Analysts Journal*, vol. 63, no. 5, pp. 69–81.

Greiner, Steven P. 2012. "The Impact of Skewness and Fat Tails on the Asset Allocation Decision: A Comment," *Financial Analysts Journal*, vol. 68, no. 3, p. 10. DOI: 10.2469/faj.v68.n3.9.

Gulko, Les. 2002. "Decoupling," *Journal of Portfolio Management*, vol. 28, no. 3, pp. 59–66.

Guo, Helen, and Niels Pedersen. June 2014. "Bond Investing in a Rising Rate Environment," PIMCO Quantitative Research and Analytics. Retrieved from https://nl.pimco.com/en-nl/insights/viewpoints/quantitative-research-and-analytics/bond-investing-in-a-rising-rate-environment/.

Gupta, Arpit, and Stijn Van Nieuwerburgh. 2019. "Valuing Private Equity Strip by Strip," Working Paper, presented at the American Finance Association Annual Meeting on January 5, 2019. Retrieved from https://www.nber.org/papers/w26514.

Haghani, Victor, and Richard Dewey. 2016. "A Case Study for Using Value and Momentum at the Asset Class Level," *Journal of Portfolio Management*, vol. 42, no. 3, pp. 101–113.

Hallerbach, Winfried G. May 2012. "A Proof of the Optimality of Volatility Weighting over Time," Working Paper. Retrieved from http://papers.ssrn.com/sol3/papers.cfm?abstract_id=2008176.

Hamilton, James D. 1989. "A New Approach to the Economic Analysis of Nonstationary Time Series and the Business Cycle," *Econometrica: Journal of the Econometric Society*, vol. 57, no. 2, pp. 357–384.

Harris, Robert S., Tim Jenkinson, and Steven N. Kaplan. 2016. "How Do Private Equity Investments Perform Compared to Public Equity?," *Journal of Investment Management*, vol. 14, no. 3.

Hartmann, Philipp, Stefan Straetmans, and Casper G. de Vries. 2004. "Asset Market Linkages in Crisis Periods," *Review of Economics and Statistics*, vol. 86, no. 1, pp. 313–326.

Hartmann, Philipp, Stefan Straetmans, and Casper G. de Vries. 2010. "Heavy Tails and Currency Crises," *Journal of Empirical Finance*, vol. 17, no. 2, pp. 241–254.

Harvey, Campbell R., John C. Liechty, Merrill W. Liechty, and Peter Müller. 2010. "Portfolio Selection with Higher Moments," *Quantitative Finance*, vol. 10, no. 5, pp. 469–485.

Harvey, Campbell R., Yan Liu, and Heqing Zhu. 2016. ". . . and the Cross-Section of Expected Returns," *Review of Financial Studies*, vol. 29, no. 1, pp. 5–68.

Harvey, Justin, and Aaron Stonacek. June 2018. "Estimating Bond Index Returns Using a Yield-Based Approach," Price Point, T. Rowe Price.

Higgins, Robert C. 2016. *Analysis for Financial Management.* New York: McGraw-Hill Education.

Hill, Joanne. 2016. "The Evolution and Success of Index Strategies in ETFs," *Financial Analysts Journal*, vol. 72, no. 5, pp. 8–13.

Hill, Joanne M., Venkatesh Balasubramanian, Krag (Buzz) Gregory, and Ingrid Tierens. September/October 2006. "Finding Alpha via Covered Index Writing," *Financial Analysts Journal*, vol. 62, no. 5, pp. 29–46.

Hocquard, Alexandre, Sunny Ng, and Nicolas Papageorgiou. Winter 2013. "A Constant-Volatility Framework for Managing Tail Risk," *Journal of Portfolio Management*, vol. 39, no. 2, pp. 28–40.

Hong, Yongmiao, Jun Tu, and Guofu Zhou. 2007. "Asymmetries in Stock Returns: Statistical Tests and Economic Evaluation," *Review of Financial Studies*, vol. 20, no. 5, pp. 1547–1581.

Horan, Stephen M. 2009. *Private Wealth: Wealth Management in Practice. CFA Investment Perspectives Book 1.* Hoboken, NJ: John Wiley & Sons.

"How Harvard's Investing Superstars Crashed." February 20, 2009. *Forbes*, https://www.forbes.com/2009/02/20/harvard-endowment-failed-business_harvard.html#4345c065312b.

Huang, Jing-Zhi, Marco Rossi, and Yuan Wang. 2015. "Sentiment and Corporate Bond Valuations Before and After the Onset of the Credit Crisis," *Journal of Fixed Income*, vol. 25, no. 1, pp. 34–57.

Hull, Blair and Xiao Qiao. 2017. "A Practitioner's Defense of Return Predictability," *The Journal of Portfolio Management*, vol. 43, no. 3, pp. 60–76.

Idzorek, Thomas M., and Maciej Kowara. 2013. "Factor-Based Asset Allocation Vs. Asset-Class-Based Asset Allocation," *Financial Analysts Journal*, vol. 69, no. 3, pp. 19–29.

Ilmanen, Antti. 2011. *Expected Returns: An Investor's Guide to Harvesting Market Rewards*. West Sussex, United Kingdom: John Wiley & Sons.

Ilmanen, Antti. 2012. *Expected Returns on Major Asset Classes*. Hoboken, NJ: John Wiley & Sons.

Ilmanen, Antti, Swati Chandra, and Nicholas McQuinn. 2019. "Demystifying Illiquid Assets: Expected Returns for Private Equity," AQR White Paper. Retrieved from https://www.aqr.com/Insights/Research/White-Papers/Demystifying-Illiquid-Assets-Expected-Returns-for-Private-Equity.

Ilmanen, Antti, and Jared Kizer. 2012. "The Death of Diversification Has Been Greatly Exaggerated," *Journal of Portfolio Management*, vol. 38, no. 3, pp. 15–27.

Israelov, Roni, and Lars N. Nielsen. August 2014. "Covered Call Strategies: One Fact and Eight Myths," *Financial Analysts Journal*, vol. 70, no. 6, pp. 23–31.

Israelov, Roni, and Lars N. Nielsen. November/December 2015. "Covered Calls Uncovered," *Financial Analysts Journal*, vol. 71, no. 6, pp. 44–57.

Jegadeesh, Narasimhan, and Sheridan Titman. 1993. "Returns to Buying Winners and Selling Losers: Implications for Stock Market Efficiency," *Journal of Finance*, vol. 48, no. 1, pp. 65–91.

Jensen, Gerald R., Robert R. Johnson, and Jeffrey M. Mercer. 1997. "New Evidence on Size and Price-to-Book Effects in Stock Returns," *Financial Analysts Journal*, vol. 53, no. 6, pp. 34–42.

Johnson, Nicholas, Vasant Naik, Sébastien Page, Niels Pedersen, and Steve Sapra. 2014. "The Stock-Bond Correlation," *Journal of Investment Strategies*, vol. 4, no. 1, pp. 3–18.

Jondeau, Eric, and Michael Rockinger. 2012. "On the Importance of Time Variability in Higher Moments for Asset Allocation," *Journal of Financial Econometrics*, vol. 10, no. 1, pp. 84–123.

Jorion, Philippe. 1986. "Bayes-Stein Estimation for Portfolio Analysis," *Journal of Financial and Quantitative Analysis*, vol. 21, no. 3, pp. 279–292.

Jorion, Philippe. 1991. "Bayesian and CAPM Estimators of the Means: Implications for Portfolio Selection," *Journal of Banking & Finance*, vol. 15, no. 3, pp. 717–727.

Kahneman, Daniel, and Amos Tversky. 1979. "Prospect Theory: An Analysis of Decision Under Risk," *Econometrica*, vol. 47, no. 2, pp. 363–391.

Kamara, Avraham, and Lance Young. 2018. "Yes, the Composition of the Market Portfolio Matters: The Estimated Cost of Equity," *Financial Management*, vol. 47, no. 4, pp. 911–929.

Kapadia, Nikunj, and Edward Szado. Spring 2007. "The Risk and Return Characteristics of the Buy-Write Strategy on the Russell 2000 Index," *Journal of Alternative Investments*, vol. 9, no. 4, pp. 39–56.

Kaplan, Steven N., and Antoinette Schoar. 2005. "Private Equity Performance: Returns, Persistence, and Capital Flows," *Journal of Finance*, vol. 60, no. 4, pp. 1791–1823.

Kim, Chang-Jin. 1993. "Unobserved-Component Time Series Models with Markov-Switching Heteroscedasticity: Changes in Regime and the Link Between Inflation Rates and Inflation Uncertainty," *Journal of Business & Economic Statistics*, vol. 11, no. 3, pp. 341–349.

Kinlaw, William B., Mark P. Kritzman, and Jason Mao. 2015. "The Components of Private Equity Performance: Implications for Portfolio Choice," *Journal of Alternative Investments*, vol. 18, no. 2, pp. 25–38.

Kourtis, Apostolos, Raphael N. Markellos, and Lazaros Symeonidis. 2016. "An International Comparison of Implied, Realized, and GARCH Volatility Forecasts," *Journal of Futures Markets*, vol. 35, no. 12, pp. 1164–1193.

Kritzman, Mark. 1991. "What Practitioners Need to Know . . . About Estimating Volatility, Part 2," *Financial Analysts Journal*, vol. 47, no. 5, pp. 10–11.

Kritzman, Mark. 2006. "Are Optimizers Error Maximizers?," *Journal of Portfolio Management*, vol. 32, no. 4, pp. 66–69.

Kritzman, Mark. Fall 2013. "Risk Disparity," *Journal of Portfolio Management*, vol. 40, no. 1, pp. 40–48.

Kritzman, Mark, and Yuanzhen Li. 2010. "Skulls, Financial Turbulence, and Risk Management," *Financial Analysts Journal*, vol. 66, no. 5, pp. 30–41.

Kritzman, Mark, Yuanzhen Li, Sébastien Page, and Roberto Rigobon. Summer 2011. "Principal Components as a Measure of Systemic Risk," *Journal of Portfolio Management*, vol. 37, no. 4, pp. 112–126.

Kritzman, Mark, Sébastien Page, and David Turkington. 2010. "In Defense of Optimization: The Fallacy of 1/N," *Financial Analysts Journal*, vol. 66, no. 2, pp. 31–39.

Kritzman, Mark, Sébastien Page, and David Turkington. 2012. "Regime Shifts: Implications for Dynamic Strategies (Corrected)," *Financial Analysts Journal*, vol. 68, no. 3, pp. 22–39.

Kritzman, Mark, and Don Rich. 2002. "The Mismeasurement of Risk," *Financial Analysts Journal*, vol. 58, no. 3, pp. 91–99.

Kumar, Manmohan S., and Tatsuyoshi Okimoto. 2007. "Dynamics of Persistence in International Inflation Rates," *Journal of Money, Credit and Banking*, vol. 39, no. 6, pp. 1457–1479.

Lam, Pok-sang. 2004. "A Markov-Switching Model of GNP Growth with Duration Dependence," *International Economic Review*, vol. 45, no. 1, pp. 175–204.

Leibowitz, Martin L., and Anthony Bova. 2009. "Diversification Performance and Stress-Betas," *Journal of Portfolio Management*, vol. 35, no. 3, pp. 41–47.

Leibowitz, Martin L., Anthony Bova, and Stanley Kogelman. 2014. "Long-Term Bond Returns Under Duration Targeting," *Financial Analysts Journal*, vol. 70, no. 1, pp. 31–51.

Lettau, Martin, and Sydney Ludvigson. 2001. "Consumption, Aggregate Wealth, and Expected Stock Returns," *Journal of Finance*, vol. 56, no. 3, pp. 815–849.

Levy, Haim, and Harry M. Markowitz. 1979. "Approximating Expected Utility by a Function of Mean and Variance," *American Economic Review*, vol. 69, no. 3, pp. 308–317.

L'Her, Jean-Francois, Rossitsa Stoyanova, Kathryn Shaw, William Scott, and Charissa Lai. 2016. "A Bottom-Up Approach to the Risk-Adjusted Performance of the Buyout Fund Market," *Financial Analysts Journal*, vol. 72, no. 4, pp. 36–48.

Li, Lingfeng. 2003. "Macroeconomic Factors and the Correlation of Stock and Bond Returns," Yale University ICF Working Paper 02-46, AFA 2004 San Diego Meetings. Retrieved from http://ssrn.com/abstract=363641.

Lintner, John. 1965. "The Valuation of Risk Assets and the Selection of Risky Investments in Stock Portfolios and Capital Budgets," *Review of Economics and Statistics*, vol. 47, no. 1, pp. 13–37.

Lo, Andrew W. 2001. "Risk Management for Hedge Funds: Introduction and Overview," *Financial Analysts Journal*, vol. 57, no. 6, pp. 16–33.

Lo, Andrew W., and Mark T. Mueller. Second Quarter 2010. "Warning: Physics Envy May Be Hazardous to Your Wealth!," *Journal of Investment Management*.

Lo, Grace H., Jeffrey B. Driban, Andrea M. Kriska, Timothy E. McAlindon, Richard B. Souza, Nancy J. Petersen, Kristi L. Storti, et al. 2017. "Is There an Association Between a History of Running and Symptomatic Knee Osteoarthritis? A Cross-Sectional Study from the Osteoarthritis Initiative," *Arthritis Care & Research*, vol. 69, no. 2, pp. 183–191.

Longin, Francois, and Bruno Solnik. 1995. "Is the Correlation in International Equity Returns Constant: 1960–1990?," *Journal of International Money and Finance*, vol. 14, no. 1, pp. 3–26.

Longin, Francois, and Bruno Solnik. 2001. "Extreme Correlation of International Equity Markets," *Journal of Finance*, vol. 56, no. 2, pp. 649–676.

Ludvigson, Sydney C., and Serena Ng. December 2009. "Macro Factors in Bond Risk Premia," *Review of Financial Studies*, vol. 22, no. 12, pp. 5027–5067.

Luginbuhl, Rob, and Aart de Vos. 1999. "Bayesian Analysis of an Unobserved-Component Time Series Model of GDP with Markov-Switching and Time-Varying Growths," *Journal of Business & Economic Statistics*, vol. 17, no. 4, pp. 456–465.

Lynch, Hailey, Sébastien Page, Robert A. Panariello, James A. Tzitzouris Jr., and David Giroux. 2019. "The Revenge of the Stock Pickers," *Financial Analysts Journal*, vol. 75, no. 2, pp. 34–43.

Madhavan, Ananth, and Daniel Morillo. Summer 2018. "The Impact of Flows into Exchange Traded Funds: Volumes and Correlations," *Journal of Portfolio Management*, vol. 44, no. 7, pp. 96–107.

Markowitz, Harry. 1952. "Portfolio Selection," *Journal of Finance*, vol. 7, no. 1, pp. 77–91.

Markowitz, Harry M. 1959. *Portfolio Selection: Efficient Diversification of Investments* (Cowles Foundation Monograph no. 16). Hoboken, NJ: John Wiley & Sons.

Markowitz, Harry M. 2005. "Market Efficiency: A Theoretical Distinction and So What?," *Financial Analysts Journal*, vol. 61, no. 5, pp. 17–30. DOI: 10.2469/faj.v61.n5.2752.

Marks, Howard. 2006. "You Can't Eat IRR," *Memo to Oaktree Clients*. Retrieved from https://www.oaktreecapital.com/docs/default-source/memos/2006-07-12-you-cant-eat-irr.pdf.

Marra, Stephen. December 2015. "Predicting Volatility," Lazard Asset Management, Investment Research.

McKinsey & Company. February 2018. "The Rise and Rise of Private Markets," *McKinsey Global Private Markets Review*. Retrieved from http://www.mckinsey.com/~/media/mckinsey/industries/private%20equity%20and%20principal%20investors/our%20insights/the%20rise%20and%20rise%20of%20private%20equity/the-rise-and-rise-of-private-markets-mckinsey-global-private-markets-review-2018.ashx.

McLean, R. David, and Jeffrey Pontiff. 2016. "Does Academic Research Destroy Stock Return Predictability?," *Journal of Finance*, vol. 71, no. 1, pp. 5–32.

McQueen, Grant, and Steven Thorley. 1999. "Mining Fool's Gold," *Financial Analysts Journal*, vol. 55, no. 2, pp. 61–72.

Mercer. 2013. "Risk Parity—Concept, Products and the Start of a Bond Bear Market?," https://www.uk.mercer.com/content/dam/mercer/ attachments/global/investments/risk-parity-bond-bear-market-mercer -august-2013.pdf.

Merton, Robert C. 1974. "On the Pricing of Corporate Debt: The Risk Structure of Interest Rates," *Journal of Finance*, vol. 29, no. 2, pp. 449–470.

Merton, Robert C. January/February 2003. "Thoughts on the Future: Theory and Practice in Investment Management," *Financial Analysts Journal*, vol. 59, no. 1, pp. 17–23.

Moreira, Alan, and Tyler Muir. April 2016. "Volatility Managed Portfolios," NBER Working Paper no. 22208. Retrieved from https://www.nber.org/ papers/w22208.

Moreira, Alan, and Tyler Muir. 2017. "Volatility-Managed Portfolios," *Journal of Finance,* vol. 72, no. 4, pp. 1611–1644.

Mossin, Jan. 1966. "Equilibrium in a Capital Asset Market," *Econometrica*, vol. 34, no. 4, pp. 768–783. DOI: 10.2307/1910098.

Naik, Vasant, Mukundan Devarajan, Andrew Nowobilski, Sébastien Page, and Niels Pedersen. December 2016. "Factor Investing and Asset Allocation: A Business Cycle Perspective" (monograph), *CFA Institute Research Foundation Publications,* vol. 2016, no. 4.

Novy-Marx, Robert, and Mihail Velikov. 2018. "Betting Against Betting Against Beta." Retrieved from https://ssrn.com/abstract=3300965.

Page, Sébastien. January/February 2013. "How to Combine Long and Short Return Histories Efficiently," *Financial Analysts Journal*, vol. 69, no. 1, pp. 45–52.

Page, Sébastien. September 2013. "Risk Management Beyond Asset Class Diversification," *CFA Institute Conference Proceedings Quarterly*, vol. 30, no. 3, pp. 52–59.

Page, Sébastien. 2016. "Risk Parity Fundamentals," *Quantitative Finance*, vol. 16, no. 12, pp. 1801–1802. DOI: 10.1080/14697688.2016.1220616. www.tandfonline.com.

Page, Sébastien, and Robert A. Panariello. 2018. "When Diversification Fails," *Financial Analysts Journal*, vol. 74, no. 3, pp. 19–32.

Page, Sébastien, Joseph Simonian, and Fei He. 2011. "Asset Allocation: Systemic Liquidity as a Risk Factor," *Trading*, vol. 2011, no. 1, pp. 19–23.

Page, Sébastien, and Mark Taborsky. Summer 2011. "The Myth of Diversification: Risk Factors Vs. Asset Classes," *Journal of Portfolio Management*, vol. 37, no. 4, pp. 1–2.

Page, Sébastien, and James A. Tzitzouris. December 2016. "Stocks Versus Bonds: Which Best Help Meet Retirement Goals?," *InvestmentNews*. Retrieved from http://www.investmentnews.com/article/20161222/ BLOG09/161229981/stocks-versus-bonds-which-best-help-meet -retirement-goals.

Patton, Andrew J. 2004. "On the out-of-Sample Importance of Skewness and Asymmetric Dependence for Asset Allocation," *Journal of Financial Econometrics,* vol. 2, no. 1, pp. 130–168.

Pedersen, Niels, Sébastien Page, and Fei He. 2014. "Asset Allocation: Risk Models for Alternative Investments," *Financial Analysts Journal*, vol. 70, no. 3, pp. 34–45.

Pelletier, Denis. March/April 2006. "Regime Switching for Dynamic Correlations," *Journal of Econometrics*, vol. 131, no. 1–2, pp. 445–473.

Perchet, Romain, Raul Leote de Carvalho, and Pierre Moulin. December 2014. "Intertemporal Risk Parity: A Constant Volatility Framework for Factor Investing," *Journal of Investment Strategies*, vol. 4, no. 1, pp. 19–41.

Phalippou, Ludovic. 2014. "Performance of Buyout Funds Revisited?," *Review of Finance*, vol. 18, no. 1, pp. 189–218.

Phalippou, Ludovic, and Oliver Gottschlag. 2009. "The Performance of Private Equity Funds," *Review of Financial Studies*, vol. 22, no. 4, pp. 1747–1776.

Poon, Ser-Huang, and Clive Granger. January/February 2005. "Practical Issues in Forecasting Volatility," *Financial Analysts Journal*, vol. 61, no. 1, pp. 45–56. DOI: 10.2469/faj.v61.n1.2683.

Poon, Ser-Huang, and Clive W. J. Granger. 2003. "Forecasting Volatility in Financial Markets: A Review," *Journal of Economic Literature*, vol. 41, no. 2, pp. 478–539.

Praetz, Peter D. 1972. "The Distribution of Share Price Changes," *Journal of Business*, vol. 45, no. 1, pp. 49–55.

Press, S. James. 1967. "A Compound Events Model for Security Prices," *Journal of Business*, vol. 40, no. 3, pp. 317–335.

Rachev, Svetlozar T., Christian Menn, and Frank J. Fabozzi. 2005. *Fat-Tailed and Skewed Asset Return Distributions: Implications for Risk Management, Portfolio Selection, and Option Pricing*. Hoboken, NJ: John Wiley & Sons.

Roll, Richard. 1977. "A Critique of the Asset Pricing Theory's Tests Part I: On Past and Potential Testability of the Theory," *Journal of Financial Economics*, vol. 4, no. 2, pp. 129–176.

Schrager, Allison. 2019. *An Economist Walks into a Brothel: And Other Unexpected Places to Understand Risk*. New York: Portfolio/Penguin.

Sharpe, William F. September 1964. "Capital Asset Prices: A Theory of Market Equilibrium Under Conditions of Risk," *Journal of Finance*, vol. 19, no. 3, pp. 425–442.

Sharpe, William F. September/October 2007. "Expected Utility Asset Allocation," *Financial Analysts Journal*, vol. 63, no. 5, pp. 18–30.

Siegel, Jeremy J. 2002. *Stocks for the Long Run* (3rd ed.). New York: McGraw-Hill.

Siegel, Jeremy J. 2016. "The Shiller CAPE Ratio: A New Look," *Financial Analysts Journal*, vol. 72, no. 3, pp. 41–50.

Stafford, Erik. May 2017. "Replicating Private Equity with Value Investing, Homemade Leverage, and Hold-to-Maturity Accounting," Working Paper, Harvard Business School. Retrieved from https://ssrn.com/abstract=2720479.

Straehl, Philip U., and Roger G. Ibbotson. 2017. "The Long-Run Drivers of Stock Returns: Total Payouts and the Real Economy," *Financial Analysts Journal*, vol. 73, no. 3, pp. 32–52.

Straehl, Philip U., and Roger G. Ibbotson. 2018. "The Long-Run Drivers of Stock Returns: Total Payouts and the Real Economy: Author Response," *Financial Analysts Journal*, vol. 74, no. 1.

Swensen, David F. 2009. *Pioneering Portfolio Management: An Unconventional Approach to Institutional Investment* (fully revised and updated). New York: Simon & Schuster.

Taleb, Nassim Nicholas. 2010. *The Black Swan: The Impact of the Highly Improbable* (2nd ed.). New York: Random House.

Treynor, Jack L. 1961. "Toward a Theory of Market Value of Risky Assets," unpublished manuscript.

Van Oordt, Maarten R. C., and Chen Zhou. 2012. "The Simple Econometrics of Tail Dependence, *Economics Letters*, vol. 116, no. 3, pp. 371–373.

Van Royen, Anne-Sophie. 2002a. "Financial Contagion and International Portfolio Flows," *Financial Analysts Journal*, vol. 58, no. 1, pp. 35–49.

Van Royen, Anne-Sophie. 2002b. "Hedge Fund Index Returns," *Hedge Fund Strategies*, vol. 2002, no. 1, pp. 111–117.

Wainscott, Craig B. 1990. "The Stock-Bond Correlation and Its Implications for Asset Allocation," *Financial Analysts Journal*, vol. 46, no. 4, pp. 55–60.

Whaley, Robert E. Winter. 2002. "Return and Risk of CBOE Buy Write Monthly Index," *Journal of Derivatives*, vol. 10, no. 2, pp. 35–42.

Wigglesworth, Robin, "ETFs Are Eating the U.S. Stock Market," *Financial Times*, January 24, 2017.

Wilcox, Jarrod W. 1984. "The P/B-ROE Valuation Model," *Financial Analysts Journal*, vol. 40, no. 1, pp. 58–66.

Wurgler, Jeffrey. July 2010. "On the Economic Consequences of Index-Linked Investing," in W. T. Allen, R. Khurana, J. Lorsch, and G. Rosenfeld (Eds.), *Challenges to Businesses in the Twenty-First Century: The Way Forward*. Retrieved from https://ssrn.com/abstract=1667188.

Xiong, James X., & Thomas M. Idzorek. 2011. "The Impact of Skewness and Fat Tails on the Asset Allocation Decision," *Financial Analysts Journal*, vol. 67, no. 2, pp. 23–35. DOI: 10.2469/faj.v67.n2.5.

Xiong, James X., and Rodney N. Sullivan. March/April 2012. "How Index Trading Increases Market Vulnerability," *Financial Analysts Journal*, vol. 68, no. 2.

Zhang, Qi J., Peter Hopkins, Stephen Satchell, and Robert Schwob. 2009. "The Link Between Macro-Economic Factors and Style Returns," *Journal of Asset Management*, vol. 10, no. 5, pp. 338–355.

Index

About the Author

Sébastien Page is Head of Global Multi-Asset at T. Rowe Price, overseeing a team of investment professionals dedicated to a broad set of multi-asset portfolios representing more than $350 billion in assets. He is a member of the Asset Allocation Committee, which is responsible for tactical investment decisions across asset allocation portfolios. He is also a member of the Management Committee of T. Rowe Price Group, Inc.

Prior to joining the firm in 2015, Mr. Page was an executive vice president at PIMCO, where he led a team focused on research and development of multi-asset solutions. Prior to joining PIMCO in 2010, he was a Senior Managing Director at State Street Global Markets.

Mr. Page won research paper awards from the *Journal of Portfolio Management* in 2003, 2010, and 2011 and from the *Financial Analysts Journal* in 2010 and 2014. He is coauthor of *Factor Investing and Asset Allocation* (2016) and is a member of the editorial board of the *Financial Analysts Journal*. He regularly appears in the financial media, including Bloomberg TV and CNBC. Mr. Page earned a master of science degree in finance and a bachelor's degree in business administration from Sherbrooke University in Quebec. He has earned the Chartered Financial Analyst designation.

Mr. Page is donating proceeds from this book to the T. Rowe Price Foundation, which is committed to supporting long-term community impact on youth empowerment, creativity, and innovation, and to advancing comprehensive approaches to alleviating hunger, poverty, and homelessness in Baltimore and other communities around the globe.

Follow him on LinkedIn: linkedin.com/in/sebastien-page.